My Love Affair

with the

State of Maine

BY SCOTTY MACKENZIE
with Ruth Goode

Down East Books
Camden, Maine

For D. B. M.

Certain names and situations
have been altered in this book.

ISBN 0-89272-407-2

Cover design by Tim Seymour
Cover photograph by Robin Lovell
Printed and bound at Capital City Press, Montpelier, Vt.

2   4   5   3   1

Down East Books, P.O. Box 679, Camden, Maine 04843

LIBRARY OF CONGRESS CATALOGING-IN-PUBLICATION DATA

Mackenzie, Scotty, 1917–
    My love affair with the state of Maine / by Scotty Mackenzie, with
Ruth Goode.
        p.   cm.
    ISBN 0-89272-407-2 (pbk.)
    1. Mackenzie, Scotty, 1917–   . 2. Goode, Ruth. 3. Maine-
-Biography. 4. Maine--Social life and customs. I. Goode, Ruth.
II. Title.
CT275.M137A3   1997
974.104'092--dc21
    [B]   97-929
                                                            CIP

CONTENTS

Where Else But in Maine?

This is the story of my love affair with the State of Maine, which, like all love affairs, ran anything but smooth.

Dorothy says it began on a night of crisp stars in early June when we were walking along the hard, chilly sand of Goose Rocks Beach with the two cocker spaniels yipping hysterically around our ankles. Madison Avenue, traffic lights, zooming elevators, and the smoke and yammer of plush restaurants were all far away, on another planet.

We had dined that evening on Albion's small tender lobsters, a new experience for me; I had eaten them big and broiled and dressed up in bread crumbs and butter, but had never seen a lobster green and wriggling, nor tasted one so young and fresh from the sea. We had listened to some Dixieland records from Dorothy's collection. And now we were giving Imp and Spike their run before bed, as delighted as they with the unobstructed length of firm white beach and the salt-sweet breath of sand and beach grass and early wild roses.

This is the life, I thought. And at that moment Dorothy said, out of nowhere, "Do you know, I'm almost tempted to buy the village store."

To give you the full absurdity of her remark, I must tell you that Dorothy and I were refugees from the polished purlieus of the advertising agencies in New York. One of us was a little over twenty-five years of age, the other a shade under. Put us on the scale together in our Bermuda shorts and Saks Fifth Avenue T-shirts and we would weigh about the same as one good-sized man. We knew how to talk business charmingly over three cocktails and lunch at Twenty-One. We knew how to spin out an advertising idea, make a market analysis, and sell a corporation vice-president a promotion campaign that would cost $1,000,000 across the board. Which is not the same as knowing how to sell twenty-four cases of canned beans, can by can, or get five cents more for one head of lettuce than another identical head. I was innocent of this difference at the time, and so I was unaware of any absurdity in Dorothy's proposal.

Correction: her idea was not quite out of nowhere. Herb Atwood had put the question to her that afternoon, when we were in Herb's accommodation store in the village. The store was in what had been the Atwoods' kitchen, and to me, coming in out of the sharp clean daylight, it seemed overheated and airless; I didn't know that Clara Atwood's rheumatism was the reason for the blazing potbellied stove and the tight-shut windows on a sunny June day. To my city gaze the old-fashioned showcases were not quaint but merely dark and crowded. Following the shelves upward, my eye picked out a cobweb in a ceiling corner and an insect corpse in the cobweb. Clara, who had been a schoolteacher before she married Herb, caught me looking at it and said, "Herb and I are too old to keep a store as it should be kept."

Herb was tall and thin and looked like Carl Sandburg in spectacles. His gold-rimmed glasses kept slipping down his thin straight nose, and he kept pushing them up all the time he was talking. He talked about the hard winter, talked about Clara's rheumatism, and asked suddenly, "Dor'thy, why don't you buy my store?"

Dorothy thinks that's when it began. My own version goes back a few weeks to a cocktail party in New York. I had had a long business luncheon with several Scotches at Theodore's, and after that a promotion party for some product or other, also with several Scotches, somewhere else. Toward evening, with a glass in my hand again, I said, "Enough. I'm getting out while I'm still in my right mind. I'm going to Arizona."

Why Arizona? someone asked. I really didn't know, except that it was far away, underpopulated, and had neither skyscrapers nor subways.

Across from me in the group stood Dorothy. She and I had been meeting on and off for some time, in that glibly social climate in which Madison Avenue does business. She waited until everybody else had thoroughly canvassed the idea of escape, and then she said, "On your way to Arizona, why don't you stop off in Maine? It's far away too, and there's a three-mile stretch of beach with no one on it. I'm opening my house there next week."

So a few days later I had quit my fine and well-paid job and was in Dorothy's bright red Packard convertible. Our luggage was stowed. Imp and Spike quivered between us in the front seat. I was on my way to Arizona via Maine.

Dorothy, as she thought, was merely leaving New York for her usual summer in Maine. But I was running away from New York, as far as I could go. I had had a bad fright. I loved my job, I loved my friends, I even loved my big, noisy, pushing, beautiful and ugly home town. But one day a man I had lunched with was dead of a heart attack at his desk an hour after we parted at my office door. Another day a girl I knew in another office, as smart, as fast-talking, as brassy-confident as I, was fired without notice—"let out" is the kinder phrase—because her agency had lost an account or two. A terrifically successful woman executive I knew took an overdose of sleeping pills. A man who had sky-rocketed to a vice-presidency went home from his analyst's office and jumped or fell from his Park Avenue apartment window. All this in less than a month.

The smooth machinery ran on without even a momentary shudder. Typewriters tapped, though other fingers touched the keys; telephones rang and other hands reached for the receivers; under the same highly polished conference tables, other well-creased Brooks Brothers trousers and other nyloned ankles rested. Those who were gone were gone, and not missed; the waters closed over them as though they had never been.

I was a girl who had no family left; I had been an only child. Home to me was one clever little apartment after another; New Yorkers are notorious movers. I had achieved that pinnacle of independence people dream about, with nothing and no one to hold me down. For a girl like me, heart-whole, fancy-free, having wonderful time and never a dull moment, it was like being hit by a Diesel-motored trailer truck to realize that if anything happened to me, nobody would really care.

I was not, of course, quite fair to my friends, but that's the way I saw it. So I was running away from that chilly, fearful, lonely independence. I didn't know it, but I was looking for a place small enough to belong to, a place where I was wanted and needed and would be missed if I went away, a place I could call home.

I was to help Dorothy open her house, enjoy her hospitality for a few days, and then go on to the West. That was the deal.

But I reckoned without the sea and the pine woods, the hot sun and the spank of the wind. I reckoned without Albion's lobsters. I reckoned without Herb Atwood's urgent wish to retire from storekeeping and the subtle ways by which a State of Mainer gets his wish. I reckoned without the gambler behind Dorothy's soft ladylike exterior and the gambler in me. Mostly I reckoned without the State of Maine, which gets a hold on you like an impossible man you can't live with and you can't live without.

2

And Bowling Alleys!

Dorothy is not a native of Goose Rocks, but she grew up on that beach. Her family came from Massachusetts. Her father, Dr. Mignault, discovered Goose Rocks Beach when he was drifting up the coast one fall, duckhunting. There was nothing but the curving stretch of unspoiled sand outlining a sheltered cove and a solid wall of pines hiding it from the highway. A rough little road stole off from the highway, running through the woods to the beach and the few scattered houses there. It was a road which the speeding traveler on his way to Kennebunkport would never see.

Dr. Mignault built a summer house, then another and another, selling each to a friend or friend of a friend as he explored a more charming house site or thought of a pleasanter plan for a house. Finally the family settled for the summers on the Point, looking out past Timber Island with nothing between their living-room windows and the coast of Spain but the pounding blue Atlantic. This was the house to which Dorothy brought the two cocker spaniels and me.

A few independent lobstermen like Albion Fisher, a few families whose boys and men went out in the fishing fleet, Herb Atwood's store, and the summer people whose houses stood along the village road and away from it, following the beach—that was all of Goose Rocks. Tucked away along the shore and in the woods there were now, after thirty years, about four hundred and fifty families. I never knew it, until they came to buy at the store.

But Dorothy knew them all. And they all knew Dorothy and loved her. She also knew all the local men, their wives and children and grandchildren. She knew which boys went away to college, to the Navy, to Portland, which girls worked in the mill town and when and whom they married. She knew who was a plumber and who was an electrician and who would come to clean for you.

For all her soft ways Dorothy has a first-rate business head. She also has a law degree and passed the bar in Massachusetts. Even before I met her I knew her reputation as a market analyst and the respect with which her judgment was received by men with Vice-President after their names. So that night on the beach, when all of a sudden she stopped running with the dogs and said, "Why not buy the store?" I stopped too.

Now, Dorothy by temperament likes to do a small job and do it perfectly, while this Mackenzie here has no time for anything if it isn't big. My first reaction to her question was characteristic.

"That crummy little store squeezed into the kitchen of a Charles Addams house? It's so little!"

Herb and Clara, in these chilly days of late spring, still dined, entertained, and slept in the parlor. What was in the upstairs rooms I couldn't imagine, but to my mind skeletons and vampire bats would have been quite at home in any house of that period. Herb had neither designed nor built it, but had taken it over as it stood when he bought the property. Inside, it was pleasant and comfortable, but from the outside it was one of those Victorian mistakes you occasionally find in New England among the austere salt boxes and Cape Cods and the many which are just houses to live in. It was topped with gables and cupolas and hung with porches, and everywhere you looked it bulged with a bay. The shingles were a liverish green and a tower on top was painted red. With a coat of white paint, however, later on, the house lost its grotesqueness and acquired a kind of ponderous dignity.

When I said, "It's so little!" Dorothy, knowing my weakness, laughed at me.

"Not that store, silly. The big one—didn't you see it? It's closed—Herb hasn't run it for five years, but when he did, it was always very successful, even in bad times. And there's the guesthouse," Dorothy went on. "And the Casino, with two bowling alleys—"

"Bowling alleys! You could bowl all you wanted for free?" I've never been able to get enough bowling.

And we were off. We walked up and down the beach, forgetting that in Maine even summer nights can be cold, and June is not yet summer. When our teeth began to chatter we went into the house to get warm. We couldn't light a fire, because in that lovely house Dorothy's mother had arranged things so that there wasn't a fireplace; she had too many of them in the family home in Lowell. We plugged in an electric heater, put coffee on, and went on talking.

I couldn't understand how Herb Atwood had come to offer the store to Dorothy. Dorothy said, "Herb's had offers for the store, but he doesn't want to sell it to anyone who may not feel the way he and Clara do about Goose Rocks. The store sets the tone for the beach, you know. I've never made any secret of my interest in it. Every chance I've had, I've pumped Herb about the life of a storekeeper. And besides, I think he thinks I'm—well—a woman of property." Dorothy looked at me and added, "Of course, I couldn't run the store alone. I suspect Herb thought you might come in with me."

Storekeeping! The thought was new and startling. But in the next breath I was wondering, Could I swing it? And what would this do to my future plans? And then I remembered that I had no future plans.

Now I'm convinced all State of Mainers believe as a matter of course that they are poor and out-of-staters are rich and New Yorkers are millionaires, or close to it. Yet I could see that in Herb's eyes Dorothy in her smart city clothes, with her smart car, her two smart dogs, and her large, solidly built, well-furnished summer home, was a rich girl. How she lived all winter in the city, how she sweated to keep her house and to preserve her very modest inheritance—this Herb didn't know and could hardly even imagine. It was out of his experience entirely. As for me, I was an unknown quantity, and for Maine people anybody who isn't obviously poor can be assumed to be rich.

I maintain this is not naïveté or provincial ignorance, but a cunning strategy. Look how well it works! In two months or so they make enough out of us self-styled city slickers to keep themselves the year round. We may scrimp and save all year for that vacation, but once we get there we pay prices and labor charges automatically multiplied by two for our special benefit. What's more, we like doing it so well we go back again and again. And they know all the while that we will.

Herb Atwood was daring us to run a country store, and I think he knew all along that we couldn't resist a dare. Only city people would accept such a challenge, people who didn't know what they were getting into and who, to tell the truth, didn't much care. The challenge was the thing.

Dorothy said, "There's nothing to buying. I've bought all over the world. And as for selling, if you and I don't know how to sell, who does?" I have mentioned that what we knew how to sell was ideas. Canned goods were different.

Dorothy pointed out that if we went into it I could spend the summer in Maine and make a living at the same time, probably a good deal more than a living. If I didn't like it, she would buy me out and I would be no worse off financially than I was at the beginning. And storekeeping was, to both of us, brand-new.

This was a clincher. Though she had not let on at the start, I knew by now that Dorothy was as fed up as I with the high gloss of city existence. At not quite twenty-six we thought we had had everything the city could offer, including success in the most glittering kind of business. We'd been lunched and dined and theatered until the sight of a marquee made us yawn. We never wanted to see another uniformed doorman or ride in another taxi. Even I, loving bigness, was tired of talking million-dollar campaigns. (But I was already dreaming in terms of an enormous supermarket; it never occurred to me that storekeepers count their profits in pennies!)

As we were climbing the stairs to our rooms a little before dawn, Dorothy asked diffidently, "Will you mind giving up Arizona?" And I realized that the thought of Arizona had not once entered my head since the day we arrived at Goose Rocks. Maine had me, hook, line, and sinker.

Herb showed no surprise when we turned up after breakfast and asked to see the property. In Maine nobody is ever surprised. Maine people are not merely poker-faced. I firmly believe they know what we're going to do before we know it.

He'd be glad to show us, of course. There was exactly an acre of land, a deep rectangle fronting on the road which was the main street of Goose Rocks. Across the road, summer homes lined the beach to left and to right, but just opposite our acre (I was already thinking, "Our acre") there were no houses and the land was not for sale. We had an unobstructed view of the beach and the sea. It was beautiful and soothing.

Herb's Victorian mansion was on the road at one side of the rectangle. Behind it, and connected to it by a covered passage, was the guesthouse, a white house in New England style but with no particular distinction. It had twelve bedrooms, some single and some double, making twenty beds in all.

"Who'll occupy twenty guest beds?" I asked skeptically.

"The art students," Dorothy answered. "They scramble for rooms, there are so few in Goose Rocks." Arthur Woodbridge, a distinguished painter, happened to have chosen Goose Rocks for his summer home years ago, and his school was a famous one.

At the back of the rectangle, reached by a short drive-in and with its own turnaround, was the Casino, with the finest dance floor I've seen anywhere, although it would take slaving to get it in shape after years of disuse. The Casino was of silvery weathered shingles; built up on stilts, it had a broad flight of ten steps leading up to a porch the width of the whole front. Inside the door was a box office. And beyond the dance floor were two beautiful, beautiful bowling alleys. I gazed at them with love and longing; I couldn't wait to possess them. Little did I know that I was not going to bowl —not even once!—until the day after the summer season ended.

Going around the rectangle's perimeter we came down its third side to a broad white building facing on the road, glittering with plate glass, and finally we were inside The Store. By this time I was thoroughly hooked and not paying much attention to Herb. I kept wandering away, looking at the orange-colored floor with distaste, but admiring the two enormous show windows fronting on the road and the sea. Dorothy would call me back: to look over the ancient mahogany and glass showcases, inefficient by modern standards but handsome even under a film of dust; to consider whether we shouldn't build more shelves, perhaps a whole wall of shelves.

Dorothy asked about vegetable bins; Herb pointed out a long table counter, not too far from the sinks at the back where you washed the vegetables. Dorothy spoke of frozen foods, dairy stuff. I had a vague notion that a store must have a pattern of some kind, but no idea what it might be. Were we going to have meats? Dorothy was asking about meat storage, whether the refrigerator cases and the big refrigerator were in working order. There was a cash register on one of the mahogany counters in the center of the store; Dorothy said how nice it would be to have a big check-out counter at the doorway, maybe shelves behind it for cigarettes, tobacco, candy, toys. Gifts! Something to buy your hostess and the children when you arrived for a week end without a present. Nice gifts, Fifth Avenue gifts—I could already see the kind of things they'd be. Display them in the show window, too, to be seen from outside.

And on that wall of shelves behind the cash register— after they've done their serious marketing and are on their way out, the expensive stuff in cans and glass jars: hors d'oeuvres, canapés, pâtés, peaches in brandy, the trimmings. Get the last dollar before they leave.

Walking around the littered, dusty store with its uninhabited dead look, we went on dreaming. Herb had had a drug counter opposite the entrance; we could recognize the remains of ancient tooth paste ads in the rubbish. We would want display space there, lots of it, Dorothy said. "How about a cosmetic bar?"

"Demonstrations, maybe?" I countered.

Dorothy nodded. "Why not?"

We looked at the dingy walls and said: White. Snowy, pure, unblemished white, if we had to scrub it clean every night ourselves (we did). Dorothy said, "And how about gray deck paint on the floor?"

Herb, waiting patiently for us to get our feet back on the

ground, called our attention to the restaurant—"with table service, and hamburgers and all that at the soda fountain—you got the kitchen for it right here."

"But who will do the cooking?" I asked.

"Cora!" Dorothy exclaimed. Cora had been Dorothy's mother's cook and came regularly in the summer to cook for Dorothy. "She's done catering for big parties—why, she cooks in a school all winter. I'll write her right away."

Now, Dorothy herself is a gifted cook, and furthermore she is the kind of cook who walks into a strange kitchen and knows without asking where everything is. But even Dorothy was floored when we made our inspection of the kitchen. Even Dorothy didn't know what half the equipment was for.

Those two deep aluminum wells with their own burners were deep-fat fryers, Herb told us, for clams, of course, and for French fries. A small gas range was there, and an enormous oil range which Dorothy saw with approval. And then there was the Blodgett oven. I had never seen a Blodgett oven or known one existed. But there it was, a solid wall from floor to ceiling, with handles as on bureau drawers to pull out racks and racks, enough to hold Lord knows how many pies, cakes, biscuits, muffins.

Herb still had a great deal more to show us. We followed him dutifully out of the kitchen, in and out of the refrigerator rooms and storerooms, but we weren't really attending. In our minds we had already bought the store.

3

We Acquire the Store—and Some Friends

From the moment we decided to buy the store we were in a terrible hurry.

On the face of it this made sense. In Maine the money you don't make during the summer you're never going to make. A day gone is gone forever, and it was already the second week in June. But we weren't being sensible. We were just in a hurry. Maybe we were afraid that if we stopped to think we would lose our nerve. Whatever the reason, we rushed poor old Herb, harried the lawyers, and sat on the doorstep of the bank.

It took a week for Herb to make up his mind how much less he would take than he had asked for, for the lawyers to agree on just what we were buying, and for the bank to decide how much of a mortgage we and the property were good for. ("We" to the bank meant Dorothy; the mortgage would be in her name. In Maine I wasn't worth a cent more than the clothes I stood in, but I was going into hock up to my neck in New York to pay my junior share.) A businessman will tell you that to do this in a week is supersonic speed for such a transaction anywhere, let alone in Maine. But to us it was like traveling by camel caravan, and with the camels balky besides.

We signed the papers late at night in Herb's parlor. Dorothy's signature was witnessed by me; Ben Beebe of Doolittle and Smith, the Biddeford grocery jobbers; and Herb's son-in-law, who was to be a prop and staff to us in the next few days. Dorothy acted as her own lawyer.

We had bought just about everything except the shirt on Herb's bent old back and the modest contents of his wife's bureau. Herb's lawyer was holding out Dorothy's check to Herb—when Herb, without warning, put his hands palms down on the table and said, "No."

The son-in-law's mouth dropped open, the lawyer shut his lips tight together, and Dorothy's soft voice asked anxiously, "Herb, don't you feel well?"

"It's not me, it's the lion," Herb said cryptically. "I never thought about the lion."

I had a wild vision of a lion caged in the attic; they keep all kinds of things up attic in Maine, including mad relatives, so why not a lion? And then, following the direction of Herb's eyes, I saw the lion on the wall. Among Herb's unsuspected gifts was a talent for penmanship, and framed on the wall was his proudest creation, a lion with full mane and glaring eyes, from ears to tail drawn in scrolls with pen and ink.

It was the biggest thing in a frame I have ever seen outside of a museum, and Herb was ready now to toss our whole transaction out of the window because he had forgotten to keep it out of the sale. It never occurred to him that we might not consider it part of the transaction, and he had no intention of being forced to buy it back from us.

Dorothy and I looked at each other, and both got up and lifted the picture off its hook and set it down beside Herb's chair.

"With our compliments, Herb," Dorothy said gravely. "We wouldn't think of taking advantage of an oversight."

It was the first and only time I ever saw Herb really smile.

He accepted the check, we shook hands all around, and then we relaxed and began to talk plans.

Herb had made up his mind to leave Goose Rocks on June 25 and would close his little store the night before.

"Then we'll open the big store the next morning," I announced brashly.

"Oh, I wouldn't try to do that," Ben Beebe, the jobber from Biddeford, suggested. "You ought to give yourselves a little time. You need to transfer the stock from Herb's old place."

"All right, twenty-four hours." What stock? I wondered. From what I had seen, I could move it myself in an hour. "What do you say, Dorothy?"

"Twenty-four hours ought to be enough time," Dorothy agreed. "We don't want to leave the community without a store any longer than we have to."

This struck me as odd. Where I came from, the word *community* was strictly corn. A New Yorker is proud of his city, even though he is always trying to get out of it. But what *community* does he belong to? I had hocked myself to go into business, not social welfare.

But for whatever reasons, Dorothy was with me in the fever to get going. I was bouncing with excitement. "Why, we've got five whole days from tonight!"

"There's quite a lot to opening a store," Ben Beebe murmured.

We barely heard him; five days was enough time to get anything done. We forgot we were in Maine, where nobody hurries and time is one of the only two things that go quickly, the other being money.

We were at the bank the next morning when it opened, but it took the better part of the morning to get all the corners of the transaction neatly tucked in to the bank's satisfaction. We drove back and straight to the store.

It was the first time we had been in it since we had gone dreamily over the property with Herb a week before. We stood in the doorway, appalled. Newspapers, old cartons, broken packing boxes, advertisements, display cards, cigarette litter, dead field mice, and a scurrying that could only mean live ones—I blanched, being mortally afraid of mice.

Had this all been here when we saw it? Hadn't someone spent the intervening week dumping all his trash here? Or was it only that we were seeing it with different eyes, now that we had to clean it up and put it in shape?

Dorothy, who is an able housekeeper along with all her other talents, went right out back in search of a broom. I followed her, stamping my feet and whistling through my teeth to drive away any small furry creatures that had the poor taste to linger.

(The big stockroom had one light in the middle so that you had to walk all the way in, in pitch dark, to pull the cord, and its floor was bare two-by-fours with cracks between, through which anything—but anything—could come up from below. Let a customer ask for a bottle of soda, and I would start for the stockroom, stamping and whistling, making like a locomotive, all the way from the counter into the stockroom and back, while the customer stared, too astonished to ask what I was doing. The dogs of course purged the place of undesirables and kept it thoroughly policed, but you couldn't convince me there wasn't a mouse lying beady-eyed in wait just for me.)

I followed Dorothy, making noises all the way. She already had a worn-down broom in one hand and a carton in the other. Her competence, added to my mouse timidity, made me feel inadequate, and I don't like feeling inadequate, so I got mad.

"Aren't there cleaning women to do this kind of thing?" I demanded.

"Of course," said Dorothy. "You get Mrs. Keene, and on the way back stop at the Cape Porpoise store and pick up a couple of brooms and some scrubbing brushes and pails. All the ones here have rusted through."

It was a glistening day. I drove up the road, took a left, the second right, and a left again, about eight miles into the woods, and found Mrs. Keene sitting rocking on her porch. Now, a cleaning woman is in the business of cleaning, and if she hasn't any houses to clean she hasn't any business. So I said, very businesslike, "Mrs. Keene, we need some cleaning done. When can you come, how much time can you give us, and how much do you charge?"

Mrs. Keene rocked a while and said, "I ain't got time."

There she was, sitting and rocking, but she had no time. I tried the ways I knew from the city, asking for Tuesday, Wednesday, Thursday, offering twice what I assumed she usually charged. She rocked and rocked and said politely, "I'd like to oblige you but I ain't got time." It was clear that she would not have time for us, now or ever. What had I done wrong?

I drove back to Dorothy and the trash without a cleaning woman. I did, however, stop at the Cape Porpoise store according to instructions. When I arrived with the cleaning paraphernalia I found Jean and Susan, the two village girls who used to wait on the trade for Herb, helping Dorothy, and the trash was collecting on the loading platform to be carted away. I was to do the carting, I discovered, and the place I was to cart it to was the town dump, a garden of noisome smells and raucous sea gulls. I found myself thinking affectionately of the New York City Department of Sanitation. City dwellers never realize what a thing of beauty is a covered garbage truck.

Chris Marble came in to measure for the shelves and counters he would build. Chris was the kind of man you automatically label a handsome devil. He stood six feet and a couple of inches and had the flat, hard-muscled physique of a young man though he was past fifty. His hair was a thick mane of snow white, his eyes a startling electric blue. High bronzed cheekbones gave his face an Indian look. Altogether, confronted with Chris, I could well believe I had really gone to Arizona: he wore, of all things, cowboy boots, a belt adorned with silver and turquoises, and on his arm a wide, Indian silver and turquoise bracelet. When I asked Dorothy how come all this Wild West finery on the coast of Maine, she startled me even more with the news that Chris was quite a fine painter—of canvases, not alone of houses. Chris's wife ran the tearoom for the art school, and Chris was the handyman and caretaker there. One day he had idly begun fooling around with some paints on a sheet of wrapping paper, and Mr. Woodbridge had taken a fancy to what he did and encouraged him, giving him lessons in return for odd jobs. Chris turned out to be a really interesting virile painter. One winter Mr. Woodbridge took him along to his winter school in Santa Fe. Chris came back from there sporting his cowboy regalia, in which, I had to admit, he looked very well.

As a carpenter Chris was first-rate when he wanted to work at carpentry, and for Dorothy's sake he worked like a demon to get the store ready. He had carried Dorothy pickaback as a child; he was the only one I ever knew who was allowed to call her Dottie. For me he had nothing but taunts—I was a New Yorker and a legitimate target. If I asked him about a door sticking, and would you sand it at the bottom or the side, he would say, "Don't have to know nothin', you New Yorkers, do you? Get everything done for you since you were born," and sooner or later out would come his favorite line about "put a nickel in a slot." I was already waiting for a chance to catch him off base.

On this afternoon he was being serious and helpful. We three went into a planning huddle which lasted a couple of hours.

It was suppertime and the girls had gone home when I came back from my last trip to the dump to find real trouble. A pipe had burst somewhere under the building.

We were city girls. We didn't realize that in the country, in a building that is not used in the wintertime, plumbing pipes are generally underneath the house, out of sight but exposed to the weather. Country people would have known that when a place has stood unused for five years—as the store had been—pipes are likely to buckle. They have hard winters in Maine.

Anyway, a pipe went, the plumbing stopped dead, and precious water went streaming away down the road. Dorothy said, "I think we'd better go down the road and talk to Andrew Austin."

Andrew came out of his house, munching his supper, and leaned on the gate. He had obviously got up from the table in the middle of his meal to talk to us. Dorothy said, "Well, Andrew!"

Andrew said, "Glad to see you, Dor'thy."

Dorothy introduced me and said, "How's Jim liking it over at M.I.T.?"

Andrew said, "He likes it fine, Dor'thy."

Dorothy said, "Did the cows make it all right through the winter?"

Andrew said, "Cost me some extra feed, but they made it all right."

There was more, about Mrs. Austin, the daughter Millie, Millie's new baby, and a neighbor's broken leg. I fidgeted.

Finally Dorothy said, "You know we bought the store, Miss Mackenzie and I. We're going to run it."

Andrew said, "I heard. Good idea."

Dorothy said, "We're having a little trouble. A pipe burst."

Andrew said, "That's too bad."

Dorothy said, "Well, I'll be seeing you, Andrew."

And Andrew said, "Come by any time, Dor'thy."

Whereupon Dorothy took me gently by the arm, turned me around, and walked me at a leisurely pace back to the store. I was ready to burst like the pipe.

"Dorothy, are you crazy? All that water running out— and so much to do—and you stand and—"

"Why," she said, looking at me with big surprised eyes, "you heard me tell him the pipe had burst!"

"But you didn't say a word about his coming, or how soon, or anything sensible. How do you know he'll come tonight, for heaven's sake?"

"Scotty, really! He knows we need him. He'll come."

But when? I groaned and went into the store. Twenty minutes later, or maybe less, I went out in back for something. There was Andrew's pickup truck in the yard, and there was Andrew under the store, with a work light, probing for the leak.

So this is how it's done, I thought. You don't ask for anything. You just let them know you're in trouble, and they "help you out."

The next morning Dorothy rented her house on the Point. We had talked about it. With the hours we were planning to keep—and we were agreed that however big and flossy, the store must still be a village accommodation store, open every evening and all day Sunday—it seemed wise to live nearer than three-quarters of a mile away. That was what we said. What we knew without saying was that Dorothy ought to take the good rental she could get for her house. In such a gamble as we were in, she might need every dollar. She also rented her cottage, Riverview, since her two maiden aunts who usually occupied it in the summer would be visiting out West.

We were going to live in our newly acquired Victorian mansion for the summer. The move added complications. We would have to get the big house ready for its tenants, get our "town house" ready for ourselves—and it needed a complete paint job as well as cleaning—and get the store ready, all at the same time. But we still had four days. We would work in the store daytimes and evenings in the house on the Point. Nothing seemed too much.

Dorothy was away most of that day, going with Herb to all his suppliers, changing his accounts to the new ownership, ordering stock for the store. She had nothing to go by except Herb's customary orders, and both of us had a taste for fancier groceries. So she bought the kind of things she normally kept in her own pantry. Her invoices were her own household shopping list—magnified.

I stayed at the store. Jean and Susan, the two village girls, had to be told what to do next; Chris and his helpers had questions which had to be answered as they worked at top speed; the utilities had to be turned on. Also I naïvely imagined that the stock Dorothy was buying would begin pouring in almost at once. I had yet to learn how long you waited between buying anything and getting what you had bought.

We reached the scrubbing stage. Though the store was bright with daylight from the big show windows in front and windows halfway down the side wall, we needed light to get in the corners, and we had no electricity. Chris helpfully looked for and found the main switch. He flipped it, and nothing happened.

I ran across the lot to Herb, who was waiting on customers in the little store.

"Could be there's something wrong with a wire. Guess you'll have to get Will."

And so we acquired Will. You could say Will went with the place, but it was more accurate to say the place didn't go without Will. I wouldn't know whether to call him an electrician or a master mechanic, but he could make things work when no one else could.

There is no doubt that the store's electrical system was complex to begin with and that Will was an authentic genius. It is also true that he alone, of all the electricians around, could follow the devious paths of wires and cables in the store. He carried in his head a map of what years of home repairs, amateur tinkering, and emergency improvisations had done to the system. We found that on those occasions when we couldn't get Will—typically, he had no phone—anybody else who came in would throw up his hands and say, "What you really ought to do is tear out that whole wall and . . ." When Will came he said not a word about what we should or shouldn't do. He brought a length of wire and a couple of plugs, and with pliers and shears he got the system running again. Each time Will picked up his tools after doing a job we had the feeling he had just saved us six hundred dollars.

Unfortunately Will also had a friend, and his friend had less endearing talents. He knew everything and he told everything he knew. He was tirelessly sociable. Will did not talk at all, but his friend talked enough for two. When Will was working in the store the sound of his friend's voice was continuous.

At first I took him for Will's helper. He handed tools and offered suggestions. Then I noticed that Will accepted neither the tools nor the advice. More often than not Will reached around the wrench his friend held out, to pick up a screw driver instead, and went on doing what he was doing no matter what his friend counseled. But the goodhearted fellow was in no way discouraged.

Will's friend was helpful. He was not only helpful to Will,

he was helpful to all of us. He was especially determined to be helpful to me. Probably because I was an out-of-stater and could be presumed not to know much of anything, he dogged my footsteps, and his friendly admonitions were a constant obbligato to all my thoughts and actions.

I was so unsure of myself in even the smallest tasks I undertook—let alone in the role of junior storekeeper—that if Imp or Spike were to offer advice I would probably have bent a respectful ear.

When I struggled to open a crate with a screw driver as I had seen men do, Will's friend came over and stood with his hands on his hips, not offering to open the crate for me but suggesting, "Why don't you go at it from the other side? Seems to me I remember when my cousin Nate used to work for Swift's he always used to tell me—"

So I obediently straightened my back and went around to insert the screw driver on the other side, and pried and pushed and tugged all over again while attending to the words of wisdom uttered long ago by Will's friend's cousin Nate on the subject of opening crates.

When I got all ready to wash the big show windows, with a bottle of prepared window-washing fluid and the softest cloths I could find, Will's friend was at my shoulder the moment I raised my arm for the first stroke.

"What you want to use that stuff for? Plain water's the best window washer there is and it don't cost a dime! Why, when my Uncle Harry's second wife used to run the boarding house down by the sawmill, I used to tell her . . ." I put down my bottle and cloth and went for a bucket of water. After fighting the grime of five years with plain water and achieving no results except a weary arm, I took up the bottled stuff again. My trust in Will's friend's counsel dimmed as the windowpane brightened.

Hurrying past Chris as he bent to put the last touch of immaculate white on the vegetable counter, I stopped to admire. "Isn't that handsome! It lights up the whole back of the store!"

Will's friend, at my shoulder, said, "Can't see why you painted that counter white. That white'll be all splashed and marked up in a week. Now a good dark brown, I always say—"

"Not brown!" I exclaimed. "It's so gloomy!"

"Why, all the stores I ever was in had good dark brown on their counters, and you know there's always a reason why people do a thing one way instead of some other way. Why, one winter when I was up to Lewiston—" And I found myself in an argument which ended only when I realized that Chris hadn't even looked up, let alone offered a word on brown versus white, and I was wasting precious time.

All the time we were working, early-comers to Goose Rocks kept dropping in to see what we were doing and express their joy at the prospect of having the big store and the Casino in operation again. Some of these, who rented their houses for the summer, had come to put things in order for their tenants and incidentally snatch a taste of Maine for themselves. Others came early to their pleasant houses—and also stayed late—because they loved the serenity of Goose Rocks out of season even more than the summer's gaiety. One of these was Mrs. West, next-door neighbor to our town house, whose hospitality, Dorothy told me, was famous in southern Maine.

"I hope you're going to have those wonderful things in cans and jars that I'm not supposed to eat," Mrs. West said to me. I walked her over to the wall of shelves Chris was putting up near the front of the store and told her about the table delicacies we planned to have there.

"Then I won't need to write and order from Boston—I'll just come in and buy everything from you!" Mrs. West ex-

claimed joyfully. With equal joy I looked over the printed
list she took from her handbag, with the most tempting items
already marked.

And there was Will's friend's head between us, and his
forefinger with the broken nail pointing to Imported Swedish
Cheese Biscuits in Tins. "You going to pay over two dollars
for them crackers from overseas? Pretzels go just as good
with beer!"

Mrs. West drew back, but instantly warmed the distance
she had placed between herself and Will's friend with a
smile. "Oh, I like pretzels, too, but these are new and I want
to try them."

"Just a waste of good money. Now I remember—" Will's
friend began, and Mrs. West smiled and said she would bring
the list over when I had more time, and quickly left.

Matters came to a crisis when the kindly advice of Will's
friend began to spoil sales. If Will happened to be working
in the store, I was never sure I could sell even a bar of soap.
Let a customer ask for Lux, and Will's friend was right there
to recommend Ivory—or more likely some little-known brand
we didn't even carry—"one cent cheaper and washes just as
clean!" And one day I was doing my best with a jar of crayfish bisque with Chablis off the fine-groceries shelves, and was
telling the customer—a newcomer to Goose Rocks—how one
of our Goose Rocks hostesses had tried it out for us on her
dinner guests and what a sensational success it had been. The
customer gave ladylike signs that her mouth was watering—
as was my own, by that time—when Will's friend's hand
reached between the customer and the jar, and Will's friend
picked up the jar and turned it over to look at the price. Naturally the price was the last subject I wanted brought into the
discussion at that point, and the number of jars necessary to
serve a dinner party of eight was the next to last. Will's
friend conscientiously drew attention to them both, and

added, "Why, this here's the same stuff made by that fellow down on the Cape, only it's got a different label and costs four times as much. Look here, that fellow down on the Cape, he sells his clam chowder for twenty-nine cents a can—"

And I found myself involved in a hopeless effort to convince Will's friend that crayfish bisque and clam chowder were not the same, while the customer quietly slipped away.

I spoke to Dorothy. She was gentle but firm. Everybody felt the same about Will's friend, but nobody did anything about him. When Will came, his friend came too. It was the general belief that he was indispensable to Will's happiness, and Will, who wasted neither word nor gesture, did not contradict the belief. Everyone was careful not to offend Will's friend, for fear of offending Will. So I coped with Will's friend the best I could. We could not get along without Will.

We endured Will's friend all that summer because Will kept us going, working miracles with the deep freezes and the refrigerator room and the meat display cases and all the other mechanical mysteries which he alone understood. He reached his creative peak when he converted three ancient ice-cream boxes into additional containers for our frozen foods. One of our art student customers painted an elegant sign: FROZEN FOOD DEP'T, which we hung over the door to the stockrooms. If any of our customers had ventured beyond the sign, they would have been horrified at the beat-up old boxes which DEP'T represented. But those boxes kept the foods frozen and unspoiled, thanks to Will.

Once, only once, did Will come alone, and then it was to shut things off for the winter. The season was ended, the store closed. We asked, "Where's your friend?"

"He's no friend of mine," Will said. "Don't know why he comes when he does. Can't seem to get that fellow off my neck. Plain nuisance to me, that's what he is." Dorothy and

I were staggered. Had we really put up with that character all summer long for nothing? When we and Will himself could have been rid of him simply by having the courage to take a strong stand? It seems we had.

Incidentally, this was the longest consecutive speech I ever heard Will make.

𝕨 *4* 𝕨

Twenty-Four Hours to Go

It was our last day. Four of our precious five had flown by. Herb had closed his store at ten o'clock the night before, and everybody had been dropping in on us to ask when we planned to open. So the first thing we did that morning when we got to the store was to put a sign in the window:

OPENING IN 24 HOURS
D. B. Mignault, G. Mackenzie

I went all prickly with pleasure to see my name there; Dorothy wasn't obliged to do it. By putting my name up with hers she automatically gave me status. People would talk to me; I was one of the owners.

"There," Dorothy said, her thumb on the one corner of the sign which wouldn't stick, "that will reassure them that they're going to have a store."

When we turned back to the store it was we who needed reassuring. Twenty-four hours!

We had come a long way. The place was shining, what one could see of it from the front, except for sawdust and shavings from Chris's carpentry. The refrigerator room and deep freezes were down to the proper temperature. Will had the machinery humming. The plumbing had shown its evil nature only once so far, and Andrew Austin had fixed it. There was ice in the ice room; you kept meats and cheeses and dairy stuff (we had none yet) in the electric refrigerator room, but you liked to keep fruits and vegetables where there was ice. Housewives, who know what happens to unprotected vegetables in their electric refrigerators, know the reason for that as well as storekeepers. I didn't, but I learned.

The stockrooms were filling up. The small one had maybe twenty cases of Coca-Cola and fifty of soda pop—eventually we kept twenty-seven different flavors—and tobaccos, candies, and other small stuff. The big one was stacked helter-skelter with cases and tins of crackers, cereals, and packaged goods I never dreamed existed. What wouldn't fit into the stockrooms was beginning to collect in the middle of the store, on our beautiful floor painted like a deck in battleship gray. It had taken gallons of expensive deck paint to cover the nauseous orange color; you could have painted the decks of the U.S.S. *Missouri,* I swore, with less. But even the *Missouri* couldn't have looked more shipshape. Incidentally, we had lost one of our irreplaceable workdays while the floor was drying.

Nothing was on the shelves because the shelves were still being painted. They and the walls and the counters were as we had dreamed them, gleaming white.

Dorothy and I looked over the stock. Something was missing, and at first we couldn't tell what it was.

"Of course, canned goods!" Dorothy exclaimed.

"Didn't you buy any?" I asked.

"Yes, and we bought Herb's too."

"We did?" I remembered the item on the legal-size sheet in the sale contract; it was one of the few in the interminable list which I had understood. But what had we bought, and where was it? Neither of us had thought to ask. "I'll go see Herb."

I ran across the lot to what we were now calling our "town house." We would be living in it the next day. Herb was in his parlor, puttering over his possessions, packing.

"Where's the stock we bought, Herb? Besides the stock in the store here?"

"My, I dunno. Guess it must be in the attic up over the guesthouse."

"How much is there? What is it, cases or what?"

But Herb's attention was wandering; he had retired from storekeeping in spirit from the moment he closed his little store.

"Well, I'll get Will to go up," I said, and ran back to the store.

Will departed to get the cases. I bent a polite but deaf ear to Will's friend, who promptly transferred his sociable attentions to me.

"Miss Mackenzie!" Susan called from the soda fountain where she was polishing chrome and nickel. The fountain was a beauty now that it was shining clean. It had twelve wells for ice cream, spigots for ten flavors, two taps each for water and fizz, and it seated twenty-one on stools.

"Miss Mackenzie, when you getting the fountain working? The ice cream'll be coming in."

Automatically I looked for Will; he was over in the guesthouse attic. I ran over there.

Will put his head down through the trap door, listened, and said merely, "Not my work."

Something Will couldn't fix? I wouldn't believe it. But he was firm, shaking his head. I went back to Herb.

"Herb, what about the soda fountain?"

Herb at once looked animated, put down the indistinguishable object he was holding, and walked spryly to his own little ice-cream wells. "Here, come on and I'll show you how to scoop ice cream—"

"You showed me yesterday, Herb." Herb was doing his best to teach us the storekeeper's trade, but there really wasn't time. "I mean, how do we get the fountain working—

the power for freezing, fizz water coming out of the taps, all that?"

The pause, while Herb pushed his glasses up and down on his nose; but I didn't hurry him. It didn't help to hurry them; they just took longer. It was the hardest thing I had to learn in Maine, I think, to contain my impatience; to ask my fast question, and then stand and wait while they got the slow words out one by one, water falling drop by reluctant drop.

Herb said finally, "The Hood's man comes to do that. Didn't you call the Hood's man?"

"No, Herb, I don't think so."

"Well, he won't come if you don't tell him. You just get the Hood's man."

Maybe Dorothy did tell Hood's when she was there ordering ice cream. Find Dorothy.

Dorothy was out in the turnaround, with a man. "Dorothy, the soda fountain—"

Dorothy, a lady even under the stress of setting up a store, introduced the man: "Mr. Riley, of Gulf. We're discussing putting in gasoline pumps again. They used to be here, you know; the tanks still are. It's a useful service—"

"To the community," I finished for her. By now I was ribbing Dorothy about the service angle, but she wouldn't rise. She merely gave me a smile, which I interpreted to mean, "You'll learn, smarty."

"It's useful to the storekeeper, too," Mr. Riley put in. "A man waiting for gas goes in to buy cigarettes, thinks he'll have a soda, picks up a magazine, remembers something his wife needs for dinner, goes home and tells his wife what a nice place you have here—and you've got a new customer."

He was a very attractive man, Mr. Riley. I said, "Sure, let's have gas pumps. Dorothy, did you tell Hood's to send their man to get the fountain working?"

"I don't think so, Scotty," Dorothy said vaguely. She had

something else on her mind, and in the seconds before she told me I guessed it was bad news. "Scotty, Cora can't get here today. Her daugher needs her."

I was horrified. No cook! "When will she come?"

"She couldn't say. Maybe not for a week or so."

I said, "Well, then we can't open the restaurant tomorrow."

"Oh, but we must!" Dorothy exclaimed. "There's nowhere else in town the art students can afford to eat—regularly, that is."

"But, Dorothy, who'll cook for them?"

Dorothy said, "I will, until Cora gets here."

I was speechless, having no idea whether Dorothy was, in her quiet way, slightly out of her mind. "The fountain," I muttered at last, and fled.

Back in the store, at the telephone, I gave no more thought to Dorothy and the cooking. I was seeing mountains of ice cream being delivered and melting on the gray-painted floor.

I told my story to Hood's. When could they put the fountain in working order?

"Oh, yes, Goose Rocks. We'll get the man there."

"When?"

"Couple of days, Miss, we'll take care of it, don't worry."

"Oh, no, you've got to come today! We're opening the store tomorrow morning—why, you're delivering ice cream to us today!" I wasn't sure they were, but I was concentrating my fire power.

"Don't see how we can help you out today. There's just one man in Maine who does that work. He's up above Portland—"

"I want a promise. You've got to find him wherever he is and get him down here today!"

Couldn't promise, but they'd try.

In Maine they boast about how they keep their word. They do keep it; they never give it! You find a little leak in your roof—stormy weather is coming—and you call and ask to have it fixed now instead of waiting until the storm brings the whole roof down. "Well, I'll try to make it. Got some other jobs—"

"Tomorrow?" you ask.

"Maybe—"

And if he does come tomorrow and you express joyful surprise, he says, "Told you I'd come, didn't I?"

But if he doesn't come for days, and the storms come first and blow your roof off, when you call up and berate him he says, "Well, now, I didn't give you my word, did I?"

There was nothing more I could do about the fountain but wait. Will came bringing cases, and I went to see what they were. I was almost afraid to look. What if they were package stuff, aged crackers, cereals full of cereal worms? I had never seen a cereal worm but I must have heard of them because the thought popped into my head. Worms to me were synonymous with snakes, and snakes belonged with mice in my private list of things to avoid at all costs.

I watched Will pry the first case open with a screw driver. On the outside of the case it said DEL MONTE CAL. PEACHES and a picture of the can, but I would believe when I saw with my own eyes.

It was peaches, and they were in cans. The next case was pineapple, the next prunes—which I would have called plums, from the picture on the label—and then fruit salad; then some vegetables, and so on. There were about two dozen cases, one variety to a case.

I took up a can and turned it in my hands. The label was brown, stained, curling off in places. I took up another and another; they were all the same.

"Herb's sold us spoiled stock," I said.

"Them ain't spoiled," Will rebuked me. "The cans ain't swoll."

Probably everybody in the world but Mackenzie knew that cans were good if they weren't swollen. Still, I couldn't see putting those shabby old labels on our bright shelves.

"Stow them away in the stockroom, please, Will," I said, and determined to be on the lookout for a way to get our money out of those old cans without selling them to our own customers.

Somewhere along there, while Will and I were opening the cases, Dorothy came in to say she was going to drive down the main road with Mr. Riley and count the gas stations. At least that's what I thought she said, and it sounded all right at the time, although later I was sure any gasoline salesman worth his commission would know how many gas stations there were in the neighborhood and whose gas they sold. She also said she might stay out to lunch. And she went away.

Things were popping too fast for me to give thought to Dorothy's departure. She'd gone to lunch with an attractive man and there was nothing unusual about that. I only wished that I were in her shoes, as to lunch especially, because I'd had nothing since a cup of coffee at six that morning.

Herb came shambling in to say he had found some negatives of photographs of Goose Rocks homes which a post-card photographer had once taken, and maybe we'd like to order post cards. The news dealer drove up with a load of magazines and wanted to know whether we would simply continue Herb's newspaper order or did we want some others?

"Send 'em all—Portland, Boston, New York!" I said grandly, with no notion of the trouble I was brewing for myself. Nobody told me that the Sunday papers would come bundled according to sections, and that we would have to assemble each paper ourselves. When you handle twelve different newspapers for four hundred and fifty families, and they all come in at once on Sunday morning to get their papers—well, you get the idea. The man who wanted the Boston *Post* sports section was sure to get the Portland classified instead, and the woman who waited breathless for the *Times* garden page was not enchanted with the financial news from Boston. But the news dealer drove away well pleased with the journalistic broad-mindedness of the new store management.

Hood's arrived, on schedule with the ice cream but without the soda-fountain mechanic. There was nothing to be done but send the ice cream back again, with a fervent prayer that it would be delivered in the morning and that the fountain would be ready to receive it.

I appeased the truck driver; I found I got along well with truck drivers. In fact, I found I was a truck driver at heart myself. I was never happier, that summer and afterward, than when I was tooling along the road at six in the morning in the lively little truck we inherited from Herb, with the back loaded with fruit and vegetables and crates of luscious Maine berries.

I had never, in my city incarnation, been up at six in the morning except after a long night of club-hopping ending with a jam session in some hep-cat dive. But six in the morning, when it's the beginning of a new day rather than the end of an old one, is something to discover, and especially in Maine. There, the world is created brand-new every morning. There is a pearliness about the sky and sea, translucent and faintly flushed like the pearly inside of a sea shell you held in your hand when you were a child, and on the other side of the road the pines march by, dark and somber and glistening, the aisles between their pillared trunks inviting you to explore. The air you breathe has a cool clarity like water from a spring, and it carries a variety of perfumes never captured in bottles labeled *Shocking* or *Je Reviens,* the smell of moist green things and the earth they grow in, the fugitive scent of wild roses and the undercurrent of tangy pine, a whiff of sawdust, mingled with lettuce and green onions and strawberries from the back of my own truck, and always the seasoning, in Maine, of the salt sea. A pinch of salt, as Dorothy maintains in the kitchen, brings out the flavor of everything, even sweet things.

And now and again there was the rank odor of lobster bait, the Chanel No. 5 of the Maine coast, but it came and went quickly as I drove on my way, and I learned to love even that essence of putrefying skate in my six-in-the-morning happiness.

At this moment I was experiencing none of the joys, only the pains, of being a storekeeper. The Hood's truckman sympathized about the soda fountain and promptly floored me with the news that the dairy branch of his company had no milk order for us.

Hadn't Miss Mignault given it?

No, Miss Mignault had not. So it was up to me.

"Tell them to double Herb Atwood's normal order," said I, thinking big as usual. "Oh, and we're going to want heavy cream." Country stores I had known generally didn't carry it; it's expensive and luxurious and it spoils fast in the summer. But I had wanted heavy cream for my coffee ever since I had come to Goose Rocks, and heavy cream I was going to have. What's the good of owning a store if you can't have the things you like to eat and drink yourself?

"Right," said the Hood's man, and drove merrily off. Behind him was the Kraft man, with cheese and mayonnaise and such. The refrigerator room, I remembered with satisfaction, was working, thanks to Will. And then a horrible thought struck me: was it clean? Jean and Susan had been scrubbing all day, but in the store. I couldn't remember sending them into the refrigerator room.

The driver brought in the cases, and I ran ahead to learn the worst: the room was cold but it wasn't clean. No litter, but the dust and stains of five years were still on the shelves. Of course it should have been scrubbed before the refrigerating machinery was turned on. Any housewife who has moved into a new house and had to stock her kitchen from scratch would know that. But maybe even an experienced housewife would have forgotten to ready the refrigerator if the carpenters and painters were still working while she was moving in, the utilities being turned on, and the repairman waiting for orders. And she would have to multiply her problems by about five hundred to compare them with ours; we were stocking the kitchen for a whole village.

The driver asked, "Where do you want these, Miss?"

I couldn't send him back, too. I said in desperation, "Put them down in the middle of the store. We'll move them in when the room is ready."

I called the two girls over and told them the difficulty.

"You don't need to put mayonnaise in the refrigerator until it's opened, Miss Mackenzie," Jean pointed out. "The jars stand on the shelves."

"Oh, that's so. But the cheeses!"

"Oh, them."

The girls sounded discouraged, and they were dropping with weariness. They couldn't last much longer. I yearned for Dorothy, but Dorothy wasn't back.

"Tell you what," I said. "You two get the refrigerator room clean, and then you stop. I'll get someone to finish in the store." But whom? Not Mrs. Keene. "Do you know anybody I could get?"

"Try Mrs. Cobb."

Mrs. Cobb lived on the same road as Mrs. Keene. But if I went up there and the girls were in the back, there would be no one in the store except Chris, who was too busy finishing the shelves to be bothered by deliveries. And the Hood's man might come to fix the fountain. Where in heaven's name was Dorothy? It was three-thirty; I'd wait until four.

The girls took their pails and brushes and went out in back. I looked down at my feet; I had been dimly aware that the dogs had been following me around, and now I saw them sitting there, looking hopeful. They hadn't been fed. And neither had I.

I reached under the counter for the box of Gro-Pup we had brought with us that morning and fed them. Without thinking, I stuffed a handful into my own mouth. It wasn't half bad, unseasoned and rather dry but clean and needing no dishes or silver to eat with. I gobbled another handful. For the next six days I lunched on Gro-Pup with the dogs, until I had sense enough to figure out a lunch hour for myself. And that's no easy one to solve. The help have their time off for lunch, but when does the storekeeper eat? Whenever the boss sits down to a cup of coffee, some customer is bound to come in who won't be waited on by anybody else. Dorothy was so forgetful of eating that her doctor punished her with giant-sized liver shots when he came up for a visit in midsummer.

I waited until four. Summer people kept coming in to say hello, to see how the store was going to look; they'd been doing that all day. It was very social, especially when Dorothy was there, but when they found only me, whom most of them were meeting for the first time, the greetings were brief though friendly. Each time I told them that Dorothy was out but would be back, I got madder and madder at Dorothy. How could she abandon me this way?

At four I called one of the girls out of the refrigerator room, and I got into the car with the dogs; fortunately Dorothy had gone off in the good-looking Mr. Riley's car, so at least I had transportation. I remembered all too well the way to Mrs. Keene's and went on past her house to Mrs. Cobb's.

Why don't these people like me? I thought as I drove. Despite my slick selling techniques, my confidence was nil that I could persuade a Maine woman to come and clean for me though cleaning was her business and I would pay. Now I can see myself as they saw me, a young woman with bare legs below and a boy's cap on top, driving around the country in a showy car with the top down and two sleek and, by their standards, useless little dogs in the front, and ordering people around. The car and the dogs were Dorothy's, but they liked Dorothy and so I took the rap for her. And however hard I tried to follow the ritual of Maine courtesy in which you never asked anybody outright for anything, I'm sure there was always that executive ring in my voice. Try as I might to go around it, I always managed somehow to come to the point, and in Maine that's what you never, never do.

I still think Mrs. Cobb would have refused me. But actually I didn't stay to find out. An unforeseen circumstance with horns and four legs intervened.

I drove halfway up Mrs. Cobb's rutted road, and there was a cow tied to a tree with its rear half blocking the way. I honked the horn, the cow snorted, and the dogs were out and after her. I leaped after them, snatched Imp with one arm, lifted Spike out of hoof's range on my instep, and got them back somewhat scrambled into the car. I was more than a little scrambled myself. I had never been that close to a cow.

With all the hubbub Mrs. Cobb had come out on her porch. I waited for her to come down, either to remove the cow or to find out what I wanted. But she stood there. So, barricaded behind the car, holding the dogs down, I had to shout my story across the cow's back and fifty-odd feet of Maine country.

She asked, with a minimum show of interest, "What kind of work is it?" And before I could reply, without provocation the cow snorted again, the dogs jumped, and I grabbed them in mid-air. Again she made no move to succor me.

"That's rather a cross-tempered cow you have there," I remarked laughingly. What I meant was, *Don't stand there —do something!*

But she stood on her porch, arms folded, and answered, "Why else do you think we keep him tied up?"

Him. I stopped laughing and was in the car and out of that driveway without knowing how.

I drove back without a cleaning woman. I'd been scared to death, and because I was scared I was angry. Strictly speaking, I had no logical excuse for anger, since the bull was tied up. But if I hadn't been mad I'd have been sunk. I was mad clear through, with no room in me for being sorry for myself. By the time I arrived at the store I was going to show Mrs. Cobb and Mrs. Keene and Dorothy and her Gulf salesman and all of Maine—yes, even the bull—that if I had to open the store all by myself I would do it, by heaven, and no thanks to anybody.

I stalked into the store. No Dorothy. Susan and Jean were waiting for me. The refrigerator room was clean, and they were dabbing at the glass and mahogany showcase, but they were tired out and their hearts weren't in it. Chris was waiting, too. FRESH PAINT signs were everywhere. Cases and cartons stood like a barricade across the middle of the floor. The dogs walked around them with a sniff and went to a corner to lie down.

I thanked the girls and sent them home to their dinner. I walked around with Chris, admiring his handiwork, absorbing a few taunts at my ignorance, and then he went home to his dinner. Through the big show windows I looked up and down the road. All over Goose Rocks, people were going home to their dinners, from the beach, from the golf courses, from sailing in their boats, from gardening in their gardens, all going into their houses to have their dinners. Only I had to stay here, alone and working, without any dinner. (I have never been able to explain why, famished as I was, I stood in the middle of a store full of food and never thought of opening a can or breaking into a box.)

I looked for the dogs, just for company, but they were asleep in their corner, curled up together. They didn't need me; they had each other. Dorothy had her Gulf salesman. Only I was alone.

But I wasn't. Up from behind the soda fountain, scaring me half to death, rose slowly a brown bald spot, then a fringe of thin white hair, and then the face of an old, old man. As he got painfully to his feet and rested his hands on the counter I saw that he held a screw driver. The soda-fountain expert!

But for me he was the *deus ex machina*, the god in the Greek plays who comes down from Olympus and puts everything right. He certainly didn't look like a Greek god, and he was cross at being kept from his own dinner, but I could barely restrain myself from throwing my arms around his wrinkled old neck and kissing him on his bald head, I was so glad to see a human soul at that bleak moment.

"How's it going?" I asked, bouncy and cheerful as though it were the top of the morning and there weren't a mountain of work ahead of me which I didn't know how to do.

"Well, she's troublesome," he wheezed. "Lots to do still before she'll run."

"Never mind, it will all come out all right," I caroled. As on wings I flew to the refrigerator room. It was clean as a pin; I could have eaten off the floor if I'd had anything to eat.

I flew back to the rampart of cases and boxes. Somewhere in that pile were cheeses. I began to root them out and carry them into the refrigerator room.

I discovered that a case of twenty-four cans is heavy. I also discovered that a case of grapefruit juice is heavier than any other. It can't be the juice, because every can that size holds sixteen ounces net whatever its contents, and it can't be psychological, though it's true I don't care for grapefruit juice, because other storekeepers have since told me the same. Grapefruit juice and all, I had to learn in the next hour how to swing those cases without breaking myself in two.

One, two, heave, and a case of tomato soup came off the top, barking my shin on the way down. One, two, heave, and beets came down, landing on my sandaled toe. One, two, heave, baked beans hit the floor, and I sat down on the beans.

This is no work for a woman, I thought, panting, and then I thought, Why isn't it? I was young, healthy, strong for my size, with plenty of tennis and golf and swimming behind me. Wasn't I the long-ball hitter on our softball team at Miss Raleigh's School for Young Ladies? Like everything else, from promoting a product to playing a game, this called for a technique.

Concentrating on working out a technique made it easier. A barked shin or a clipped toe still made me jump, but it also made me figure out where I had missed. When I finally got to the cheeses I was aching in every bone and muscle, and you could have wrung me out, but I was getting my back into it. I did have the rueful thought, as I carried the cheeses which now felt light as feathers, that when I next got into a strapless evening gown they'd take me for a lady wrestler. By the end of the summer I could swing a case of soda bottles by the hand-hold at one end, in one motion from the car to the loading platform, a spectacular skill which I performed not to show off but to get the unloading done in a hurry because there was so much else to do. By that time I also had a muscle in my right forearm like Big Bill Tilden's, though tennis to me had become part of a paradise inhabited by everybody who didn't keep store.

When I had the cheeses all put away, I went to the soda fountain and peeked over. I hadn't heard a sound from the ancient repairman for ever so long. He was so very, very old that I thought he might just lie down behind the fountain, fold his arms on his breast, and go peacefully to his reward, and I'd never know it.

He was there, quietly turning screws and splicing wires and doing whatever mechanics do to make things work. He turned his gnomish face up with a querulous look.

"Just checking," I said brightly, and went back to my task.

On one side of the store the paint, being yesterday's, was dry on the shelves. I might as well begin putting up the stock.

But which to put on what shelves? There must be a system; everything has a system. There must be some reason why canned fruit goes one place in a store, canned vegetables in another, crackers in another; why sugar, flour, cereals, soaps, and cleansers all have their right places. Even Herb's little store must have had some sort of pattern. If I'd ever shopped for a household I'd have some idea what the store pattern ought to be. If Dorothy were here she could tell me. But I'd never shopped, except once in a while at the delicatessen, and Dorothy was not there. I had to do it myself.

5

Night Shift

The only way I know to do a thing I don't know how to do is to plunge in and do it. Right or wrong, you're doing something about it and that's better than standing around biting your thumbs, asking yourself questions you can't answer. If you're right you're pleased with yourself, and contrariwise, events will show you soon enough if you're wrong. So I began tearing boxes open and putting stuff on the shelves.

An elementary sense of order dictated that like should be with like, at least, and it seemed simple enough to put all the peas together, all the beans, all the tomatoes, fruits separate from vegetables, cereals from soap powders. Simple. But I had no idea what tangles even such simple rules could get me into. I had no sooner got all the tomatoes up, with the peas on one side of them and the beans on the other, the labels all uniformly facing front, than a new crop of tomatoes came up from another canner. Down came the beans, up went the tomatoes, up went the beans again, and then I discovered tomato sauce. And tomato juice. Should tomato things go together, or should sauces go with sauces, juices with juices?

My orderliness had also misled me into beginning with the top shelf so that I could work down. I quickly discovered I could save climbing the ladder with every pair of cans by stacking them first on the highest shelf I could reach from the floor. And then, after I had a whole top shelf filled, it dawned on me that high shelves should be used only for things infrequently demanded or for things light enough to get down with the gadget on a long handle I had seen in Herb's store. Down came the cans again, and up went breakfast cereals, and presently paper goods like tissues and towels. By this time I wondered how I had ever managed to get through first grade.

Dinner in Maine is supper, and luckily for me it's over early. I had been at this arduous game of putting up and taking down no more than three-quarters of an hour when Dr. Curtis, Herb's son-in-law, bustled in at the door.

"All alone? Where's your partner?"

It was on the tip of my tongue to tell him where I thought she deserved to be, but I refrained. "She'll be along. Did you come all the way down from Biddeford to help us?"

"Well, I've had you girls on my mind. My wife's over helping the old folks with their packing, but I guess you need help more than they do." He was looking at the stock piled higher than his head. "Takes more work than anybody'd think, to set up a store, doesn't it?"

He took off his coat and laid it neatly across the soda fountain where he was sure there was no wet paint. The ancient popped his head up and said, "Good evenin'," and vanished again below. Dr. Curtis started, but quickly recovered and went right to work. He pulled the top carton down and attacked it briskly with his pocketknife. He was a dentist and a very good dentist too, but I doubt that he would have many patients if he attacked a tooth with the fiendish vigor with which he attacked those boxes.

Jean and Susan, bless their loyal hearts, came in. They had had their supper and were quite restored, but they had also changed to fresh dresses. I was aware that the kitchen hadn't yet been touched, the stockrooms were a shambles, and the ice room was in no condition for the fruit and vegetables which I assumed would be arriving in the morning. But I hadn't the heart to put them to scrubbing again. They weren't cleaning women, they were store clerks. And they had to be fit for work in the morning.

Jean said, "Oh, Miss Mackenzie, you can't put things on the shelves that way. First place, they have to have the prices on them!"

Prices. With all my strictly business mind I had forgotten that this stuff was to be sold—and at a profit or we'd soon be out of business. But how do you set prices?

We looked at each other blankly. The girls remembered a good many prices, but from the summer before, and they were reluctant to take responsibility in so vital a matter. Once more I longed for Dorothy, but even Dorothy wouldn't know the answer to this one.

"Herb would know," I ventured.

"Herb's gone to bed by now," Dr. Curtis said. And then through the door came Ben Beebe.

This was pure human kindness. It's true it's good business for a jobber to be helpful to his customers, especially new ones, but there's no call for him to give up his evening and most of the night to setting them up in business. He had come down from Biddeford to look in and see how we were getting on. When he saw, he rolled up his sleeves like Dr. Curtis and prepared to stay to the end.

"Prices? You need Herb's old invoices for that," he told us.

I looked at Dr. Curtis, who smiled and shook his head. "We'd be all night trying to find them."

"Well, then, we'll just price everything ourselves. Take the wholesale price on a case, divide by twenty-four pieces in the case, add a cent each for delivery—you're entitled to that—and seventeen per cent markup, and there's your price. For instance, the peaches—"

Now I'm no worse at arithmetic than most people. My check stubs match the bank statement at least fifty per cent of the time and my income-tax returns cause only a slight increase in the sales of aspirin each year in March. I lifted the new invoices off the spindle where they'd been accumulating with each delivery and stood there holding them helplessly in my hands. Finally Ben took them from me and fished a pencil out of his pocket.

In a little while we were organized like an assembly line. Dr. Curtis would rip open a crate. The girls and I, sitting on the floor with stubs of black pencils—we had hunted all over for marking pencils without success, and at last cut one Ben had in his pocket into three pieces—scrawled the price on each can or box as Ben called it out. Then one of us, whoever wasn't too stiff to get up, would put them on the shelves while we tackled the next batch.

The mountain on the floor had diminished to one case, and Dr. Curtis and I were surveying the confusion in the big stockroom, when Dorothy came waltzing in.

I hadn't thought of her once for the past hour, and it was with some surprise that I saw her standing there. Oh, yes, Dorothy!

She was glowing, whether from a day of sun and wind or from romance I couldn't tell, and she didn't offer any information on the subject. She had the tact not to ask, either, how I was doing. She calmed the dogs, who were wild with happiness to see her, and then she said, "I'll be back." And she was gone!

Not knowing what to make of this odd behavior, I dismissed it and went back to the stock.

When I looked around again, something new had been

added; our graveyard shift of workers had been sizably increased. Voices came from the kitchen; there was Dorothy, directing three—count 'em, three!—robust cleaning women. She had brought back good-natured Abby Peace, who had been working in the house on the Point all day, cleaning it for the tenants. And not only Abby, but Mrs. Keene and Mrs. Cobb. Abby greeted me like a long-lost daughter, Mrs. Keene looked up from the sink and said, "Good evenin'," and Mrs. Cobb bobbed her head and bent to the gas range.

Dorothy said to them serenely, "If there's anything you need, call me," and put her arm around my shoulders and walked back with me into the store.

Things moved along in an agreeable blur for me after that. We went on writing prices and putting things on shelves. Dorothy's Gulf salesman—who was Jack to us all by this time—relieved Dr. Curtis at carrying in crates from the stockroom. Ben continued his lightning calculations, and the shelves filled up. Abby Peace and Mesdames Keene and Cobb went from kitchen to ice room to stockrooms, and back to the store to sweep up sawdust and painters' mess and the litter of our unpacking. And I have a distinct picture of Dorothy sitting on the floor, opening boxes of chocolate marshmallow cookies one after another and passing them around, like a hostess at a party.

Sometime during the evening the aged genius—whom we had all forgotten—emerged from behind the soda fountain. We watched him gravely while he put on his coat, assembled his tools, accepted a chocolate marshmallow cooky from Dorothy, said "Good evenin'," and disappeared into the night.

Gradually the emergency staff melted away. Dr. Curtis, having hauled and opened the last crate, said good night and went to collect his wife, who had been waiting for hours at her father's house to be taken home. Ben Beebe, that good man, shook our limp hands, wished us luck, and departed. Jack Riley offered to drive Jean and Susan home, and then Dorothy pressed him into driving the three women home. When he came back, I was lying flat on the floor with my mouth open, and Dorothy was feeding me and herself the last of the chocolate marshmallow cookies.

"You girls need some solid food," said Jack, and persuaded us up off the floor and into his car. It was past two in the morning, but the thought of food got me half awake, anyway. We had to drive to Biddeford, where the all-night diner was the only place for miles open at that hour. I remember that as I stuffed hamburgers Dorothy said confidently, "Ours will be better," and Jack Riley said, "I'll be there to sample them."

We slept that night for the last time that summer in the big house. Abby Peace had left it in good order, and we were ready to move out the next day; we had spent every night, after working in the store, getting Dorothy's possessions packed away and taking the things she wanted for the summer down to the garage to be moved. I, having come almost literally for a week end, had little more than a pair of shorts to pack.

As I fell into bed Dorothy said, "It was nice of Dr. Curtis and Ben Beebe to come over and help." She said not a word about Jack Riley, or where she had been all day. When the gas pumps came they were not Gulf but Mobilgas! Dorothy just shrugged.

🌺 6 🌺

Open for Business

I woke at five-thirty to the smell of coffee and the feel of Imp licking my face. We'd gone to bed at four, but Dorothy was already dressed and downstairs, and she had not only coffee but a fire going in the oil stove—mornings in Maine can chill you to the marrow. I popped under the shower, scrambled into shorts and a shirt, and ran downstairs. Today was the big day.

It was going to be quite something to synchronize the activities of that day. Dorothy's tenants would be arriving. Chris Marble and his crew were due in the "town house" with hammers and nails, paints and brushes, and simultaneously the cleaning women would be cleaning the house for us. We had to clear out the last of our belongings from the big house and find time to move—but not until Chris and the women had made some kind of livable order for us in our new home.

And we were opening the store! With all the other things we had to do, I had almost forgotten that the moment we had been working like steam engines to be ready for was upon us. When I thought of it I had butterflies.

It was difficult drinking my coffee, because the dogs were up and down and all over the place in their own canine super-excitement. Did they know what an important day this was?

We finished our coffee fast, rinsed the cups and the pot

and stuck them away. We stripped the beds, hauled the last laundry bag down to the kitchen entry, collected our overnight things and put them into our overnight bags. Then I drove Dorothy to the store and went to pick up the three cleaning women.

When I got back it was past seven o'clock. I had Abby Peace and Mrs. Keene and Mrs. Cobb in the car. Chris's truck was there, and Chris and Dorothy were in the house deciding on paint colors and shelves and urgent repairs. Deliverymen had begun to arrive at the store.

The breadman had already carried in his load of bread and rolls and was waiting for a signature and the next day's order; having no notion what the next day's order ought to be, I told him to repeat until we let him know otherwise. The cigarette man dumped a load of cartons on the cash counter and held out his pad for me to sign. Hood's drove up with milk, cream, cottage cheese, cream cheese, and, thank heaven, the ice-cream truck right behind. I'm not superstitious—that is, not very—but somehow this was a good omen. The ice cream was there before we opened the store, and the fountain was ready for it. O little old man from north of Portland, blessings on your bald brown head, I thought, and I knew exactly what I would do as soon as the dairy stuff and bread and cigarettes were stowed where they had to go.

When Dorothy came in she found me behind the soda fountain, madly scooping ice cream and tossing it back, patting it down and scooping again and tossing it back. It's quite a trick to scoop ice cream quickly and efficiently; if you don't think so, try it sometime. At the end of a busy evening at the fountain my right hand and arm would be numb up to the elbow, and the veins would stand out in little knots.

At the moment I was not practicing the technique of ice-cream scooping, however. I was doing something I had wanted to do ever since the days my family had a summer

place in the Adirondacks. The village storekeeper there had
our pigtail set in a state of helpless fury all summer because
the gobs of chocolate and vanilla he slapped on our ice-cream
cones were big and round on the outside all right—but inside
they were hollow. What I was doing, at last, was breaking
the secret of the hollow ice-cream scoop.

"Look!" I called to Dorothy. "This is how that stingy old
ice-cream pincher did it—scrape around the sides, cover the
edges of the scoop, and inside it's *hollow*! And this is how
we're going to do it!" I dug in and filled the scoop full and
hard and overflowing. "Ten cents' worth of ice cream in a
nickel cone. Give the kids double their money's worth—and
make up for all the hollow scoops I got when I was a kid!"

"Good," Dorothy agreed. She came around beside me and
began practicing with a scoop too. After a while she thought
we'd better figure out how to make a soda; we'd had thousands of sodas in our lives but had never watched how one
was made—have you? So we practiced making sodas. All
that day, whenever there was a lull in the store, one or the
other of us would be behind the fountain, making sodas of
every possible combination we could think of, and tasting
them. We sickened on sodas, but by the end of the day we
had the formula for the best soda we had ever tasted. (One
of our secrets was that we used light cream in them.)

In the middle of my third attempt at a black-and-white—
there was always too much sirup or too little—I thought of
something I had been trying to remember since the night
before. It came to me that the imagined music of money
clinking into a drawer was the last thing I had heard as I
fell asleep.

So I asked, "Dorothy, may I please take the cash register
this morning?"

"Of course," said Dorothy, and we came out from behind
the fountain and walked to the register.

"But, Scotty!" Dorothy exclaimed suddenly. "There's no cash!"

There were two old-style registers, one at the soda fountain and the other back in the grocery department. They were nothing more than drawers for cash, with keys you hit that registered the amount of the sale where the customer could see it, but they didn't add up for you or keep a record. Still, the drawer made a satisfying clang as you punched it open, and for now we thought these would do until we could afford the several hundred dollars for a really efficient one. It was a case of penny-wise pound-foolishness. We never knew the amount of money we lost, and particularly frustrating for two owners with market-research and promotion experience in their background was the fact that we never could tell which department was paying off and which needed a booster shot of some kind.

And we were shamefully careless with money. After all my loving care of the cash each night after closing, my counting up and separating bills and coins, like with like, I would carry it up to our rooms in the town house and wearily dump it into, of all things, a cigar box. Not until all the cigar boxes we could lay our hands on were filled to overflowing and wouldn't close, would I make the time to go to the bank. Furthermore, Dorothy and I habitually carried a roll of several hundred dollars in our jeans for cashing checks. At night, getting out of our clothes, we would empty our pockets of cash and checks onto the dresser, into a drawer, or into whatever handy receptacle we happened to be near when we undressed.

Once when I was driving to the bank all the checks blew out of the back of the open car. I had with me our friend Charmaine, who, like many of our city acquaintances, came up to see what we were doing and stayed to lend a hand. Charmaine had a Gallic respect for money, and it was at her

perfectly reasonable insistence—when she saw all that cur-
rency lying around—that we were on our way to the bank
that day. We were in a hurry to make it before the bank
closed at three, and I hadn't been able to put my hands on an
envelope, or even a rubber band, so I had stuck the checks
loose in a manila folder and put the folder on top of the
dashboard.

We were bowling along, I talking a streak to Charmaine
about the store, the people, the wholesalers, when a gust of
wind came into the car, flipped up the edge of the folder, and
carried the checks sailing out through the back. Charmaine
screamed in pain, and I jammed on the brakes. When I had
made sure she was hurt in spirit only, I began to back up.

"There! There ees one!" Charmaine pointed wildly. A
check was still fluttering across the field on our right. I pulled
over and we got out.

The wind was prankish that day. Some checks had blown
to one side of the road, some to the other, over weeds, into
brambles, even up into trees. Luckily I had taken the time, in
the rush before leaving, to write out my deposit slips; they
were in duplicate, and on the edge of the road we found one
of them. Now at least we knew how many checks we had to
retrieve, and Charmaine was unshakable in her determina-
tion to retrieve them all. We did, too, every one of them. But
we never made it to the bank that afternoon.

It was typical of our joint heedlessness about money that
on this first morning, the feverishly anticipated hour when
we would open our doors and become storekeepers in fact,
neither of us had remembered that we needed money to open
with. To drive all the way to Kennebunk to the bank was
impractical; there would be customers in the store, we fer-
vently hoped, and we would need to make change, long before I could get there and back. And I would have to wait
for the bank to open, too. Our pockets were empty; one

doesn't normally carry much cash around a summer village. You charge at the store, pay by check for the services, and when you make a shopping trip to town you cash a check there for what you expect to spend.

"The Cape Porpoise store," I suggested. "They don't know me but they'll cash your check, won't they?"

"I'm sure they will," said Dorothy, and wrote out her personal check for fifty dollars. I drove to Cape Porpoise.

Not until I was inside the store and had to meet Mr. Jenkins' eye did I realize that I was asking a considerable favor from our nearest competitor. It was a little store, much like Herb's but with gas pumps added, and here I was to take fifty dollars in cash, including all the silver and singles he would part with.

He didn't know me but he knew Dorothy well, and as I explained sheepishly how we had come to open our store without money in the till, I could see by his sidelong look that he didn't think we were going to be serious competition. He counted out the money ungrudgingly, silver and singles and fives and a couple of tens, and I thanked him with all my heart and went out of there hoping we wouldn't quite put him out of business.

That hope was just too big-hearted to stay with me long. With all Dorothy's capital sunk in this venture—to say nothing of my own small security and the credit which I had spent the years since college accumulating—who were we to wish a competitor well? It was more suitable to pray that we wouldn't go flat broke, let the competitors fall where they might. Perhaps Dorothy had already suffered in private the bleak thought that we might not make good; I hadn't, not until this moment. Not until I stood in the presence of Mr. Jenkins, in all the security of his well-established little business, and read in his wise face the certain belief that we weren't much for him to worry about. I made the last turn into Goose Rocks, swung in to the back of the store and parked, suffering from a real case of the shakes.

Inside the store I found the perfect cure for my jitters. Customers! Quite a few were walking around, just looking. Dorothy was serving coffee at the soda fountain. A woman was standing at the cash register, waiting for someone to take her money.

Someone to take her money—that could only be me! I slid in behind the cash register, clanged the drawer open with pride, and emptied Mr. Jenkins' cash into the compartments.

"I think I have the honor of being your first customer," Mrs. Sergeant said. Fran Sergeant was originally a summer resident who now lived in Goose Rocks the year round. Her children and grandchildren, too, had grown up on the beach. She was seventy-four that summer. I would have loved our first customer if she had had two heads, but Fran had the wittiest and wisest—and probably the handsomest—head it has ever been my good fortune to admire. She was a tall woman and at seventy-four she still walked like a queen, her hair a white crown above her distinguished face, and when she was in the store I used to like to watch the men and boys. All sizes and ages, they gravitated toward her, and if they didn't actually go up to her and speak their eyes kept turning to her wherever she was.

I said, "I'm so glad it's you," and I meant it. I wished I had a present to give her, but there wasn't a thing. The fancy groceries I had dreamed of had not yet materialized; the big wall of snow-white shelves which would hold them was still bare. I made a mental note to ask Dorothy if we could pick out the first fine jar of pâté and present it to Mrs. Sergeant when it came.

"Soap, cleanser, canned tomatoes, three soups, bread, butter, cottage cheese, coffee—" I ran down the list, checking the items, totted up the bill, and handed it to her with a feeling that I had been mighty efficient. My pride was due for a tumble. She paid, I made change, and the transaction was complete. I said, putting the finishing touch to it, "Thank you."

Then she asked, "How shall I carry it home?"

Not until then did I realize that we had opened the store without any paper bags!

I ducked under the counter, mainly to hide my red face, because I knew there were no bags there, no bags anywhere. If Herb had left any, they had been thrown out with the trash. And we had not thought to buy any. I didn't even know where one bought them!

Emerging once more, I said with a handsome gesture, "You don't need to carry it home. I'll deliver it, of course!"

Mrs. Sergeant said, "How nice!" and started toward the door. Halfway there she turned and called to me, "I did want some lettuce, but you don't seem to have any."

"It hasn't come yet," I fibbed readily. "I'll bring it with the order."

This was another jolt. Had Dorothy ordered any lettuce, or any fresh vegetables or fruit at all? I ducked around behind the fountain.

"Lettuce," I hissed. "Fruits and vegetables. When are they coming?"

"Dear heaven!" Dorothy murmured, and turned around to hand a cup of coffee to a customer, smiling and continuing her conversation with him unperturbed. "Yes, it is a lovely day to open the store, thank you," and to another, "I'm so glad you like the coffee—would you care for another cup?" and back to me, stage whisper, "Maybe you'd better run up to Biddeford while it's still early and we're not so busy."

I ran up to Biddeford and made the rounds of the retail markets. It was quite natural that Dorothy should not have thought of lettuce and things. Dorothy had been ordering from Herb's suppliers, and in his winter store Herb did not have lettuce; it was expensive and quick to spoil, and anyway the local people thought lettuce was for rabbits and there was no accounting for the stuff summer people would eat. But we were after the summer trade. Furthermore, we wanted lettuce for ourselves.

The lettuce in Biddeford that morning was not even fit for rabbits, and the fruits and vegetables were hardly better. This wasn't the quality of produce we wanted in our store. I telephoned Dorothy and told her.

"You'll have to go over to Kennebunkport. Try Mr. Baumgarten. He's expensive, but he carries the best. He supplies the best hotels and all the big houses."

"What shall I buy, and how much?"

There was a silence. I hadn't yet tumbled to the fact that Dorothy, who had bought all over the world—there's nothing to it!—was as perplexed as I when she had to order in quantity. Then her voice came, a little faint, "We're getting busy here—I really mustn't stop to give an order now, Scotty dear—use your judgment—"

It was stuffy in the booth. "Right, I'll take care of it," I said, and hung up. I drove over to Kennebunkport.

Mr. Baumgarten had a great big beautiful wholesale market, with trucks that went up and down the Maine coast to the big hotels, and alongside his market he had a tiny jewel of a store where he sold produce and fine groceries at retail. I learned in time that the prices he charged in his exquisite little store bothered nobody but me. The cooks in the big houses did the ordering from Mr. Baumgarten, and often they didn't even bother to come in but ordered by telephone, or sent the chauffeur. And nobody worried about the bill; it was paid automatically. A few cents on an item, a few dollars on a week's marketing, a few hundred dollars on a year's food bills were not noticed in the big houses with their staffs of servants as well as house guests and big parties to feed. An inferior piece of fruit or a poor head of lettuce might be remarked on, but not its price.

Mr. Baumgarten would be with me in a moment, said the clerk who had tried to persuade me that I didn't need to see Mr. Baumgarten. I walked around the little store, admiring and observing for future reference how beautiful fruit and vegetables could be beautifully displayed. I strolled into the wholesale market and watched the market men slicing the outside leaves and brown tips off the lettuce with two strokes. Finally Mr. Baumgarten was free.

He was short, round, rosy, and kept an ancient flat straw hat—the kind they used to call a boater—on his head all the time, as I've since seen many market men do. His hair was pure white, his cheeks pink as though they had just been scrubbed—and in fact they had, as I learned when I began to come in early in the morning for my order later on and found him with a little gray stubble on his face; market men get up in the middle of the night to go to the city and buy their produce, and don't shave until the store is open and they have to meet customers.

He smiled and showed even white teeth which probably had never needed a dentist in a long happy life with fresh fruits and vegetables. He was Grandpa, he was Santa Claus, and I wanted to put my hot little hand in his and let him lead me through this bewildering world of wholesale produce.

So instead I drew myself up to my full five feet three and one half and made him a very businesslike speech about keeping store in Goose Rocks. "We want to make money and we want you to make a fair profit, but don't charge us so much that we have to charge the customers too much and they won't buy from us."

He listened and smiled and nodded comfortingly and said, "Of course. Now what can I do for you today?"

There was a bushel basket of the most beautiful peaches

at our feet as we talked, and he saw me looking at them. I
had seen them in little baskets of three in the retail store,
nested in green leaves. He reached down and picked the
rosiest of them.

"Try it and tell me if it isn't the finest peach you ever ate,"
he said.

I ate it. I bought a basket—I think he charged me twelve
dollars for it, but I wouldn't have known the difference if
he'd said twenty or even thirty dollars. I bought cherries
and strawberries and oranges and grapefruit and bananas.
I asked for apples and grapes, but he advised me against
them. "The new ones are not in yet, and you don't want the
cold-storage ones now that it's warm weather." I thought,
here's a man to trust. I bought fresh peas and green beans
and spring onions and radishes and celery and tomatoes. And
I bought lettuce. I had stopped asking prices long before;
they didn't mean anything to me anyway.

The men loaded it all in the car, some in the trunk, the
rest in the back seat. Mr. Baumgarten made them put brown
paper under the crates on the back seat to protect the up-
holstery.

"You shouldn't use your car this way," he rebuked me.
"Haven't you got a truck?"

"It's in Portland today," I lied. I hadn't yet tried to start
Herb's truck, which had stood in the yard behind the store
for years and looked it, but I could see I was going to have
to. It was nice of Mr. Baumgarten to worry about the car,
and I didn't like to give the impression that we couldn't
afford a good truck. At least not on my first visit.

I drove back to the store in triumph. I had a load of
matchless produce and a wonderful new friend. Dorothy
came out to help me unload; the store was full of customers
—yes, it was, because I peeked in to see—but Jean and
Susan were there to take care of them. Dorothy exclaimed

with gratifying enthusiasm over my purchases—she didn't ask the prices, to my relief—and I went to work preparing them for sale.

This was more complicated than canned and packaged goods. You counted grapefruit and oranges, but you weighed peas and beans, and scallions and radishes were to be sold by the bunch. Also, most vegetables had to be hosed down to wash off the soil and trimmed of bruised leaves and broken stalks.

As to pricing, I had figured out a trick. While walking around admiring Mr. Baumgarten's display techniques in his retail store, I had carefully registered his prices. I had also taken note of the prices in Biddeford when I tried to buy there, earlier in the day. Ben Beebe's formula—divide what you paid for a case by the number of pieces in the case, add seventeen per cent and one cent for delivery—was too complicated for me. I was in no mood to study Mr. Baumgarten's invoices or go into higher mathematics when there were customers in the store who might buy this lovely produce right out of my hands.

Get the stuff where they can see it while there is still someone to buy it, I muttered. So I hit a level somewhere above Biddeford and below Mr. Baumgarten and wrote the price tickets with a flourish. Later, when I knew prices and what I could expect of Mr. Baumgarten, I found we could sell many items for only a penny more than the chain stores in Biddeford and still make a modest profit. But that morning, staggered by the maze of wholesale and retail, luxury goods and chain-store prices, I plunged in and made up prices as fast as I could go.

As soon as I had them ready I carried the fruit and vegetables out to the big table and laid everything out in the neatest order I could—all but the peaches. Those luscious peaches I saved until last. I had bought two dozen of Mr. Baumgarten's little baskets and some of his green leaves too. When everything else was done I sat down on the floor and began filling the baskets, three peaches to each and a fringe of green leaves.

Mr. Baumgarten had charged thirty cents for each of his baskets. I settled for twenty-nine cents a basket, nine cents a peach and two cents for the trimmings. It sounded like robbery, but they were beauties and it was only a little more than a quarter, which wouldn't make anybody go broke. What I didn't dare try to figure out was whether, at twelve dollars a bushel, *we* wouldn't go broke.

I finished the first layer of the bushel, carried out the baskets to the front of the store where customers would see them no matter what they came in to buy—everybody did see them at once and came over to admire—and I went back to tackle the second layer. I was working fast now, taking peaches with one hand and leaves with the other, not looking except at the basket I was arranging. I carried out the second batch of baskets and came back for the third. Then I looked into the bushel basket and saw that from the third layer down my exquisite peaches were mush!

Poor Dorothy! At this rate my carelessness would ruin her in a week.

I washed the peach pulp off my fingers, wiped my hands on my good flannel shorts without thinking (later we both had sense enough to wear jeans for the early-morning dirty work), and walked into the store. Dorothy was taking cash, chatting happily with all her friends of the beach, the mothers of the kids she had grown up with—establishing good customer relations, we would have called it in our Madison Avenue days, but Dorothy with her flushed smiling face was looking as I was certain she had never looked on Madison Avenue.

I wasn't going to spoil her innocent joy. I sidled up to her, said, "I'll be gone for about an hour," and went back to face my shame alone.

I lifted the bushel basket back into the car, whistled for the dogs, and set off down the Kennebunkport road for the third time that morning.

I said not a word, merely brought in the basket and put it down at Mr. Baumgarten's feet.

"My dear child!" he said in genuine horror. "Who sold you that garbage?"

"You did," I answered in a small voice.

"I did?" Not until then did it dawn on me that it was not Mr. Baumgarten but one of his helpers who had put a basket of peaches in my car. He beckoned one of the men. "Bring me a basket of peaches!" he commanded. When it came, he turned to me. "In this business we never know what's underneath. We must always look. Remember that."

He lifted a few out at a time, one layer, two layers, three layers; underneath they were a little greener, a little smaller, but they were whole.

"The ones that are not fancy enough for your trade, you can sell them by the pound and still come out," he counseled. "The green ones you can keep a day or two in the back before you put them out. Put the peaches in Miss Mackenzie's car," he said to the man. "No charge."

I thought of my beauties, which now cost me nothing but the price of the baskets and the leaves. "What about the good peaches that were on top?" I asked.

He waved a pudgy hand. "In this business we have to take the loss; you will take your losses too. Nature is not kind. Peaches lose their bloom, old men lose their hair"—he lifted his straw hat and showed a shining pink pate—"and become soft like putty in the hands of pretty young ladies."

A tubby Sir Walter Raleigh in an apron, he bowed me out to the car.

✿ 7 ✿

When Is a Customer?

Sometime late in the afternoon it came over me that we were having a tremendous day. The store was constantly full of people. All the local women had come to look us over, of course, and a good many of the men. Only about a fourth of the summer population had arrived for the season so far but they had all come complete with families. More summer residents were coming all afternoon, and they were stopping at the store before they even went to open their houses. Outside, their cars stood loaded to the gunwales with luggage, pets, babies, and nursemaids.

What with waiting on customers, accepting stock as it arrived, seeing salesmen of every kind of thing from kitchen gadgets to dirty post cards (but the post-card salesman also had a dollar pen which we thought we could sell), Dorothy and I had not had time to exchange a word as we flew past each other on our varied missions.

Finally I cornered her in the refrigerator room. It was a chilly place for a meeting of the board, but my excitement was more than I could keep to myself. I shut the door so we could have a moment alone (and also to keep the room's temperature—I had an obsession about this) and said, "Dorothy, doesn't it look to you as though we're in?"

She stood for a moment, with a bar of butter in one hand and half a dozen eggs in the other.

"I wish I could say so," she answered me diffidently.

"You mean they're just sight-seeing?"

"Well, look. They don't buy a pound of butter, but a quarter-pound. They don't buy a dozen eggs, just half a dozen. We're the biggest news in Goose Rocks in the past ten years, so they come in. But what they're buying is just samples."

I'd been high as a kite, and now I slid down sickeningly. The sales I'd been making, too, were piddling.

"Why, Scotty, don't look so undone!" Dorothy said, at once forgetting her own doubtful feelings to comfort a fellow creature. "It just means we'll have to work harder to get them."

"Work harder!" My bounce had gone at a stroke, and I knew for the first time how tired I was.

"I mean, think harder, work it out like a problem in merchandising. That's what it is, really, and that shouldn't floor a couple of experts like us. Listen, these people who are coming in to look around—they're the ones who can tell us what we need in the store to get their business. We have to pump them for information. And the ones who are stopping off before they go to their houses—we have to try to get them to stock their pantries here instead of in Biddeford or Kennebunkport—you know, the first big order of the summer—"

I didn't know, never having opened a house except Dorothy's, with her, but I saw what she meant.

"Our job is to break them of their old buying habits—they're accustomed to go to town for their staples and buy just what they need today from Herb, a few eggs, a stick of butter to tide them over until next shopping day. We've got to get them to buy their big orders here."

"That's right," I said. It was a challenge, and what does one do with a challenge? One rises to it. "We ought to have things they can't even get in Biddeford or only in the best shops in Kennebunkport, maybe even things they'd send for to Boston or New York. Look, I'll keep a pad and write down things they ask for that we haven't got. The girls ought to keep lists too. I'll tell them."

I opened the door and skinned out to the stockroom in search of pads, not omitting to warn the mice. It's remarkable how much better you feel about a problem the minute you find a little bit of a handle to it, like pads to write lists on. Dorothy went out to the store with her quarter-pound of butter and half-dozen eggs.

She had given me a good deal to think about, in those few well-chilled minutes, and as I went to wait on customers the argument continued in my head.

What makes people buy? We could reel off a glib Madison Avenue answer to this, full of long words and fancy theory. This was no time for theory but a matter of survival. If you have what people want, of good quality and at reasonable prices, they'll buy it. (Laugh, you clever advertising boys in your skyscraper offices. Have you ever sold a can of beans?)

Prices could be the key to the whole thing. I shuddered, remembering the hit-or-miss way we had been setting prices, especially the way I had priced the fruits and vegetables.

But prices weren't the factor in Mr. Baumgarten's store.

No, I could hear Dorothy saying, but he wasn't out to do a volume business. His wholesale market was his real business. His store was just a flower in his buttonhole. Our store was our whole stake.

The more I tossed it back and forth, the more I realized how complicated it was to set a store policy—and by the wisdom of your policy you could live or die. Storekeeping wasn't just putting things on sale, not by a long shot.

"They don't trust us," Dorothy had said in passing. I had scarcely heard her at the time, but I watched now, and I saw.

Though the store was nowhere near the chic establishment we dreamed of making it, it was already different enough from any country store they had ever seen to make the customers curious, and also apprehensive. The white walls and shelves, the floor like a deck, the shipshape look of the place, resembled Herb's little emporium about as much as Dorothy and I resembled Herb.

If under their surface politeness the local people resented us, why shouldn't they? They had lost their kind of storekeeper and their kind of store. It would take us a long time to convince them that we were there to serve them as well as the summer people—if we ever could convince them. The summer people were a subtler proposition. They shook our hands and bought a little of this and that, and all the time they were asking us, with their eyes and their pauses in conversation and the meagerness of their purchases, "What are you up to, you two smart girls? What are you trying to put over on us?"

When I came to deliver the day's orders I knew we had a real tussle ahead. "Our paper bags haven't come yet," we had been apologizing all day, and most people bought so little they could carry it home in their hands. So there weren't many cartons, after all, for me to deliver.

And there wasn't an awful lot in the cartons, either. One head of lettuce, one quart of milk, and one loaf of bread can rattle around something awful in a box meant to hold twenty-four cans. My spirits threatened to take another nose dive.

But I made an effort to keep up a front. Driving up to people's back doors and carrying the groceries into their kitchens, I affected the cheery briskness which seems to be the professional manner of delivery boys. Pretty soon I began to believe it myself, and by the time I got back to the store and saw that the trade hadn't slackened, had even increased, I was feeling both cheery and brisk. People were coming into the store, weren't they? And as long as we could keep them coming in, we would find a way to make them buy. Dorothy (I amended more modestly) would find a way.

As the evening business began, there could be no mistake about the soundness of our ice-cream policy. We had taken Jean and Susan behind the fountain early in the day and demonstrated to them the generous scoops of ice cream, and every cone a double one—they gasped at that. All afternoon whoever was on the fountain was a natural ambassador of good will to the community. The kids stared at their cones, lapped up the overhang like starved kittens, and ran out to spread the good tidings. The evening business was mainly soda-fountain business, and it boomed.

Dorothy served dinners, too. Somehow she had managed to put together two dinner menus. You could order hamburgers or—of all things—veal *scaloppine,* and Dorothy would whip it up. She had coaxed a special price for quantity out of her Kennebunkport butcher, and she was using wine in the *scaloppine,* too, out of a bottle she had brought from her own pantry. Dorothy's *scaloppine* happens to be one of her culinary triumphs. Green salad came with your meat order, and since she hadn't got around to baking yet, dessert was a choice of sundaes from the fountain. I had two helpings of *scaloppine* for my dinner. Not only was I that hungry, it was that good.

During the evening Ben Beebe came in. Sometime in the midst of the day I had phoned him and asked desperately, "Ben, for heaven's sake, where do we buy paper bags?"

"Why, from me, if you like," he answered, and it is to his credit that if he was laughing at us, then or later, he never let it show. When he arrived in the evening he quietly carried a supply of paper bags into the stockroom, and then he made his appearance at the fountain and ordered a chocolate fudge sundae. This was his standard order; he was an addict.

We huddled with Ben over the lists of things people had asked for that we didn't have. At some of them he shook his head.

"Herb vinegar, olive oil—not salad oil, I take it, but the imported Italian—some of these canned items—young ladies, are you planning to serve a luxury trade or just ordinary people like me?"

"Can't we do both?" we asked.

"It hasn't been done that I know of, in a community store."

"Does that mean it can't be done?"

"No-o, no reason that I can see. You'll run into some problems."

"Like what?"

"Well, people won't generally go into a de luxe store to buy potatoes, or else they'll buy a pound or two for tonight's dinner and wait to go to the chain store for a ten-pound bag."

Dorothy asked, "Can't we sell a ten-pound bag at the same price as the chain store?"

He looked at us. "If you can, it will be the first time I've ever seen it."

Dorothy looked at me. "Scotty, are you game to try to meet chain-store prices on some staple things? I've been thinking—it's probably one of the ways we'll get them to buy their big orders from us."

"I'm game," I said

Ben shook his head. "I'll help you girls all I can, but—well, I dunno."

We left it at that.

Near midnight Dorothy and I decided that the customers who were then drinking sodas at the fountain should be the last of the day. Jean and Susan had long since gone. I closed the doors, went to the cash register, and clanged open the drawer.

All that lovely money! I had put fifty dollars in, this

morning—long, long ago—but there were easily several hundred there now, besides some checks we had cashed. I was dying to count it, but there was the soda fountain to clean, and Dorothy was already in the kitchen doing a stack of dishes. The dishwashing situation was one we had not yet faced. Herb had left us a huge supply of dishes, and we had been using them all evening as at the March Hare's Tea Party, not washing, simply bringing on the clean ones as long as there were any. I shut the cash drawer after a yearning look and went to help Dorothy, putting off the fun of counting up until the dirty work was done.

I took a dish towel and said, "Looks like there's quite a bit of money in the till."

"Mm, how nice!" She rinsed another dish and then she said, "I can't remember what I did with my jewelry."

"Your jewelry! What was it in?"

"A little steel box, with a handle on top and sides that open. I was going to take it to the bank but I never got around to it. Can you remember seeing it when we were packing?"

Now, Dorothy packs like this: she opens a drawer to empty it, picks up a paper or letter she finds there, begins to read it, goes on to read everything in the drawer, and then decides she can't really part with any of it and a place will have to be found for it. I, having almost nothing of my own to pack, stood ready to help her. I would wait and wait for her to finish going through a cupboard, and then I'd start polishing a mirror Abby Peace had already polished, or rub down a table already rubbed. Finally, as time ran out, I succeeded in persuading Dorothy not to try to throw any more things away at all—old bills, check stubs, even old advertisements—but just to pick out what she wanted to take along to the town house for the summer and let me stuff everything else in trunks and boxes in the attic. Otherwise we'd never have finished.

So as soon as Dorothy had a bag packed for the town

house I would cart it down to the garage, and as soon as she had finished taking what she wanted from a drawer I'd pack the rest away in the attic. One way or another, I handled just about every one of her belongings.

I had carried bags and boxes, and finally odd-shaped bundles and packages, up to the attic and down to the garage. The whole operation was by now thoroughly scrambled in my mind—remember, all of it had been done in the late hours of the night, when we were both dazed with weariness after the long day's work in the store. Search as I might through the blurred images of what I had carried up or down, I could remember no little steel box. I had also taken one overflowing carton to the dump. Had it got in there by mistake?

"Was it important jewelry?" I asked.

"Reasonably important."

By this time I knew Dorothy's brand of understatement. Dorothy said "reasonably important" when anyone else would say, "It's a matter of life and death." I went hot and cold. Dorothy didn't really know much about me except through business and mutual friends. For all she knew I could be anything, even a thief.

I couldn't say a word. I dried the dishes and put them on the shelves. I went to clean up the fountain while Dorothy finished in the kitchen. I said an absent-minded good night to the customers, who were inclined to stay and chat about how exciting the store was, what fun to run a store—isn't it just wonderful? I was in no mood to encourage them. At last I went to the cash register, dumped all the money into a cigar box I found under the counter, first dumping out a mess of thumbtacks and rubber bands, and took the box under my arm. We turned off the lights, locked the store, and went to our town house.

I had brought all our things from the big house late in the afternoon, after I had finished delivering the orders, and piled them in the kitchen. The kitchen was still a store, but stripped; odds and ends remained to be sorted out and then the room would be closed. We weren't going to need a kitchen. We wouldn't have the leisure to use it.

Herb's parlor was just a parlor now, the table with the kitchen chairs standing neatly around it, and Herb's shabby, comfortable Morris chair in a corner looking orphaned. We went upstairs. The bathroom and the two back bedrooms had been painted; their beds had been taken apart and were standing in the hallway while the floors dried. One of them would be my room. We opened the door to the big front bedroom.

It was not uninhabited. There was a large, florid lady in a frilly housecoat, sitting in a chair, sewing a hem. The beds Dorothy and I were to sleep in that night were made and turned down.

"I beg your pardon," Dorothy said, and introduced herself and me. "This is our room."

"It can't be," said the lady. "Miss Hattie Black put me here herself. This is my room."

She was (she told us in not a few well-chosen words) Mrs. Belle Brobach, she had just returned from Rome, she had arrived a few days early for Mr. Woodbridge's school, Miss Black had put her in this room this very evening and here she was going to stay. She said a great deal more, but I hardly heard her. I was interested in the beds.

"You will have to take the matter up with Miss Hattie Black," she concluded, and sat down again with an air of great permanence in the chair.

Miss Hattie Black ran the bookshop. She was born to be Madame Chairman of a ladies' club dedicated to art appreciation and good works, but fate had cheated her, and so she followed instead a destiny created by herself. She was convinced that all artists were children, helpless, impractical, and in constant need of her protection. She would take Dorothy or me aside during the summer and suggest, "Could you put a little extra meat in their sandwiches, dear? They're so undernourished!" Or sometimes, "Perhaps you could charge them a little less for their breakfasts—they sacrifice everything for their art, you know!" Now and then her motherly heart led her to meddle; obviously this was one of those times. One imagined her, small and bosomy, in her little high heels and her large flowered hat, leading this lady artist twice her size into a house where she had no business whatever to be, settling her in the best room with comforting chirps—"Now don't worry about a thing, dear, just hop into bed and get a good night's sleep!" With only the slightest encouragement I'm sure she would have stayed to tuck Mrs. Brobach in.

Dorothy's temper never rose, no matter what the provocation, but now two little round red spots came into her cheeks, and she said, "I'll take nothing up with Hattie Black. This is our house, this room was prepared for us to sleep in tonight, and I must ask you to go now."

The lady artist stared defiance, but Dorothy can be very firm when necessary, and it was the formidable Mrs. Brobach who folded. "You can't do this to me! Where shall I go, at this hour, in a strange place?"

"Why don't you go to Miss Hattie Black?" I inquired sweetly. Dorothy threw me a reproachful look. She was already melting, and I could see those beautiful beds, with their white pillows and their white sheets turned back, receding by the minute.

Dorothy said, "Please don't be upset. We can't let you keep this room but we have twenty rooms in the guesthouse. I'll have one made up for you right away, and if you'll pack your bags I'll have them carried over there. You don't need to dress—there's a covered passage."

The beds came back into focus. But then I thought, Is Dor-

othy mad? Who's going to make up a room? Who's going to
carry bags? Where am I to find bed linens, for heaven's sake?

I didn't wait for the final surrender. I went scurrying
through the house in search of bed linens. I opened every
door, every cupboard, every closet. I looked in the sideboard
in the parlor, and even in the little old music cabinet. I saw
something interesting in there but it wasn't bed linens, so I
closed the doors and went on into the kitchen.

There on a shelf was a package like a laundry package.
I opened it; it was bed linens. Somehow, sometime, Dorothy
had brought it over here for Abby Peace to make up our beds.
I took two sheets and a pillowcase and went down the passage
to the guesthouse. I still had the car flashlight in my hand—I
had never even turned the light off.

The things Dorothy managed to attend to in her unob-
trusive way! The first bedroom I came to in the guesthouse
was clean and there were blankets folded on the bed. I made
the bed.

I had just about finished when Dorothy came, lugging one
of the lady artist's bags, a whopping big one. The lady artist
click-clicked after her in her high-heeled mules and her frilly
robe, carrying two small ones. We ushered her in, said good
night, and withdrew. She was quite pleasant, finally—Dorothy's magic—and we almost forgave her for delaying our
longed-for bedtime.

I had carried the last of our things up to our room and was
undressed and ready to drop into bed. Dorothy came in from
her bath looking well scrubbed and fresh. She said, "Scotty,
are you hungry?"

"Famished. But there's nothing to eat."

"Yes, there is. Can you walk downstairs, or shall I bring
it up?"

I thought I could walk downstairs. Dorothy said, "I
brought it over from the store today, just in case." She went

to the music cabinet in the parlor and took out of it a thing I had seen there. It was a small picnic box, and in it she had a thermos bottle of coffee, a box of crackers and a jar of peanut butter, which she knows I have a passion for and can eat even in my sleep.

Despite my transports over the peanut butter I still remembered a glimpse of something more in the music cabinet, something I had seen behind the picnic box when I was looking for the linens. I reached in for it—it was in the farthest corner—and brought it to the table.

"Dorothy, what's this?"

Dorothy put her hand over her mouth. "I remember now. I brought it with me this morning—you were too busy with the dogs to notice, probably. I put it in the music cabinet because I wanted a safe place, with all the people going in and out here all day. I put the picnic box there for the same reason, I suppose."

What I had found was, of course, the little steel box. She opened it, and I saw a collection of heirloom jewelry to dazzle the eyes. I couldn't guess its worth; Dorothy doubted if it had much money value, though there were some good precious stones. But it was antique family jewelry, irreplaceable, full of associations for her, and some of it truly beautiful.

She had remembered without trouble where she put the peanut butter—for me. But she couldn't remember what she had done with the "reasonably important" jewel case. Funny girl.

I was falling asleep when it came to me that I hadn't counted our first day's take, after all.

8

Dorothy Has a Way

How Dorothy would cook and bake three meals a day for the restaurant and fountain customers, along with everything else, I couldn't imagine until I saw her do it.

I had been eating her cooking since we arrived at the house on the Point, and I knew she was not only a fine cook but also one of those happy natural cooks who do what they do without effort, like breathing. She is the kind of cook who can give a cocktail party for twenty people, stay in the room being hostess the whole time—or at least you never see her leave—and afterward serve a superb dinner you haven't seen her cook. That she cooks it, right down to the chocolate soufflé, I know. But I can be in the same room with her and never know when she's done it. Under her tutelage I've learned to cook. Ham that I am, I concentrate on *spécialités*—no reliable daily craftsmanship for me—and I lock myself in the kitchen for four hours to turn out a dish. My performances are full of temperament, stage fright, and a need for applause. Not Dorothy's. She does things to food in passing, apparently without measuring, tasting, or timing anything, and everything is wonderful. She never looks at a clock, but when she opens the oven there are the pies, the biscuits, the layers, golden and perfect.

On the second day she began baking, and each day the racks in that remarkable Blodgett oven filled with more kinds of things as she fed her enormous repertoire into it, little by little. And the racks filled with quantity as Goose Rocks and then the neighboring communities discovered Dorothy's baking. People came for her corn muffins fresh every day. She baked oatmeal bread, which nowadays a good many people bake, and shredded wheat bread, which I never knew anybody but Dorothy to bake. Pretty soon we found we had to build a special set of shelves to hold the outgoing orders of Dorothy's baked goods. All of this, of course, was only temporary, only until Cora arrived. Or so I kept reminding Dorothy. And Dorothy nodded and smiled and said, "Yes, of course, only until Cora comes," while at the prompting of her mysterious, built-in timer she turned from scrambling the art students' breakfast eggs to take the pies out of the oven.

With Dorothy happily attending to the cooking, I naturally took over the management of the guesthouse. It began in a small way; Mrs. Brobach, rushing the season somewhat, was our only guest for two nights, and then another room filled, and another. We arranged with Abby Peace to do the thorough cleaning one full day a week. To dash over every morning after the breakfast rush and do the rooms in the guesthouse, along with our own two rooms in the town house, seemed to me hardly an extra chore at first when only a few of the rooms were occupied. It would take more effort to find a part-time daily chambermaid, just then, than to do them myself. Dorothy protested, "—only until we can get time to find someone—" and like Dorothy on the subject of Cora and the cooking, I said briskly, "Yes, of course," and flew to make the beds.

The day after we had bedded down Mrs. Brobach in one of the guest rooms, I checked the linens and found gratefully that Herb had left us an ample supply. When Mrs. Brobach asked for a key, however, I discovered that there were no keys to any of the guest-room doors.

"In Goose Rocks people never lock their doors," I assured Mrs. Brobach blithely. Dorothy and I hunted for keys but never found any. "In Goose Rocks people never lock their doors," became my stock reassurance to any guest who thought he would like a key. I learned that it was literally true. In Goose Rocks people took the Tenth Commandment seriously and did not covet anything that was not theirs. Down on the beach, on a post that held a life preserver, a jeweled wrist watch and a solitaire ring were displayed for nearly a week with a sign reading: "Found on beach—owner please claim." There they stayed until the owner came again the next week end and retrieved them. Once they got used to the unaccustomed sensation of living with unlocked doors, our lodgers never had cause to feel uneasy.

My routine in the guest rooms would have been simple enough—make the beds, empty the wastebaskets, dust the tops of chests, change the towels twice a week (Abby Peace changed the beds)—but I made the mistake of feeling responsible and housemotherly like the head of a college dormitory. I hung up their clothes. I looked at their canvases— and it become a matter of personal satisfaction to me to see how the tight, tense brush strokes of the first days gave way before growing freedom and imagination under the beneficent influence of Goose Rocks and Mr. Woodbridge.

Students as a class are not the tidiest people in the world, and art students are even less orderly than other kinds. No private family who could avoid it would take them as guests. On the other hand, they were up and out early for nine A.M. class, and some even earlier to paint before breakfast, so there was no waiting around for late risers—as in a hotel— before one could get at the rooms.

There was a washroom and shower on each of the two floors; the showers had the most wonderful needle-sharp water pressure, but they were walled with grim gray rough-surfaced cement; we had Chris paint them white, and though they were just as rough, they looked more inviting. Some paper-goods salesman turned up with disposable paper bath mats; I put a fresh one in each room every day.

Dorothy and I discovered we both detested prissy little signs that said PLEASE PUT USED BATH MATS IN WASTEBASKET and PLEASE DO NOT WIPE PAINT BRUSHES ON TOWELS. So when I found the soggy, soaking mats tossed on the floor outside the shower I bought the two biggest trash cans there were and put them where a guest would practically fall into them if he forgot to stop and throw in his mat. I hung rolls of paper towels on each floor for wiping brushes, and when the towels were smeared with paint anyway I simply clucked disapprovingly and put in fresh ones even though it wasn't the day to change; I couldn't bear to leave them the paint-stained ones to wipe their faces on.

There were a bed, chest, mirror, chair, and night table in each room, two of everything in a double room. We decided to go along with Herb's much-laundered white voile curtains and green cotton bedspreads for the time being, but we put bright paper scarves on the chests and, because we both like to read in bed, we hung a pin-up lamp on the wall above each bed. The fine old hardwood floors were neither painted nor varnished, and a good thing too. Abby Peace attacked them vigorously with scrubbing brush and paint remover each week to get the paint stains off.

Contrary to my—and the popular—impression, most of the art students were a sober, hard-working lot. They were in Goose Rocks, not to carouse, but to paint and to learn. Older ones like Mrs. Brobach and many of the younger ones were up with the first light and went to bed at nine regularly on weekdays and some the week through. It followed that the store noises and clattering of dishes, later the bowling and the Saturday night dances in the Casino, were disturbing.

During the very first week I found it advisable to fore-stall complaints with a little spiel to newcomers about the store's being "the center of activity, and there's the fountain and restaurant just across there where you can eat inexpensively and well"—I did not mention dishes rattling—"and some kinds of noises you get used to, you know. . . ."

I wasn't exaggerating about the store's being a natural center, not only for the beach people and the local folk, but especially for the art students. Three times a day at meal hours they cluttered the front steps comparing their work, arguing about composition and color—and making dates. Dorothy and I usually knew who was dating whom, simply because as we flew out of the town house early in the morning we saw them go down the beach, two by two, carrying their color boxes and canvases for a before-breakfast stint in the lovely light of the new day. A couple of hours later they'd come back together to camp on the steps, starving, waiting for us to open the store and give them breakfast.

I was supposed to get the full rent in advance for the two or three or four weeks each of them stayed, but from the beginning I found this impossible for me. Consequently I suffered each day that someone's rent was due—oddly, that particular person was usually extra diligent with the painting that day, out at dawn and too absorbed to come into the store even for meals. When someone was about to depart I had cold chills for fear he would leave his bill unpaid. But nobody ever did. Poor as some of them undoubtedly were, and squeezing out the last dollar for Mr. Woodbridge's valuable classes, they paid up.

From the beginning, of course, something was always going wrong with the facilities, in the guesthouse as in the store. On the very first morning, hurrying along with an arm-load of towels, I was scared out of my shoes by an ominous rumbling from a closet in the hall. As I listened, shaking, there was a POP! and silence. I dared at last to open the door and discovered the water heater, which Herb had optimistically described to us as "automatic." By blowing on it with my hot breath and lighting a dozen matches, I got it going again. Technically, the hot-water heater was automatic, going on and off when needed except when it went off altogether. It was the most frequent subject of Mrs. Brobach's friendly little memoranda, one of which greeted me from atop the bureau nearly every morning as I ran in to make up her room: "Dear Miss Mackenzie, So sorry to trouble you but there was no hot water again this morning. . . ."

Complaints and all, from the first I got along beautifully with the art students. I was also fine with the truckmen, the salesmen, the produce men, the summer people, and especially the summer customers, male. But I was completely and utterly undone by the local people.

It was Dorothy who knew how to talk to Andrew Austin when the pipe burst and knew also, with sublime confidence, that he would come and fix it the moment he had finished his supper, though she hadn't even asked him. It was Dorothy who, long after working hours on the night before opening, went up and got Mrs. Keene and Mrs. Cobb, who had rebuffed me (strictly speaking, whose bull had rebuffed me), as well as Abby Peace, the best-natured woman—and with the most uninhibited speech—I have ever known. The three of them worked most of that night and then came every day for nearly a week until all the houses were in order. (Mrs. Keene never bothered to explain to me about the other engagements, for which, presumably, she had turned me down.)

Then, we had hired Harry, a boy from one of the near-by towns, to help with the heavy work and behind the fountain; he'd had experience as a soda-jerk. Before the end of his first day Dorothy said, "Scotty, we can't keep him. He talks to the customers, forgets their orders, and he's not clean."

I nerved myself to speak to him. I went into the store the next morning at starting time with no other purpose. There was Dorothy behind the soda fountain with him, giving him vitamin pills from the drug counter, talking about changing his hours so he could eat more frequently because he looked pale and tired all the time. There was no firing that day.

Eventually we both spoke to him separately. Dorothy said, "I'm so terribly sorry, but you know we have to keep expenses down at first. The minute we have a place, we'll call you back. Do keep in touch."

I said, "Sorry, but you just aren't in the right job here. I'll be glad to see if there's something for you somewhere else. Here's your pay, and good luck."

Harry went away saying, "She's a fine girl, that Miss Mignault," and "You know that Miss Mackenzie? She fired me!"

Any time of the day, if you walked into the store, you had to step over the kid population strewn all over the floor reading the comics. When I came in they'd jump up and stuff the comics back in the rack. When Dorothy came in they'd say, "Hi, Dorothy, did you see what Superman did in this one?" and go right on reading.

Back on Madison Avenue I would have said sagely that there was something wrong with Mackenzie's public relations. At this point in my new life I wondered occasionally about my frequent frustrations, but most of the time I was simply grateful for Dorothy's astonishing ability at getting things done, either through her own seemingly effortless talents or through her magical way with people. The local people especially would drop everything and come, no matter when, if she needed them.

But right at the start there was one time when they didn't come, when no one would come. And it was my fault.

❧ 9 ❧

Albion

I committed what was, in Maine, the unpardonable crime. And I committed my crime against the patriarch of Goose Rocks, the lobsterman Albion, whom I admired inordinately, as did everybody else.

This is Albion. In the middle of the twentieth century, when machines do everything and a lobsterman has a motorboat to take him out to his lobster pots, Albion still goes out to gather his lobsters, halfway to Europe, or so it seems, in all weather, standing up in his boat, facing the bow, *rowing.*

Albion used to have a telephone. About three years before I met him the phone company sent him a bill for more than he thought he owed. People were coming into his house, said Albion, and using his phone. The telephone company said they were sorry but it was his phone and his bill and he would have to pay it. Albion delivered an ultimatum to the New England Telephone Company. He told them they had just one hour to come down and take their telephone out. He stood beside the phone with his dollar watch in his hand, and on the stroke of eleven, when they hadn't shown up, he tore the instrument out by the roots and dropped it into the sea.

Albion is a family man. He has six children living at home and he's a loyal and devoted father.

And Albion has his principles. A model T Ford stands up

on blocks in his front yard. It is a monument to Albion's dedication to principle.

It belonged to his cousin Coleman, of whom he is not fond. When Cole went off to the wars he sold the Ford to Albion. The day Cole came back, Albion put the little car up on blocks, stripped it, took off the wheels—and it has stood there ever since. That was eight and a half years ago. Albion simply wanted to make sure that Coleman never could ask him for the loan of his car.

Albion makes his living, of course, catching and selling lobsters. But he is choosy about whom he sells his lobsters to. If he doesn't like you, he'll give them away to someone else rather than sell them to you. The whole community rates you by whether or not you are one of Albion's regular customers. You may never know, though, that you are on his black list. He is invariably courteous and even, in a Maine way, friendly. There just aren't any lobsters the day you want them. The wind has been high, or the tide low, or the lobsters aren't coming to the pots for reasons of their own. Or someone has been there five minutes before you and taken the last of the lot. If you are persistent, he says sadly, "Lobstering is not what it used to be, you know," and predicts an early end to Maine's leading industry.

Albion spends the winter reading Voltaire and every current book of importance, especially the controversial ones, as fast as they come off the press. When the season opens he puts on his lobsterman's uniform—a pair of faded dungarees and a checked flannel shirt—assumes a Down East twang and allows himself to be considered a "character." Transients discover him with glad cries and snap his picture, and the art students are forever after him to pose. They love his powerful shoulders, his big, hamlike hands, and his face carved the way the sea carves a rock. He doesn't mind posing, so long as he can sit in the sun and carry on that form of communication—a sentence, and then a three-minute pause, and then another sentence—which in Maine passes for conversation.

Naturally it took months to gather even this meager knowledge of Albion. At the beginning of that first summer I knew him only by his lobsters. He always had lobsters for Dorothy, and I was the beneficiary thereof. I had never eaten anything like them, and in the first fine glow of falling in love with Maine I was inclined to broadcast my new gustatory experience. I was talking about food a good deal anyway, it seems to me, and eating an awful lot too (only until we became storekeepers; storekeepers don't have time to eat). I, who felt stuffed on a shrimp salad and a cracker in the city, was putting away meals a stevedore would find ample. I was working like a stevedore, to be sure. But that appetite and that muscle power are well-known by-products of the State of Maine.

In those first days, too, a good many things went clear over my head. I suppose people talk as much in Maine as elsewhere, but they don't say much. It seemed to me that a vast amount of what I heard did not mean what I thought it meant when I heard it. I felt like a not-very-bright child trying to follow the conversation of adults who didn't want me to catch on.

Anyway, late—oh, very late—on the night after the opening of the store I was driving Mrs. Keene and Mrs. Cobb home. We went past Albion's house with the Tin Lizzie enthroned in the yard, flimsy and frivolous in decay, a ghostly Blithe Spirit of a little car in the starlight. I asked, "What in heaven's name is that little Ford doing there?"

They told me about Albion and his cousin Coleman. When I got through laughing I said, with feeling, "What a man, that Albion! And what delicious tiny little lobsters he sells!"

The climate in the car turned suddenly chilly. Had I said

anything? No, probably the two of them were just beat. They had every right to be; we had worked like oxen that night. I drove them on home and thought no more about it.

Early the next morning Chris Marble came by for gas. I was proud of my newly acquired technique of pumping gas; I had got our first customer to teach me how it was done. So I pumped him five gallons with a flourish, and then as he was shifting into gear, he said, "What'd you do to Albion?"

"Me? Do anything to Albion? What do you mean, Chris?"

There was the Maine pause before he answered, and by this time I had learned to wait instead of pressing. Then he said, "Doesn't do to be careless with what you say around. Could make trouble." And at the continued blankness of my face he made a gesture—lifted an eyebrow, that is, a fraction of an inch—said, "Well, forget it," and drove on. Chris, as I say, had already begun his campaign of baiting me; all the while he was building shelves he poured it on: "You New Yorkers—all you know is how to put a nickel in a turnstile." He said nothing like that, this morning. Only something really serious would put a Maine-style leash on his teasing tongue.

That afternoon the deep freeze died on us. We had by that time hundreds of dollars' worth of frozen foods in it, and to lose them could be a major tragedy. To add to our worry, Maine did us the dirty by giving us an opening-of-the-season heat wave.

Dorothy called the man who had originally installed the deep freeze. He was sorry, he couldn't make it, but he recommended another man, who was sorry and recommended a third man, who was also sorry. Dorothy turned to me.

"Scotty, did you do anything to Albion?"

I bristled. "For heaven's sake, Dorothy!"

"Or say anything about him? Try to remember."

"You mean those men won't come to fix our deep freeze because I said or did something to Albion?" The cryptic exchange with Chris at the gas pump that morning came back to me. "Has Chris Marble been talking to you?"

"No, I haven't seen Chris. But one or two words have been dropped—Scotty, listen, this is serious. We're dead pigeons here if Albion is angry with us. Nobody will fix a leak or drive a nail. Think, Scotty. When did you last see Albion?"

"Not since the last batch of lobsters. You were there. Yesterday, or rather last night, I naturally had to drive past his place taking the women home, but I didn't stop. Mrs. Keene told me about Cousin Coleman and the Ford."

"Did you say anything about Albion? Anything at all?"

"I may have. But nothing to hurt him. You know what I think of Albion!"

Dorothy looked unhappy but she said nothing more. I waited on the next customer fast, cutting short the chitchat. Then I told Dorothy I'd be back in an hour, put a bottle in the front seat beside me, and drove down to Albion's place. I don't know any way to right a wrong, real or fancied, whether I'm the doer or the done, except to go straight to the interested party and face up to it. It can be unpleasant, but it's better than waiting until the roof falls in on you.

I drove past Albion's place slowly, went up the road to turn around, came back, and stopped the car. And sat there, waiting.

Now, Albion has the only place along there for quite a stretch of road. He knows the sound of every car in the community, and if one stops, whether he's in the house or out in back tinkering with his gear, he hears it and comes out to the gate. He knew perfectly well who it was that had gone by once and come back and stopped.

He kept me waiting a good five minutes. Then he came out of the house, walked across the yard to some lobster markers he had piled up there, and stopped with his back to me.

I got out of the car and went over to him. He didn't turn around.

I said to his back, "Albion, they tell me I may have said or done something I shouldn't't."

No answer.

"Albion, you know I think you're a wonderful man and I'd like you to be my friend. I wouldn't do anything to hurt you if I knew about it. I don't know what I've done. I'd like to know what it was, and I'd like to tell you I'm sorry."

He didn't turn around even then, but he moved a shoulder and said, "Well, Gawd knows, there's a law in Maine."

I supposed there were laws, even in Maine, but all I said was, "Yes, Albion?"

"Well, Gawd knows, if people go around telling people a man is sellin' short lobsters, he could have a little trouble."

Short lobsters. I'd heard the phrase and thought they were some special breed or variety of lobsters, like shorthorn cattle, maybe. Then it came out of nowhere, my own voice in the car, going down this road last night—"And those delicious tiny little lobsters!"

Late last night, not twenty-four hours ago, and Albion doesn't even have a phone. Yet today one man had spoken to me, more than one to Dorothy, and three had refused to come and fix the deep freeze. Talk about message drums in the heart of Africa. In Maine they don't even need drums! Thought transference, that's the only explanation I could think of.

"Albion, you won't believe I could be so stupid, but I don't know what short lobsters are. I remember saying something about your delicious little lobsters to Mrs. Keene and Mrs. Cobb last night in the car. It's the only time I ever used anything like the term. I didn't know what it meant and I'm pretty sure I still don't."

By this time Albion had turned around. His carved face was severe, but at least it was his face I was talking to.

"Listen, Albion, can't most things be settled over a drink?"

He followed me back to the car. We got in the front seat together and I opened the bottle, took a sip, and handed it to him. He held it up to his open mouth and poured. Then he wiped it carefully, put the top on, and set the bottle down on the floor.

"Short lobsters, Albion. Tell this dumb girl what they are."

When he got through telling me about the law, and how you had to throw back lobsters shorter than so many inches—just like trout, I thought, and I knew about trout from the sport films in the movies—we handed the bottle back and forth once more and I said, "Albion, we've got a little trouble over at the store. The deep freeze quit."

"Why, how much stuff have you got in that thing?" I told him. "Well, you'd better get somebody quick!"

"We tried, but nobody seems free to come over."

"Who'd you call?" I told him. "Come on, let's get back to the store and start phonin'." I put the car in gear and off we went.

On the phone I heard Albion say to the first man Dorothy had called, "Well, Gawd knows, Ozzie, the girls are going to lose a pile of money if you don't get here right away."

Ozzie was there in fourteen minutes flat.

Just for the record, Albion never did sell short lobsters. I'm sure he never took a ruler to them—he didn't need to—but once to settle an argument with a guest from New York I did. The smallest was one-quarter inch better than the law's three and one-eighth inches of body shell, measuring from the back of the eye socket to the beginning of the tail.

🌺 *10* 🌺

Buying? There's Nothing to It!

I don't think I was so very dumb about it. Dorothy performed so impressively in areas where I was helpless, like cooking and baking, planning for the restaurant and short orders, the sheer housekeeping of the store, handling the staff. At predicting and interpreting the needs of the community she was positively brilliant, and incidentally the word *community* was already becoming less and less corny to me, also the word *service*. With all this competence she was tossing around like nothing at all, it never occurred to me to doubt her when she said she knew about buying. It's true that after her initial trips with Herb, some buying always seemed to fall into my lap. I thought it happened that way because she was so busy doing other things. And heaven and I knew there were enough other things—the things she never boasted she could do, but could, while I couldn't—to keep her busy from dawn to midnight.

Even after the incident of the fruits and vegetables on our opening day, when she couldn't give me the order on the telephone and I had to learn from Mr. Baumgarten how to buy produce, I didn't get it. When it came to the meat order—that was when I knew.

We had been open several days, the big Fourth of July week end was coming up, and we still had no meat in the store. We had tried everywhere to get a butcher, but butchers are expensive, and a good one, it seems, is almost never looking for a job. Even for a hundred and fifty dollars a week we couldn't find one in Maine—or Massachusetts, for that matter—who was free to come to Goose Rocks for the summer.

That morning Dorothy said, "We've got to have meat. They won't come here with their big week-end grocery orders if they have to go to town for their meat." We were still wrestling with that problem of getting the big orders. We were busy all the time, the store was never without customers from eight in the morning until closing, but the business we were doing was still small. With the same number of customers we could have been selling four or five times as much and making four or five times as much money. (We didn't know, yet, whether we were making money at all, and wouldn't really know until the bills came at the end of the month.)

I said, "Let's get meat, then. What do we do?"

Dorothy pondered. "Well, it's either Armour or Swift, and around here it seems to be mostly Swift. So run up to the Swift branch in Biddeford and pick up an order."

"What shall I buy?"

"Oh. Well, you go ahead. I'll phone them while you're on the way."

I ran up to Biddeford and parked outside Swift's. I waited; someone would come out and ask and then they would bring out our order. That was the way it was done. But nobody came. So I secured the dogs in the car and went inside.

A man, soft around the middle and hard around the face, sat with his hat on his head and his feet on his desk and merely turned his head when I walked in.

"I'm from the store in Goose Rocks. Miss Mignault phoned in our order. I've come to get it," I said.

"Miss Mignault didn't phone in any order," he answered. "She just called and said I was to give you good meat."

That was when I got it. She had had plenty of time, and she hadn't been particularly busy as she was when the fruit-and-vegetable matter came up; even if she had been busy, this was the meat order for the July Fourth week end, the order which would bring all Goose Rocks to do their big week-end shopping in the store. Dorothy, who had bought all over the world, nothing to it. . . . Oh, Dorothy, Dorothy!

So it was up to me. I wasn't offered a chair but I sat down. I said, "Good enough. Here it is."

And I, who had never bought so much as a lamb chop in my life, who in the city normally ordered dinner by talking it over with my maid—and then only on the rare occasions when I wasn't out to dinner but was having people in—I ad libbed more or less as follows:

"Let me have twenty-five pounds of lamb chops, one and a half inches thick—I mean, that thick *after* they're broiled. And twenty-five pounds of filet mignon, say two inches thick. Give me twenty rib roasts, about ten pounds each—well, maybe ten smaller ones and ten larger. Steaks—twenty-five sirloin and twenty-five porterhouse, assorted sizes. Twenty-five legs of lamb."

My head was beginning to go round. Four hundred and fifty families, four hundred and fifty dinners times four days of the week end—how many was that? But some would eat fish once or twice, and all of them would have at least one lobster dinner, seeing they were in Maine. What else did people eat besides steaks, chops, and roasts?

"Hamburgers—fifty pounds, all beef, please, and no fat. Frankfurters"—must remember, frankfurter and hamburger rolls from the baker, an extra supply—"say fifty pounds of franks. Oh, and chickens—twenty-five broilers, and split them, of course."

I stopped, unable to think of anything else.

"Want any turkeys?" he asked.

Did people eat turkey all year round, or was he selling me a gold brick? "Twenty turkeys"—no, that was surely too many for the odd people who might eat turkey other times than Thanksgiving and maybe Christmas—"make it ten."

"We carry eggs, too."

"Good." Think, now, of all the scrambled eggs and fried eggs and omelets for four hundred and fifty times four breakfasts. "Eighteen hundred eggs," I said.

He squinted an eye at me briefly. "You mean seven crates, don't you? They come twenty-four dozen to a crate."

Oh, Lord, how many eggs was that? I gave up. "Seven crates, of course." I got out of the chair. "I guess that's it."

"No bacon, no ham?"

Of course, bacon and eggs, ham and eggs. "Twenty-five pounds of each."

"Smoked meats keep, you know."

"That's true. Double those."

"And hams for baking?"

Baked ham—that's a natural for a week end with lots of company. "Twenty-five hams will do it."

He hadn't written any of it down, but that didn't strike me as odd. Either he was a mental giant or, more likely, I was giving a pretty standard order. Anyway, I was having my own troubles, mentally speaking, at the moment.

"You want me to wrap it up?" he asked.

"Yes, I'll wait for it."

I went out and sat with the dogs in the car. That egg order still bothered me. I got out pencil and paper and did some arithmetic. It seemed to me that not every family on the beach would eat eggs every morning for breakfast, but to allow an egg per family per day for four days of the week end —eighteen hundred eggs—left a safe enough margin. Now how many did he sell me? Seven crates, twenty-four dozens to a crate, made a hundred and sixty-eight dozens. My estimated eighteen hundred eggs would come out to a hundred and fifty dozens. Good Lord! What would we do with eighteen extra dozens of eggs? Then I thought of the hungry art students swarming over the fountain and the restaurant every morning for breakfast, and I relaxed. They'd eat up eighteen dozens without a bit of trouble.

I felt pretty darn pleased with myself—especially for those one-and-a-half-inch lamb chops and the two-inch filets mignons. I'd shown that flint-faced man he couldn't put it over on me. He hadn't guessed for a minute that I was shaking in my sandals and didn't have a notion what I was doing. Well, maybe for a minute there, with the ham and bacon, my slip showed. But otherwise—

"We handled that one, didn't we, girls?" I said to the dogs, and the three of us settled down again in the sun.

At last two men came out, heaved an enormous bundle over the side, and dropped it into the back seat. The little car shook as with an ague.

"Hey, careful—this isn't a truck!" I protested.

"Sorry, Miss. It ain't feathers, you know."

"Right. Have a nice Fourth!" I called cheerily, and stepped on the gas.

Dorothy had put up a sign advertising the opening of the meat market for the Fourth. She had anticipated a crowd and planned how to serve people in turn—she had the bright idea of writing little slips with numbers; this, we learned afterward, is routine in supermarkets, but as far as we were concerned she invented it. Anyway, when I drove up to the store there were all the housewives in Goose Rocks, or maybe half of them, hovering around the entrance to the store.

I drove around to the back and pulled up smartly at the loading platform. Here were all these good folk wanting meat, and I was bringing it to them! Steaks, chops, the works! I felt like the huskies who carried the serum to Nome.

Dorothy came out. "Thank heavens, Scotty—they've been here for hours!"

I was too happy to scold her for her "meat order." "Where's Walter?" Walter was the boy we had hired on the second day to handle heavy stuff for us.

"I'm afraid he's gone home to lunch." It seemed to me that people were always out to lunch when there was hard work to do. "Can we lift it? I couldn't bear to keep those people waiting any longer!"

"Sure." I did not dwell on my memory of two husky men, staggering as they carried it to the car and dropping it so that the car shook. We tackled it.

Finally, with me flat on the back-seat floor pushing, and Dorothy on the platform pulling, we got it up. "Better undo it here and carry it in piecemeal," Dorothy suggested. I looked at her strained face, listened to my own heart pounding, and agreed. We couldn't move it an inch farther.

She ran for a knife and cut cords frantically. I tore away paper. We got it open at last, and when I saw what I had brought I sat down on the loading platform as though I had been hit.

Whole animals. Animals without their fur on. Maybe they were sides of beef, or quarters of beef, and halves of lamb. But they weren't chops one and a half inches thick, or two-inch filets. They were skinned, bloody carcasses.

That man. He had sat there with his hat on and his feet up and let me go on about steaks and roasts, knowing all the time this was the way the meat would come. "And split the broilers, of course!" No wonder he hadn't written down the order; he didn't have to be a mental giant if he wasn't going to remember anything but a load of whole animals.

Dorothy said, after a long minute, "What are we going to tell all those people?"

"We'll just have to tell them the truth, that's all. We won't have any meat today." Would we have it tomorrow? I couldn't think that far ahead.

Dorothy was looking at me in her appealing way, and I knew what she meant. After placating them all morning, cajoling them into waiting, she couldn't bear to go out and disappoint them. I would have to be the heavy, as usual.

Well, this part was my mistake. And it was easier for me to be tough. I went out and told them the nicest way I could.

"I'm so sorry but the meat order came all wrong. I'm so sorry, we can't have the meat ready today. I'm so sorry, you'll have to excuse us today. I'm so sorry . . . I'm so sorry . . . I'm so sorry . . ."

Some were cross, some inclined to argue, but most took it with good enough grace, although I could see them shaking their heads as they left. Those girls, really——! Maybe some were kind enough to say, those girls, they must have their troubles. But at last they were all gone, and I went back to Dorothy and the carcasses.

She had begun to carry them into the refrigerator, and I helped. She must have noticed, as I did now, that we could have sold the hams, which came ready and wrapped, and the bacon in pound packages, maybe even the ham for slicing, since we had a slicer (but not the poultry, which came without feathers but with all its insides inside). She didn't mention it, and neither did I. We hadn't the heart to try to sell any meat at all, not now. Later, I noticed, she carried the hams and bacon into the store and put it all into the refrigerated meat display cases; she'd had Will turn on the refrigeration in the morning, as soon as I left for Biddeford.

But meanwhile we were carrying the animals into the refrigerator room. Our electric refrigerator was about twenty feet square, with shelves for cheeses, eggs, dairy stuff, and hooks in the ceiling for which now, for the first time, I knew the purpose. Those hooks—you hung animals on them, that's what they were for.

But we no longer had the strength to lift and hang them. What's more, we didn't care. We just dumped them on the floor in a heap, closed the door firmly, and walked into the store to wait on the trade.

All day long, going into the refrigerator for this and that, we stepped over those animals, walked around them, averted our eyes from them. In a little while I found we had another problem. When we ran out of local eggs, I opened the first of the crates and found the eggs weren't in boxes. How do you sell eggs without boxes? Where do you buy egg boxes? The things a storekeeper has to think about!

We got egg boxes, by dint of begging them from our local egg man and telephoning to his supplier for the next day. The day wore on, a very busy day before the week end. At eleven-thirty that night I closed the doors after the last chatty customer and came back to Dorothy.

She was clearing counters, putting things back on shelves. I leaned on the counter and said, "Well?"

No use kidding ourselves, we had a lot of money invested in those carcasses, and we had customers anxious to buy meat. We had walked around them all day but we couldn't keep our minds off them.

Dorothy said, "Scotty, I've been thinking—and I'm game if you are." And as I looked at her blankly she went on, "There are all the tools for it out in back—you've seen them." So that was what they were for, the saws and cleavers and big murderous knives.

"But how will we know—?"

"The old OPA charts. We can follow them."

Herb's OPA charts had been hanging on the wall of the refrigerator room when we bought the store, and they were still there, nobody having thought to take them down and throw them away.

And that's what we did. We took down the OPA charts and we stood over the cutting block and cut up lamb and beef until it looked like the pictures. One of us would point, "Cut here. Now here. How about here?" When we came to bone, we sawed with the saw, or clove—if that's the word—with the cleaver. The first job was not very neat, but the next was better, and we improved with each one. Each time we finished cutting up an animal we weighed and labeled it.

We hadn't, of course, thought how to price our meat—it was a habitual failing of ours to forget we had to sell the stuff for money. Naturally the OPA prices were only a fragrant memory. Dorothy said that would be no difficulty—she herself would call that man at Swift's in the morning and get him to price the whole lot for us. (This she did, and no hesitating either.)

By five-thirty A.M. we had chops, steaks, roasts—and also pot roasts, stew meat, hamburger, all kinds of incidental stuff neatly labeled and lying in trays on the refrigerator shelves. The nicest-looking cuts we put in the showcase for display. Then we scrubbed the cutting block, cleaned and dried the tools—going back every few minutes to look at our handiwork with justifiable pride. We were bloody from head to foot, haggard—but we weren't missing any fingers and we had meat!

We went home, cleaned up, had breakfast, and went back to open the store. And the first thing we did was to paste up a big sign in each window: MEAT TODAY!

We sold out our meats that week end; Dorothy just barely remembered to save some for ourselves and the hungry art students who by that time were eating in our restaurant. Nor did we hear any complaints about the way the meat was cut, although some of the first tries were a little ragged. But we gave true weight, and it was the best quality meat, so Goose Rocks enjoyed its dinners that week end after all. And we had hundreds of dollars in the till that wouldn't have been there otherwise. I felt we had earned that money, every penny of it.

We never did get a butcher that summer. Early every Saturday morning, Dorothy and I cut up the meat for the week. Dorothy was skillful from the start with the poultry; probably every really good cook can clean a bird if she has to, just as most fishermen can clean fish. Ever since, Dorothy and I have reveled in a fine sense of security; any time we need a job, we know where we can get one. A good butcher is almost never unemployed.

II

Big Week End Coming Up

The dance floor in the Casino was finished. It had been scraped and scraped, and waxed and waxed, and now it was like glass and yet with a grip to it so you wouldn't fall on your face. I tried it solo, humming a little jive, and it was dreamy. I thought, This can't go to waste another minute.

Dorothy had said, "We ought to start the Saturday night dances." People had been asking us when we would. They hadn't had the dances for five years.

We had been open all of four days. There were so many sides to this operation—and all to be started at once; Dorothy and I were the ringmasters of a circus that kept jumping into new acts every minute. Or we were like the sorcerer's apprentice who set the broomstick fetching water for him, and more and more broomsticks kept fetching water until he nearly drowned. The store was sprouting broomsticks all over, and each one fetched water—that is, business—like mad. It was wonderful, it brought customers, but we could drown, too.

On this particular day the store was running smooth as cream; we hadn't had a crisis yet, and it was nearly noon. People wanted the Saturday night dance and we ought to give it to them—though if you'd told me this was community service I'd have hooted; I had no notion how Dorothy's philosophy had already taken me over.

I went back to the store and began asking everybody who came in, "Where do you get a dance band?"

The local people said, "You got to see Robie Smith."

"Who's he?"

"Why, he works for Sellers—you know Sellers."

"No, I'm afraid I don't. Where is he and what does he do?"

"Why, Sellers is a plumber over to Kennebunkport."

I drove to Kennebunkport and found Sellers.

"You have a man named Smith working for you? I hear he plays an instrument. We want to give a dance—"

Sellers said, "Well, sure, Robie Smith, he plays the cornet. But he ain't here now. He's over to Good's—there's a pipe went in the basement—"

"When will he be back? Tonight? Will you give him a message?"

"I dunno. Likely he won't come in tonight. Likely he'll go straight home."

"Tomorrow morning, then?"

"I dunno as he'll come in tomorrow—"

"Doesn't he come in to report? Doesn't he come in to get his jobs?"

"Well, I dunno. He just hears around who needs him and he goes out there. Might see him Sat'dy."

"That's too late. The dance is Saturday night. How do I find Good's?" Of course I had all day to run around the country finding musicians, but there seemed no other way.

He told me, and I found it. No sign of life except a faint tapping from underneath the house. I looked under and then crawled under. There was Robie Smith.

Yes, he played the cornet. Yes, he'd be glad to play for the dance over to Goose Rocks. But he couldn't play without Pete Charbon. Pete, he played the fiddle.

Where would I find Pete?

Oh, he would be down the Biddeford Pool road, had a filling station there. Why, Gawd, you couldn't miss Pete's place.

There were half a dozen filling stations on the Biddeford Pool road, but to Robie his friend's was the only one. Anyway, I found it. Pete was a genial French Canadian who didn't understand half of what you said but laughed and made out as if he did.

"Sure, sure, I play—if Wallie Mead play piano," he agreed. So now I had to find Wallie Mead. He was an appliance salesman, working for Stover's agency.

I found Wallie. Certainly he would play. "Unless"—he winked broadly—"I happen to get stiff. It's Saturday, you know."

I begged him not to get stiff until after the dance and went on back to the store, nervous but ready to report to Dorothy that we had a band, and she could make the announcement: There would be dancing Saturday night.

When I got back with my news I found Dorothy had news of her own.

"Meet our new assistants," she said. She had hired the two prettiest girls on the beach, Marg Cromwell and Liz Carter. They were friends; Marg was at Wellesley and Liz was going the following fall. Marg was a blonde who took a terrific tan; she was tall and long-legged and really beautiful, and she had an air of disdain for the boys which fetched them drooling after her like puppies. Everybody was in love with Marg, but Marg wasn't in love with anybody. Liz was only a little less spectacular but she had enough and to spare. Both the girls looked smart and cool-headed, with a poise that promised to carry them through any situation.

Dorothy and I had talked about hiring additional staff. It was obvious from the first day that we wouldn't live long without more help. Jean and Susan, our faithful pair, looked very trim and were quick and efficient at the fountain and waiting on tables in the restaurant, but we were not using them as store clerks. An occasional customer is overbearing, and these girls were too loyal to us to lose a customer by giving her the Maine brush-off; on the other hand, we didn't like to see them pushed around. City girls, we thought, presented a less vulnerable surface—a harder varnish, as on a table that has to look handsome and yet take rough use.

We were besieged by the sons and daughters of the summer residents, especially the daughters; most of the sons of college age had jobs in the city and came down week ends only. The girls went to the best New England schools and colleges in the winter. They were bored lolling on the beach all summer. They wanted to work. But they didn't want to work hours that would mean no beach or tennis or sailing, no time for boyfriends.

"And an eight-hour stretch," Dorothy had pointed out, "would tire them in a week, so we'd have to get a new staff every few days."

That's where we had left it, a few nights before. There hadn't been time to finish discussing the subject; there never was time to finish anything. Now we had two new assistants, though, and we'd have to work out shifts.

I shook hands with Marg and Liz and wished them luck, as seemed appropriate, and followed Dorothy out to the ice room. This had become our top-level conference room. It was cool and reasonably private. We could perch on a shelf or a crate, reach for a pear if we were hungry, and talk undisturbed.

"They look wonderful," I told Dorothy. "How about their hours?"

"That's what I wanted to talk about. We've got to plan a schedule for these kids that will give them a good balance of work and play."

So we worked it out, a vacation-work schedule of shifts; I'm pretty sure it was an innovation in personnel planning. We kept changing it until it fitted. It was full of special arrangements to meet individual needs and peculiarities. For instance, take Jean and Susan. Jean didn't mind getting in at seven-forty-five for the breakfast rush, but Susan was terrible to get up in the morning, so we let her come in a half-hour later. Also they were double-dating a pair of Biddeford boys; we gave them some evenings off together. Sunday afternoons their aunts and uncles and cousins came visiting from all over Maine—so they both worked a long day Saturday and all morning Sunday and went off at two for the rest of the day.

Marg, the most popular girl on the beach, needed her evenings for dates; we scheduled her for daytime shifts all week.

Liz, on the other hand, didn't care about her hours; as to dates she could take them or leave them. But she was only sixteen, and we thought she ought to have plenty of afternoon time to sun and swim and play tennis. Also she had a quiet way of managing things which the other three somehow did not resent, and she was willing to take responsibility which they on the whole would rather dodge. It was Liz, for example, who finally got us to sit down for dinner. They all begged us to, but Liz arranged it so we could. If people asked for us while we were eating, she stopped them cold by saying firmly, "Dorothy (or Mac) is having her dinner now and you will have to wait or come back later."

So we gave Liza full morning shift, morning being the time when Dorothy was busy in the kitchen and I out on errands, another shift in the late afternoon and early evening, and one whole day off to sleep late and just loll.

It added up to a forty-four-hour week for each of them. I'll guarantee it was the most individualized work schedule ever devised, and it became increasingly complicated as the staff grew. I wrote and rewrote time sheets, posted them in the stockrooms, gave each girl her own to take home and stick in her mirror. And it worked, probably because it was so individual. We had virtually no labor turnover. It's true there was one more reason why it worked: Dorothy and I were always on the job and always ready to fill in for one of the staff who wanted or needed unexpected time off because a boyfriend was visiting or the tennis tournament was on. Knowing this, the kids were all the more considerate. They never even asked us for extra time unless they were really in a spot; they switched back and forth among themselves.

Later that summer Marg did fall in love, with a nice GI who was taking the art course. I knew because I saw Marg come along the beach early in the morning, to sit beside him while he painted the beautiful six-in-the-morning scene. Later that summer, too, Liz began to date the boy who was driving the bus to Kennebunkport, and the only time she really wanted off was his ten-minute stopover. Somebody always ran to take cash for Liz the minute Steve honked the horn outside.

But to go back to the beginning. Before the end of her first day Liz was in trouble. It was a funny kind of trouble; at first we didn't know what to make of it. She was taking cash, and we first noticed that the customers were going away looking puzzled or uncomfortable or outright displeased. We couldn't tell what Liz was doing wrong. She was very quick and her manners were unimpeachable.

Finally Mrs. West's cook Annie, who had bought an enormous week-end order, caught Dorothy on the fly and drew her into the kitchen. Annie had been cooking for Mrs. West for ten years, and she was devoted to Dorothy. She was also a very outspoken woman. "That child is sweet and pretty, but you sure she knows what she's doin' ?" Annie demanded. "Either she overchargin' me or she cheatin' you. She don't write nothing down !"

And she showed Dorothy the charge slip : $32.38, in clear neat figures; no items, only the total.

Dorothy said, "Have some ice cream on the house while I see to this, Annie," and went over to the counter near Liz to observe. It was true. Liz would look at some of the prices on cans and packages, glance over the rest, write down a figure, and hand the duplicate to the astonished customer.

Fran Sergeant came to the register. Fran's order was not so big—she wasn't having guests over the Fourth—but there were lots of little items. Fran said, "How's the job going, Liz ?"

Liz frowned and didn't answer at once. She gave the groceries her quick look and said, "Eight sixty-three. Thank you, I just love it, Mrs. Sergeant," writing the total down as she spoke.

Dorothy said, "Liz, I need you a minute," and drew her away. I slipped behind the counter, glad of a chance to talk to Fran, and meanwhile I wrote down her order, item by item, with the prices. I totaled them up : $8.63.

When Fran was gone Dorothy and Liz came back. "I know your secret, Liz," I said. "You're a mathematical genius."

She turned pink under her tan. "Well, no. But I was just telling Dorothy, I add it up in my head."

She was a lightning calculator! I said, "But, Liz, you don't look at each item for the price, only some of them."

"I know a lot of them by now. When I've seen them once the price stays in my head."

I showed Dorothy the slip for Fran's order. "Liz had the total absolutely correct."

"But it always is. It can't be wrong," Liz said. She wasn't

boasting, just stating a fact. She took her gift for granted, like being able to speak English.

Dorothy said, "We know that, Liz, but the customers don't. I know it's inefficient and a waste of time, but please, dear, write it down for them, item by item, so they can add it up themselves afterward in the normal, plodding away. Will you?"

She blushed again and promised she would. So with Liz we acquired an adding machine, at no extra charge, and much more decorative and companionable than the usual kind.

❧ *12* ❧

Fourth of July

I don't know how the rest of the country celebrates the Glorious Fourth; New Yorkers, I know, spend most of it jammed bumper to bumper on the roads, either trying to get away from the city or trying to get back again. But all up and down the coast of Maine, and perhaps of all New England, people spend the night of the Fourth on the beaches. They've collected driftwood for days, and they light huge bonfires, shoot off fireworks over the ocean when it gets dark, and then sit around eating too many frankfurters and toasting marshmallows and singing in close harmony until the fires burn down and it's too chilly to sit out any longer. By then it's time they were home and in bed.

So it was the night of the Fourth, and there wasn't a soul in the store but Dorothy and me. Everyone was at the beach fires, and we had dismissed the girls at nine so they could go too. We would close early, Dorothy said hopefully, and go home and rest our feet and get some sleep. The next day was Saturday of the summer's biggest week end, with every house on the beach full and overflowing with week-end guests. It would be a big day in the store, and we had the dance at night on top of that.

The Fourth had been quite a day too. People were getting accustomed to having a big store they could go to any hour of any day to get almost anything; they hadn't had a big store in Goose Rocks for five years, and they were really using us. At this quiet moment Dorothy was checking stock for the next day, and I was adding up the cash, when Fran Sergeant came in at the door.

Because Mrs. Sergeant had been our first customer I would have had a special feeling for her if for no other reason. I had seen her in the store every day since then but hardly to talk to. Still, once you'd seen Fran Sergeant you didn't forget her, and you didn't get her out of your mind, either, for hours. When she walked into the store it was like Queen Elizabeth walking in—not the young queen, the original one—or maybe Sarah Bernhardt. She had the drama and dignity of both of them, plus her own special magnetism.

I had asked Dorothy about her. She had lived at a pace that would kill most women off young, but at seventy-four she was just beginning to slow down. Even up to the summer before I met her, she would still suddenly take off for Paris to pick up the threads of her varied and distinguished friendships. She had been pursued by many men—"including my three indiscretions, whom I married," as she liked to say.

Unlike a less secure beauty, she never found it necessary to boast of her conquests. It was not from Fran that you learned of men who had been mad about her. She could never talk of her own deepest experiences with any seriousness. To Fran it would be in poor taste to reveal either a great love or a great loss. She would cloak any profound emotion with a glib phrase.

Her first husband she never mentioned. Dorothy thought that might have been an unforgettable first love, and we never learned what had happened to end it. Her second was a manufacturer of a very powerful, very expensive car; again taking refuge in the light touch, she would explain that she married him only because she loved to drive fast cars.

Fran cherished her friends. No exertion was too much for

her when there was a chance to give them hospitality and enjoy their companionship. Like Fran, her friends were vital, dynamic people, and most of them accomplished things, often on a world scale. One of her lifelong friends was a distinguished scientist who made perilous trips to far places in search of knowledge. I'll call him the Commodore, because you would know his name if I mentioned it. It is a name attached to some rare species of early reptiles whose fossils he found, and to ice-clad polar shores which he charted. He is said to have been one of those who ate mastodon steak, that time they found whole mastodons which had been frozen in Siberia for hundreds of thousands of years in nature's deep freeze; some of the party got sick on it, but not he.

From his pictures and the stories about him he was a huge, handsome man, like a Viking. One story, which Chris Marble told Dorothy, was that once the Commodore's ship, which had been following ice floes, put in at a Maine port, and Fran received a telephone call. Her husband would normally have gone to fetch him, as there was a wild blizzard through which it was impossible to drive a car, but he was in Boston that day. Fran, nothing daunted, persuaded Chris to get a sleigh and drive her up through the blinding storm to bring the Commodore back to the warmth and comfort of her house.

Fran married her third husband, she used to say, because he was the most respectable man in Maine and she wanted an aura of respectability to dignify her old age. What she really wanted, Dorothy said, was serene companionship for her declining years. Hal Sergeant was a mellow, quiet, thoughtful man with whom it would have been a joy to grow old. He was terribly proud of Fran and deeply in love with her. But he innocently cheated her of the beautiful old age she had planned by dying, five years ago that summer.

"I am punished for my sinful life," Fran said to us once,

"by being left alone to end it among dim-witted clods." She never forgave Hal for dying and leaving her alone. Though, of course, if the question of living or dying had been up to Hal, he would have asked no greater boon than to have a little more of life with Fran.

That was Fran Sergeant, who came to see us that quiet evening of the Fourth when we were all alone. She stood in the doorway leaning on her cane, her knitting bag over her arm, looking magnificent, and said, "All those clacking hens and their old roosters are on the beach, thank God, and we can have a little peace. It seems I have to call on the village storekeepers for some intelligent conversation. How are you, dear?"

Dorothy came out from behind the counter to greet her. Dorothy told me she thought Fran was really lonely this summer for the first time in her life, that for the first time she admitted to herself that she was getting old. I saw that; when we went out of the store together at night she would say, "Take my arm, child, I don't want to fall." But that was the only sign she gave that she felt old. And she wasn't old in any way that mattered. Her talk always sparkled. It might be acid, and she could destroy an individual with one sentence, but she was never slow or dull or tired. And she had a zest for enjoyment like a child's.

"I've come for my ice cream," she said in her deep resonant voice. Every evening Fran came for her ice cream, a dish of strawberry, with whole strawberries frozen in it. And this reminds me of one scene in the store I'll always treasure. I must tell you, first, that the ice cream comes in five-gallon containers, which you drop one on top of another, three deep, into each of the wells in the fountain. When the top one is empty you lift it out, and the two under it—there's a gadget like a pair of pliers which catches the wire rims of the containers—scrape out the empty and slap its leftover ice cream on top of the next full one. Then you put the empty upside down at the bottom of the well and the two full ones on top. When a second is empty you do the same, so that the full one is always at the top of the well. We never had time to scrape out the empties, though, and when Dorothy was on the fountain, if she had an empty she would look around for any kid who was in the store and give it to him to scrape out for himself with a long-handled soda spoon.

Fran was in the store one evening when Dorothy took out several empties and began calling the kids to the fountain to finish them.

Fran said, "Oh, Dorothy, let me, too! I've always wanted to do that!"

So Fran got a strawberry and sat up at the fountain with the kids, each one scraping away at an enormous container with a soda spoon. The store was full of people, and they stared and smiled, but nobody dared make a crack to Fran. Nobody ever tangled with Fran who could help it. You couldn't win in a word duel with Fran.

She got up on a stool tonight, and I ran around behind the fountain to serve her. "Strawberry as usual, Mrs. Sergeant?" I asked.

"Yes, and isn't it time you called me Fran? Dorothy, sit down, dear, your poor feet! And you too, child."

Dorothy got some cookies off the shelf and I came around the fountain, and we sat there nibbling and talking while Fran ate her ice cream. When she finished, she took out her knitting. She was finishing the toe of a beautiful cable-stitch sock; the wool was soft as feathers. "I know Dorothy's size —what's yours, child?" she asked me. She had begun a project for the summer: she was going to knit socks for us, the softest—"Your poor feet! They deserve the best socks." Fran never went to bed before five or five-thirty in the morning. She sat up all night, with the radio on, reading and

knitting. She read three newspapers a day, all the book re-
views, the several serious magazines, and all the new books
worth reading, and she was a tireless radio listener. She slept
until one; the sky might fall, but nobody would knock at
Fran's door to tell her until one o'clock.

That summer she finished a pair of socks for us every
three days or so, and we wore holes in them almost as fast.
Every week or two she collected them, made sad sounds over
our poor feet, and took the socks home to darn. She darned
as she did everything, exquisitely. She was a beautiful housekeeper and a great cook. Dorothy was the only one she allowed to cook in her kitchen because Dorothy was as beautiful a worker as herself. She gave Dorothy many of her
recipes, which she really kept, as many people say they do but
don't, in card files indexed according to French, Italian,
German, Swedish, and a dozen more nationalities. The
proudest day of my life was when Fran undertook to teach
me how to make a French omelet and was so pleased with
me as a pupil that she went on to show me variations—cheese
omelets, omelets with onion sauce, shrimp omelets with lobster sauce.

Fran said, "I'm going to haunt you two this summer. A
storekeeper gets all the village gossip and gets it first, and
can't tell anybody for fear of losing customers. But you can
tell me, because I don't talk to anybody." She was right, as
we discovered before very long. Everybody whispered the
latest tidbits of beach scandal to us first, and we told nobody, not only because it was impolitic to talk to customers
about other customers, but also because we had no time for
idle prattling. Not even with Fran; when we could snatch an
occasional hour with her we had all too much to talk about.

Dorothy asked seriously, "Fran, what do you really think
about our running the store?"

"What I *really* think? You'll break your silly little necks

and probably ruin your health but you'll have great fun.
That's what I think. You're the only people I ever meet any
more who dare to do anything at all. And I think"—she
looked around the store appraisingly—"I think this year
you'll have a good store, but next year it will be a great
store."

Dorothy laughed. "I hope you're right, Fran."

Fran said, "Why, Dorothy, you know I'm always right."
It was like saying, "You know the sun will rise tomorrow."

I think Fran liked me because my voice is deep like hers
and I talk fast and arrogantly and as though I had confidence
like hers, which I wish I had. She said to Dorothy, "Scotty is
very like me at her age." I wanted to ask, "Will I be like you,
at your age?" But not many people are, and who am I to hope
for such splendor at seventy-four.

And so the time passed, until suddenly Dorothy gasped
and said, "Good heavens—customers!"

There were just three people, and then two more, coming
in for a soda, and we thought maybe they were the few who
hadn't gone to the beach fires. But before Dorothy and I
could slip off our stools and get around behind the fountain
they began streaming through the door, four and five and six
at a time. In ten minutes the store was jammed, people were
waiting three deep for their orders at the fountain, and
Dorothy was telling others to sit at the tables in the restaurant and she would come and take their orders there.

"Fran, dear, would you mind taking the cash, just till the
girls get here?" Dorothy asked, and Fran went to the cash
register. We two were spinning behind the fountain, doling
out sundaes and sodas and hot coffee. When somebody took
a notion to order a hamburger, and six others piped up that
they would like some too, Dorothy darted into the kitchen,
and I was alone. One of the art students, a nice girl but she
wore the longest earrings and the highest heels I ever saw,

came with an order for her table, and I filled a tray and she teetered back with it. In a minute others came with the orders for their tables, and people were waiting on people, carrying trays, narrowly avoiding spills. What had brought them back from the beach to us we had no time to figure out. It was a fine evening, chilly, but evenings always are chilly in Maine. With a fire it must have been beautiful on the beach. Finally I asked one of the art boys.

"But this is the pleasantest place in town!" he said, and added, "You know you're getting to be an institution, don't you?" I didn't, but I was glad to learn.

Meanwhile people were wandering through the store, and I heard Fran's voice commanding, "Come back, please, the grocery department is closed." She grabbed three men who had finished and stationed them to see that nobody walked back to the shelves.

It went on for a solid hour. All of Goose Rocks streamed in from the beach, all, that is, except Jean and Susan, who never thought to come back from their unscheduled evening off to see if we might need them. Dorothy flew in and out of the kitchen, I scooped ice cream and punched spigots and poured coffee without a stop, trays wobbled overhead in the hands of amateur waiters. And Fran was stuck with the cash register. Halfway through the insanity she appeared at the kitchen door, looking distraught as Fran never looked, holding up a dollar bill with a trembling hand.

"How do I make change for a dollar, Dorothy dear? I haven't any more in my own purse!" We hadn't remembered to show poor Fran how to open the cash drawer.

When we finally closed up that night and staggered to our rooms, we agreed that Fran's prophecy was unassailably right on two counts: we'd kill ourselves, and it would be fun.

13

Saturday Night Dance

Since the day I had succeeded in hiring the band, Dorothy and I kept reminding each other at odd moments of the many details that had to be attended to for a dance. Tickets—did one get them printed? There wasn't time, and Dorothy said it wasn't usual. We foraged in the supplies and found a box of those price tags with strings on them that you loop around the neck of a toy. The girls could wear them on their wrists, the boys in their lapels. Later we tried the rubber stamp which many country dances use. You stamp the customer's wrist after he's paid his fifty cents, and he is free to wander out and come back any time during the evening. Ticket stubs are no good—the little ones lose them. But the customers complained that the ink wouldn't wash off and they went around tattooed all week, so eventually we did have tickets printed. By that time we knew which youngsters would try to crash and which wouldn't, and it didn't matter about the lost stubs.

I spent a couple of hours in the box office Saturday, cleaning, polishing up; I would be cashier and Dorothy would stay in the store. We brought in the cooler for soda pop and set up a counter inside the entrance opposite the box office. Our boy Walter agreed to take the pop counter.

It seemed the part of wisdom to have the strong arm of the Law in case of need. I called the police station and asked if they could send someone. They couldn't—it was the big week end and all their men were on duty. So we hired a well-muscled local youth to act as our bouncer.

We anticipated that there might be trouble. Dorothy had mentioned, and other summer people had hinted, that there were feuds of long standing in the neighborhood. The mill-town boys hated the lobster-boat boys, but both hated the summer boys and would join forces against them when necessary. And on Saturday night all three factions were likely to be on the town.

We announced the start of the dance for seven-thirty. Dorothy said that all the children, down to the age of four, normally came to the dances for the first half; around nine there would be an intermission, when they would be collected in flocks and taken home to bed, and the young people thereafter had the floor to themselves. If trouble had to start we hoped it would wait at least until after the little ones were gone.

But it didn't wait.

My three musicians arrived, all in good order, and began tuning up. The crowd began coming at seven-fifteen. By seven-thirty nearly every family in Goose Rocks was represented and they were still jamming the doorway. I took money, made change, handed out my price-tag tickets, listened for the first notes from the band. I had time to note that the girls looked enchanting, every one of them a beauty, or so it seemed, in their wide, bright skirts and flat-heeled dancing shoes, their faces and throats just turning summer gold, glowing above white frilly blouses sometimes pulled down to show their young shoulders, and some with a narrow black ribbon tied around a slim young neck. The boys came in everything from tweed jackets, collar and tie, to dungarees and T-shirts, but they all looked unnaturally scrubbed and clean. The kindergarten set was there in strength; at this hour they made about a third of the crowd.

Then the band began—thump-thump on the piano—and it was square! Nobody was surprised but me. Pete, the fiddler, did the calling; I couldn't understand a word, but everybody else seemed to. The first dance was a Virginia Reel; everybody got into it and we were rolling. They Ducked for the Oysters, Dove for the Clams. They were Birdies in a Cage. They were Mountain Gals and Buffalo Boys. The place was jumping when Dorothy came over to see, and went behind the counter to relieve our boy Walter so he could go over to the store and get a couple more cases of Cokes.

And right then—it must have been about quarter to nine, fifteen minutes to intermission—they came in. There were three of them, off the lobster boats, and they were just off, the way they looked. They had on their dungarees and stained checked shirts, stubble on their chins, and they smelled of lobster bait. Have you ever smelled lobster bait? Also they smelled of liquor. I could take the lobster-bait smell if I had to, but the liquor was something else again.

I looked for our bouncer. No sign of him. I went out onto the porch. There were several people there smoking and chatting. Someone said, "If you're looking for your bouncer, Mac, he went over to help Walter with the Cokes."

"Gosh, just when I need him—those characters look like trouble—"

"Why, we know those boys—they don't mean any harm—" But they'd been drinking and the place was full of children. I went back inside. While I watched, one of the bully boys went up to a dancing couple, whacked the man on the shoulder, and grabbed the girl. That was enough for me.

I waded onto the dance floor and clutched the boy by the arm. "Out. Right now. I don't want you here."

He let the girl go and stood staring at me. People in the sets to left and right stopped dancing, watching to see what I would do. Always, I knew, we were under observation;

summer people and local people both, at the beginning, watched every move we made, waiting to see us make a mistake. This was the toughest spot yet.

Still no bouncer in sight.

I took the boy's arm more firmly; he was a kid, not much past eighteen, but big and husky and his face was mean with liquor. None of the three was too steady on his feet, and this one swayed when he stood still. I got him turned around, talking to him all the time under the music; the music was going right on, and people beyond the range of those right around us were still dancing, unawares. I got him halfway to the door. Then one of his pals put a foot out, and he tripped and fell full length on the floor.

The second one, the one who had tripped him, began to laugh. The third one, who had been standing by, suddenly lifted a haymaker from the floor and hit the laughing one. That one fell against the soda-pop counter, toppled backward over it, and landed on top of Dorothy.

Then I really saw red. I ran around behind the counter, hauled the boy up by his shirt, and without knowing at all what I was doing I made a fist and swung at him. He went back over the counter and landed, of all things, on his feet on the other side. I went after him.

By this time the first one was getting to his feet. He and the third one glowered at me; the one I had hit was quite fuddled by this time. I said to the two, "Get out now and take your friend. Go on, beat it!"

They took him, one on each side, and went out on the porch. He was muttering and feeling really mean, having taken two punches and two falls. At the edge of the steps he shook himself loose and turned, lurching forward to get past me and go back in, shouting the offensive words he had only muttered before. I was squarely in his way. This time I was conscious of swinging—as I remember, it was something between a golf swing and a bowling motion, and it was a perfect strike. He went over backward down the ten steps and landed on his head on the ground.

I can't claim all this success for my punch. He was staggering anyway and he had already been down twice. A light slap, I dare say, would have knocked him over. But I *had* hit him and at that moment I didn't care if I'd killed him, I was that mad. Everything we had and had put into the place, this drunken fool could spoil. I was angry with our friends and neighbors, too—our customers, who were coming out through the door now to see. To see, not to help! And for all I knew Dorothy was lying behind the soda-pop counter with a fractured skull.

His friends went down after the boy and picked him up; he was dazed and shaken but all in one piece. I followed them down and all the way to the parking space.

"Which is your car?" I demanded. They showed me. "Open the door." One of them opened it. "Get him in there and get in yourselves." They did. "And now listen to me. Don't any of you, or any friends of yours, show your dirty faces around here again! Because next time I'm going to have my gun here, and I know how to use it. Understand?"

The gun was only fifty per cent bluff. Dorothy and I, on good advice, had bought a .22 and were going to learn how to use it. We hadn't yet had time, but later on we practiced diligently. When we became skillful we used to go down to the beach where everyone could see us, throw cans in the air, and plug them as they fell. Two girls alone, with so much stock and so much cash around, were sitting ducks for anything, people had told us. But it got around that we could shoot, as we wanted it to, and the truth is that we were never molested, even later during the really bad time when there was looting and worse.

Anyway, my three pretty lads drove off, and I went back to the Casino. People ran along beside me, I remember, and one or two of the men seemed to be trying to apologize, but I wouldn't stop and I wouldn't listen. I was still churning inside like a volcano, and if the truth were known I was shaking too. What I wanted most urgently, though, was to get to Dorothy.

She was on her feet, still brushing herself off, bruised a bit but not damaged. People were clustered around her, asking what had happened; it had all gone so quickly that on the far part of the floor they had been dancing the whole time. The men shouted at me as I came in, "Let's see that fist! Where'd you learn to fight, Mac?" and there were some corny jokes about my going in training for the flyweight championship. But some of the men took me aside and rebuked me. "You're too much in a hurry, young lady. You don't give a man a chance to help."

Afterward I asked Dorothy, "Why in heaven's name does it have to happen to us—that just when we need a strong man he's out carrying Cokes!"

Dorothy said, "Since it turned out all right, I'm sort of glad. He cuts ice with those boys in the winter. I never thought of it, but if he really bounced any of them it might be on our consciences if they got even next winter by pushing him in."

Well, Maine water is chilly for swimming in winter. So we never again tried to hire a private bouncer, but arranged in advance with the police to have a deputy at the dance.

That evening went on without further incident. The dance was a smashing success. As for the next Saturday, people shook their heads.

"Those were Cape Porpoise boys," they said.

I'll tell you about Cape Porpoise. You drive down the twisting, winding road from Kennebunkport, go around a corner, pass a store—and you're through Cape Porpoise. I remember getting gas there one day and Sam Jenkins, the storekeeper who is also the selectman for Cape Porpoise, stopped to talk. (In Maine the conversation is about so-and-so's breaking his leg and so-and-so's boat going aground or his roof caving in. They'll drive nine miles to tell you Joe's wife left him, but if someone has a fall of good fortune you can live there for ten years and nobody will mention it.) As I say, Sam was talking, and a very showy convertible pulled up and the man at the wheel interrupted Sam. In Maine, as I have mentioned, you don't interrupt a man when he's talking. You wait, however long, until he's finished. But this man didn't wait.

"Hey, Bud, how do I get to Cape Porpoise?"

Sam did not say, "This here is Cape Porpoise." Sam said, "You go down the road fourteen miles straightaway and turn around and drive another fourteen miles and you'll be in Cape Porpoise."

"Thanks, Bud!" The convertible shot away, and Sam went on talking, while I pictured that man, maybe eight or ten miles later, suddenly asking himself, "How's that again?"

But the point about Cape Porpoise is that it is the lobstermen's port. And when they get off their boats, they're looking for fun. Many of them are young kids. Lobstermen are supposed to like a drink or two, and the young kids don't always know when they've had enough. Also, as stated above, although they snub the mill-town boys, they scorn the summer people more. And they travel, quite naturally, in crowds.

So people shook their heads and wondered what would happen at next Saturday night's dance. Some of them, I imagine, were not inclined to come. But then they wanted, too, to see what would happen, so they came anyway.

At that second dance the mill-town kids showed up; word had got around that the dances were on again at Goose Rocks. But all was peaceful this time until after the intermission. I had left the box office and gone to speak to Pete the fiddler about something, I forget what, when one of our local youngsters came up to me.

"Miss Mackenzie, a man out there wants to see you."

"Who is he? Do you know him? What's he want?"

The boy clammed up. So I went out onto the porch.

It was my friend from Cape Porpoise. But he was clean and shaven, in a pin-striped suit and a white button-down shirt and a tie, and there was no breath of liquor on him. Also, he was alone.

He said, "I hear you knocked me down twice last Sat'dy." He was looking me over for size, wondering, no doubt, how I had managed to do it.

"I'd have killed you if I could," I said.

"I hear you said we was not to show our faces here again."

"That's right too."

"Then—well—" He tried several beginnings, and finally he made it. "I hear I didn't behave so good, and I come back to apologize. And I'd like if you'd let me go inside for a while."

I thought a moment, and said, "Look, anybody can come here just so he's clean and decent, minds his manners and his language, and stays sober."

"I don't care about dancing at all. I just want to go in and watch for a while."

"You can dance with anybody who wants to dance with you," I said, and led the way inside. I went into the box office, he stood at the window and paid his fifty cents, and he went down the side of the dance floor and sat down on one of the benches. I think he danced once or twice, though I didn't see him myself. In fact, I forgot he was there, the rest of the evening.

And that was the end of it. The Cape Porpoise boys came more or less regularly from then on, but nobody ever came in drunk again, and I had no occasion to try my bouncer technique then or afterward. Or my Sunday punch.

14

Henry and the Goose Rocks Kids

It was a lucky day for us when Henry Peters agreed to stay and run the bowling alleys. We nearly didn't get him. He was Clara Atwood's brother, and naturally when the store went out of the family he no longer had any interest in it. But, like Clara and Herb, he had a deep love for Goose Rocks.

Henry was born on his father's clipper ship when Captain Peters was in the China trade and Mrs. Peters, a young bride, went along. Henry had made money in a succession of businesses but he was not generically meant for business. He was a poet.

I mean, he really was a poet. Professionally, if one can speak of a professional poet. He had had three books of poems published. He would speak a couple of lines of verse now and then in the middle of a conversation, to illustrate a point or express a feeling. Not only his own: Tennyson, Browning (he was very fond of Browning, an old-fashioned taste), Shakespeare, hardly ever the much-quoted passages, and now and then a little Horace in Latin, which he quickly gave you in his own verse translation before you had to admit an embarrassing ignorance of Latin; he had done a good deal of Latin into English verse. He knew an ode from an epode, a quatrain from a triolet, and when he spoke poetry in his soft cultivated voice without a trace of Down East twang, nobody ever so much as snickered.

Henry was certainly past seventy. He looked, however, like a young and vigorous sixty, and you'd say sixty only because his eyebrows were white, also what little he had left of hair. He was tall and straight and thin, even gaunt. His face had a healthy glow of youth and his eyes were China blue. Perhaps it was because he had no unkindness in him that Henry wore his age so lightly. Or perhaps it was that, besides being a poet, he was also an athlete. He still consistently broke eighty on the golf course and for years he had held the regional bowling championship.

The night Dorothy put her signature to the papers, Clara Atwood spoke to us as we were leaving Herb's house. Clara had not pushed the sale. Much as she wanted to be rid of the store, she had told Dorothy over and over, "It's such hard work running a store, such hard work." When she saw she couldn't stop us—nothing could—she held her peace. But after the signing, saying good night, she said, "Why don't you speak to Henry? I think he'd kind of like to stay on at Goose Rocks."

Dorothy spoke to Henry. He said, without cracking a smile, "I have never worked for a lady before, and you are two, and quite young ones." He looked at Dorothy as though she were still the little girl with curls he had known all her life. As for me, I was still in rompers. It turned out he did want to stay on at Goose Rocks and would be delighted to take charge of the bowling alleys and keep the Casino slicked up and the dance floor waxed, for a small salary and commission. He would have his old room over the store where he had slept when he worked for Herb, and that was as good as having a night watchman. Henry became a comfort to us all around. Any time one of us got really frothy with frustration—and that was principally me, because Dorothy had sources of calm inside her that never seemed to run dry—all we had to do was run over to the Casino and have a quiet word with Henry, with maybe a line or two of appropriate philosophical verse.

Henry got to work right away putting the alleys in working order. He was ready for business the day the store opened, and if we hadn't been running in circles all day in the store we would have been over there with him, just to enjoy the show. For all his modesty he was proud of his bowling, and he opened the alleys with great éclat, putting on an exhibition of plain and fancy bowling. Henry invariably wore a pair of Army khakis, pressed with a knife-edge crease, and a shirt wonderfully white and crisp, open at the neck but with the sleeves always down and the cuffs buttoned. Covering his smooth bald head was a golfing cap of spotless white linen which he never removed, indoors or out, except to greet a lady. When expressing disbelief or a negative opinion, he had a way of pushing that hat up by the peak to the back of his head, putting his hands on his hips, and looking at you out of his clear, childlike eyes, that was more eloquent even than poetry.

In the kitchen of the store we had put up a mirror for Jean and Susan—and ourselves, if we ever had a moment—so we could tidy up before going out to serve customers. The mirror was bright with daylight pouring through the side windows of the store, and on fair days the whole kitchen was cheerful with morning sunshine. Every morning before opening, Henry came down from his room to shave at the kitchen mirror. He walked through the store, fully and spotlessly dressed, a towel over his arm, a straight razor in his hand, his white golfing cap on his head—and under the cap his face already covered with lather. I never dared to ask him why he lathered before he came down, but I suspect he did so because it offended his sense of propriety to appear before ladies unshaven, even for the moment it took to walk through the yet unopened store, even though the only ladies present were likely to be Dorothy and myself, who were far too busy to look up when we answered his pleasant good morning.

On opening day Henry had no trouble getting an audience at the Casino. Everybody who came to look over the store that day, and that meant all of Goose Rocks, went right around to the Casino to watch him bowl and stayed to bowl a few strings. The kids stayed all day, that day and thereafter.

There was one particular gang of six, ranging from ten to fourteen years old. Individually they were bearable, even nice kids, but together they were devils. Dorothy and I used to watch them, but we never could figure out how they made the jukebox play thirty records for one nickel, or got a pinball machine to jump for a penny.

From the beginning they had us on the ropes with the deposits for soda-pop bottles. No matter what rules we made, they figured out an angle. Mike, for instance, would walk in with an empty Coke bottle, put it on the counter, and say, "I won't take the two cents—I'll have a pop now in the store." He'd put down three cents, the difference between the deposit he was entitled to and the nickel for another bottle to drink in the store. He'd go over to the cooler and pick out, not another Coke, but a soda, on which the deposit would have been three cents (if he were taking the bottle away with him) in addition to the five cents for the contents. He'd open it, start to drink it, and then run out on the road to call somebody who might be going by. Or he'd run over to the Casino to watch the bowling while he drank his pop.

Half an hour later Mike would be back. He would go, not to Dorothy or me, but to one of the girls who knew nothing about the transaction, and get three cents for his pop bottle.

The whole deal cost him nothing but an empty Coke bottle he had picked up on somebody's back porch, and we were out a bottle of soda.

Mike Cary was the ringleader, a golden-haired, blue-eyed cherub who knew all the angles. Ham Erdman was the mechanical genius. Ham was a plump boy, and the gang would have kidded him, rolling along like a little barrel, but that they needed him for the inventive side of their devilment. We ourselves were inclined to forgive Ham whatever he did, for it was he who got our little pickup truck started, the one which had been standing out back of the store for five years, more or less.

It was a 1932 Ford half-ton, and it looked in good enough shape, but it just wouldn't start. After my first visit to Mr. Baumgarten I never walked past the truck without thinking I ought to get it running, to save Dorothy's convertible; trucking meat and produce was doing her nice new car no good. I finally got around to calling, and then I went down the whole list of garages in the township. One after another, they came down and tinkered with it, to no avail. They couldn't even find what was wrong.

Ham stood and watched them work and never said a word. When the last one said, "Sorry, Miss Mackenzie," and departed, Ham piped up in his squeaky voice, "Can I try?"

I said, "I don't see why not, Ham. Everybody else has."

Ham lifted the hood and studied the situation for about forty seconds. He reached inside and turned the ignition. He went back to the motor, fished a bobby pin out of his pocket, and did something with it. He put down the hood, got behind the wheel, stepped on the starter. He tried it a few times and nothing happened. I turned away.

I hadn't got halfway to the back door of the store when I heard that motor cough, sputter, and turn over. And before I could get back to the truck to congratulate Ham, with a wild bound the truck started forward, and Ham drove out and down the road with his pals scrambling up the tailboard and into the truck, howling with joy.

They were gone for hours. Dorothy phoned the state troopers and the boys' parents, and I drove all the way to Kennebunkport looking for them. But they got hungry, and on the stroke of noon the truck reeled into view around the bend. Ham made a three-point landing, scraping the gas pumps, but the kids were all in one piece. And from then on the truck ran!

The other kids were followers: Kenny, Red, and Bib, and Kenny's little brother Joey made a seventh, but they didn't count him. The sixth was Georgie Randolph. Georgie was the oldest. He was small but he had the largest hands and feet I ever saw on a boy, and his ears were as big as bats' wings. His mother called him "Darlin'," and this was something the boys never let him forget. Carrie Randolph's husband made a good living in Boston, and she had a nice house. She said proudly, "I'm just a Southern belle, honey—never had a dustcloth in my hands till I came up No'th!" Nor since, as one could plainly see. Carrie ran into the store half a dozen times a day, her hair losing its curl in the sea air, trilling, "Dorothy, honey, have you seen my darlin'?"

"Darlin'" was what the boys called Georgie when they called him at all. Mostly they ignored him. It is clear that Georgie had a great deal to overcome, and he did his best. Anything Mike Cary did Georgie had to do and outdo. If Mike rolled bowling balls at the other kids' legs to make them jump, Georgie threw balls at their heads. If Mike hid the scoreboards in the Casino box office, Georgie sneaked them out of there and buried them in a refuse barrel back of the store, so that Henry not only had to find them but also to clean them before they could be used again. If Mike went sliding on the newly waxed dance floor, Georgie scraped along right after him in his big shoes, carving his initials with gouge marks a quarter-inch deep.

I had an early encounter with this bunch of young hellions. One day during the first week of the store I saw them playing ball out front. There were all their parents' lawns to play on, there was a mile and a half of hard sand beach, but they had to toss and bat a ball in front of the store, with two hundred and thirty square feet of expensive plate glass. I went out and spoke to them.

I addressed myself to Mike, but from the side I wasn't looking at, someone—and I'll bet it was George—threw the ball at me, hard and fast. On the softball team at Miss Raleigh's I used to play third base, the hot corner, and a hard liner straight at me was no surprise. I put up my hand and caught the ball, and threw it right back just as hard and just as fast. Georgie ducked and then had to run halfway to Biddeford to retrieve it.

When he brought it back I said, "Let's see who can throw highest." I used to be the highest thrower on my block. We took turns throwing the ball up. When we stopped, the kids had to acknowledge they had met their master. I couldn't serve an ice-cream cone the rest of that day, or even punch the cash drawer open, but I threw the ball higher than any of them. They went away quietly after that, and their attitude toward me thereafter was respectful.

Henry, however, had them underfoot all day. Dorothy said, "One more week and they'll wear poor Henry out. I'll have to do something." She asked Henry to let her know the next time they started anything.

The very next morning Henry marched them into the store, five of them plus little Joey.

"Where's Georgie?" Dorothy asked. Mike looked around.

"I thought he was here," Mike said, and the other kids echoed, "Yeah, he was here."

Henry said, "Probably young George found he was needed at home." I thought the pink in Henry's cheeks was a little pinker than usual.

Dorothy said, "Well, let's have our meeting without him." She sat them down at the big table in the restaurant, which was enjoying its midmorning lull. She gave them a brisk lecture on citizenship and community spirit, said, "Now I know I can count on you boys to keep order," and appointed them Henry's assistants and the guardians of the Casino. She shook hands with them all around and sealed the contract with free chocolate sodas.

When the sucking noise of his straw signaled there was not another drop in his glass, Mike said, "Come on, you guys." They trooped back to the Casino.

Henry came over at lunchtime reporting success. He had left Mike and Bib in charge while he had his lunch. The morning's mischief had been set to rights, and Mike had put Joey out for rolling a ball on the dance floor.

"You will have a proposal of marriage, Dorothy, from Master Michael Cary, if you can wait a few years," Henry said gravely.

"But what happened to Georgie?"

Henry said, "That is George's secret, which I may not divulge." He finished his lunch. As he was leaving, he handed Dorothy a shiny new hunting knife. "This is George's property. Please return it to him—but not until the last day of the summer."

George did his best to keep his secret because it was too mortifying to tell anyone. But Joey, who wormed his way into odd places and found out odd things, somehow found out what had happened to George, and Joey's big brother Kenny told me some days later, riding into Biddeford with me in the truck.

I must explain that, although we had modern plumbing in

the store and the houses, the Casino had a Ladies' Room and a Gents' Room out in back which bore those names by courtesy. That morning George had arrived with his new hunting knife and begun practicing knife-throwing, missing the other boys by fractions of an inch, or so it seemed. Henry chased him clear out of the Casino and around it. When he found himself grasping George outside the door marked "Gents" he did the logical thing. He took him in there and held him up by his big feet, head down over one of the apertures.

"The next time," he promised, "I'll drop you in."

George was needed at home for several days afterward, and when he did come to the Casino again he was a much-subdued boy.

15

Bookkeeping, Mackenzie Method

From the start it was understood that the bookkeeping was to be my job. I was a graduate of the finest secretarial school in the country and without question was prepared to keep the books in the most stylish manner. There came a moment, about ten days after we opened the store, when the Mackenzie Method of bookkeeping was revealed in all its originality, not only to the world, but also to Mackenzie.

The climax arrived in the most routine manner, with a question from Dorothy. As we flew past each other in opposite directions between counter and refrigerator or counter and stockroom, Dorothy called to me, "Scotty, when are you planning to send out the bills?" Since almost all our conferences now were taking place in mutual rapid transit like this—in the morning we were too rushed, at night too tired to talk, and there was no time in between—there was nothing unusual about the question. It was only the consequence that was unusual.

The story of my bookkeeping really began on the second day of the store, when I was sitting at the cash register sometime late in the afternoon. I liked the trick at the cash register. My joy in looking at money, handling money, counting money, was almost sinful. I had earned some very pretty sal-

ary checks in my city incarnation, but what's a check compared
with real money, green folding money in bills from one hundred dollars down, mounds of shiny coins! Sometimes I found
myself flipping open the drawer just to look at it. I am accustomed to paying my bills like everybody else, but the recollec-
tion that there would be bills to pay out of this money never
seemed to taint my pleasure in it.

To me the joys of the storekeeper's day were these three:
driving the truck to market at six in the morning, taking cash
in the afternoon, and counting up at night. When I flipped
open that drawer to add up the day's cash, I forgot how much
of it was owed, forgot we counted our profit in pennies. I forgot everything except that lovely money. Here it was, and it
hadn't been here that morning! I was compensated for all the
toils and frustrations of the day when I sat and counted that
money at night. There was something about having all that
ready cash, within reach of my hand, that seemed to allay a
basic human anxiety. With it, I felt serenely confident that no
alarm, no crisis, could arise, in our own lives or the lives of
Goose Rocks people, that I would not be prepared to deal
with. Never in my life have I felt so secure as I did when I
knew all that cash money was in the till.

The cash register stint had other joys, too. You exchanged
greetings and news with every outgoing customer; for Dorothy and me this was about the only way we saw our friends
all summer. Best of all, you took cash sitting down—ah, that
was luxury! Except for dinner—which, despite Maine custom, we still ate at night—this was the only time Dorothy
and I sat down from six in the morning until after midnight.

No sooner did I climb up on the high stool than Imp came
to keep me company. Imp is the all-black one of the two cockers and a very mischievous and endearing character. She
would jump up and melt into my lap, her chin on the counter,
and never move for the full four hours of my stint unless I

had to get down off the stool for something. When the drawer clanged open it came within a sixteenth of an inch of her nose, but she never flinched, never even batted an eye. The customers used to stand and watch her. Both the cockers were the town pets, but Imp, being of the more social temperament, had slightly the edge on Spike in popularity. One day, when Imp chased a butterfly into the path of a car and was hit and thrown twenty feet or so, the whole of Goose Rocks stopped dead until it was known that she was only stunned, not hurt.

So Imp and I were taking cash, that afternoon of the second day, when Mrs. Carter asked if she could charge. I called Dorothy over. We hadn't talked about charge accounts, but I hoped Dorothy would say we could handle them. It seemed to me one of the important ways you made steady customers. And though I myself knew stores where I charged and bought no more than an occasional lipstick or pair of stockings, still I thought people were inclined to buy more when they charged.

"Hello, Agnes," said Dorothy, who knew all the summer people by their first names. "We can handle charge accounts, can't we, Scotty? Scotty is the firm's secretary and treasurer."

Feeling important, I made a note of Mrs. Carter's purchases to be charged. When she had gone with her groceries, Dorothy came back. "Scotty, anybody who asks for a charge account, let's give it, shall we? These people are accustomed to charging at the store, and they're good for any amount."

"Absolutely," I agreed. "Should we offer them charges in case they don't ask?"

Dorothy thought so, and went away about her tasks.

Then I thought, Charge accounts—you need something to write them down on. So when my stint was over I took time off and ran up to Biddeford, to the stationer who had sold me my bookkeeping books.

"I need charge-account books," I told him.

He brought out those pads with a little bit of carbon paper which you put between the sales slip and the duplicate. They looked familiar enough, but I had only seen them from the customer's side of the counter. I took a load of them back to the store, studied them, and in a lull in business I called the staff together and gave them a little lecture.

"Now I want you to study these, and then I want you to write them up very accurately for each charge, give the duplicate to the customer, and put the original on this spindle here. Don't lose them, don't let them lie around on the counter. Put each one on the spindle the minute you've written it up. Name—address you don't need—quantities, prices, total—get it all down. And with a nice sharp pencil. Bobby, mind you keep us all supplied with sharpened pencils." Bobby had been hired that morning to sharpen pencils three times a day in return for all the ice-cream cones he could eat. He turned out to be very conscientious, both as to pencils and ice-cream cones.

The staff listened seriously to my instructions. All the next day, since the policy was now to encourage charge accounts, the slips on the spindle grew steadily. Everybody ran punctually to the spindle with each slip.

After closing that night, even before I counted up for the day, I went straight for the spindle. I lifted the pile of slips off, looked them over with great satisfaction, noted how much money had been charged that day, how much stock was gone from the shelves—and then I dropped the slips in the wastebasket.

Well, what do *you* do with a sales slip? When you've brought it home or had it delivered, you open the package, examine the contents to see if it's what you bought—and throw away the slip. Don't you? I always had.

This went on, night after night, for nearly two weeks. Then someone asked Dorothy, "When are you billing us? Every two weeks? It's more than a week now."

And Dorothy, passing me on the fly, asked, "Scotty, when are you getting out the charge-account bills?"

Bills? Oh, of course, bills. People charge, and then when you give them the bill, they pay. I knew about bills.

And then it came over me, what I'd been doing every night: throwing away the charge slips! So many hundreds of dollars, and I had no record of it.

That night I took the day's slips off the spindle and wrote out a bill for every charge customer who had made a purchase that day, for the amount of that purchase. Mrs. Carter, $2.23; Mrs. Hunt, $1.40; Mrs. Singer, $0.47. I put the bills neatly on top in the cash register drawer. And then I confessed to Dorothy.

She was wonderful. She didn't even wince. She said, "Well, it can't be so much. Forget about it."

But I had looked at the charge slips each night, and I had a very good idea how much it was. It was too darn much to have thrown away. I said so to Dorothy.

"Anyway, forget it," she said again.

The next day, or whenever Mrs. Carter, Mrs. Hunt, Mrs. Singer, and the rest came in, I diffidently handed each one her bill, unable to utter an explanatory word. They took them and went away.

The day after, they began coming back. "Miss Mackenzie, I bought much more than this!" And handed me the duplicate sales slips, neatly totaled and up to date. Every blessed one of them.

I said, "Look, it was my mistake. We were ready to take the loss."

"But I owe you this money!" they answered.

So we were not out any money after all. And something else came of my blunder, something nobody could have predicted, the reaction of the summer people.

The local people said it was just what they expected of those two girls; too bad, they were nice girls, but they wouldn't last the season, making such mistakes.

With the summer people it was quite otherwise. They had been, as we felt clearly from the first day, a little suspicious. They had expected us to be a little too smart, somehow—to overcharge them in ways they might not spot. Even though we had been revising our prices steadily downward—our new policy, which we were painfully working out day by day, until we were charging only a penny more per item than the nearest chain store—still, in our shorts we were so unstorekeeper-like, and the store so slick looking, that they didn't altogether trust us. The majority of them were still driving up to Biddeford to do their heavy shopping, getting their staples in the chain store there. They were buying no more than ten or fifteen dollars' worth a week per family from us.

But after my boner with the charge accounts they began coming to the store for everything, staples and all. They weren't sorry for us; we didn't look like two characters in need of charity, nor were we. But for the first time they trusted us. We might be smart, but we were also inexperienced, and we were honest. We made mistakes and admitted them. We were ready to take our lumps. They began really pitching for us after that. And the average weekly bill jumped from fifteen to fifty dollars.

Not such bad results, from a bonehead play. But people are funny. You learn a lot about people, running a store.

16

Storekeeper's Day

Our days began to settle into a pattern. We hired two more girls, Sally and Carol, and worked out shifts that would take care of the busiest hours, but Dorothy and I still seemed to be working just as hard. Only now we knew what we were doing at least half the time, and the crises were frustrating or funny but no longer threatened disaster several times a day.

We crawled out of bed at five-thirty A.M. Dorothy took her bath at night, so while I bathed, dressed, and made our beds, she was already over at the store starting the coffee. "Dressing" is a big word for getting into bra, pants, shirt, jeans, socks, and stepping into loafers. Lipstick, a comb through the hair, and we were ready—I doubt if it took much longer to do it than it takes to read these lines. Dorothy began the summer with beautiful long hair which she wore upswept in an elegant coiffure. Before the first week was out she begged me to cut it off. I had never cut hair, but neither would she ever find time to go and get it done, so I took the scissors to it. I found I liked cutting hair so well I nearly scalped her. Luckily she has a natural wave, and what I inadvertently produced was a forecast of the Italian cut, real cute and sassy. She should have been grateful; her hairdo took her even less time than mine in the morning.

I followed Dorothy to the store, tossed a cup of coffee

down if it was ready, called the dogs, and was off to market if it was one of my market days; by now I bought produce enough for two or three days at a time. Dorothy meanwhile would wet-mop the store floor—until Henry offered to do it, about the middle of the summer. That done, she began on the breakfast setups. From eight o'clock on she could expect about a hundred art students to come rolling out of bed or back from the beach and into the store for breakfast. Class began at nine, and these kids were paying their good money for it. "Come on, Dorothy darling, Papa Woodbridge won't wait!" they would call, and Dorothy would fly to serve them.

Preparing the breakfast set-ups was a ritual, swift but exact; she could never have got the students off to their class in time if one detail were overlooked. She separated the strips of bacon, put the butter out to soften so it could be spread on toast with a pastry brush, and stacked the sliced bread beside the toasters. She poured cream into the individual cream pitchers and filled the paper marmalade cups. She brought eggs in from the refrigerator and put them into the wire baskets. She had the Silexes going on every burner and extra ones in the kitchen.

Meanwhile I was back from the market and ready to greet the milkman bringing in the day's milk and cream and cottage cheese and cream cheese and taking the empty bottles, the bread man bringing in fresh bread and taking out the stale and giving credit for it, and I was signing their books and putting the milk and things in the refrigerator and bread on the counters. When I was free I carried the crates of fruit and vegetables in from the truck—I had learned to carry them on my hip to save my arms and back and insides—and ripped them open with my pinch bar. No makeshift screw driver for me—by this time I had me a beautiful shiny tool just for opening crates. (I was still New Yorker enough to have ordered it from Hammacher Schlemmer, the fancy hardware store on Fifty-seventh Street where Fifth and Madison and Park Avenue people go to buy a hammer and box of nails or a fine set of kitchen knives.)

I hosed down the vegetables, priced them and the fruits, and put them on display in the store. The last thing we did at night was to put the perishable produce in the ice room, so now I got it all out again, sorted it for spoilage, trimmed outer leaves off lettuce, and put all that out, too.

At seven-thirty it was time to open the store, and I had to drop whatever I was doing, set up the cash register, and unlock the doors. As soon afterward as I could I got out of my jeans, which were streaked from the crates and spattered from the hose, and into fresh shorts, and I was ready for customers. I began each day with forty-three dollars; enough pennies, nickels, dimes, quarters, and half dollars to make change, plus dollar bills and fives and one ten, happened to add up to that odd amount. I had it down to an exact science by now. The morning I had run to Sam Jenkins' in Cape Porpoise for fifty dollars to open the store was barely a memory.

At quarter to eight Jean came on to join Dorothy behind the fountain, and soon afterward the art students began pouring in. At quarter after, Susan was there too, waiting on the crowded tables. While it lasted it was like being washed away in a flood, but soon enough the students were out again, flying to class. And if they didn't go fast enough we had some customers who could be counted on to hurry them.

There was dear Mrs. Hippenhouse, a small round butter tub of a woman, who arrived promptly at twenty to nine every morning, squeezed into the first empty place at the fountain, and asked in her high sweet voice, "What can I have that's really yummy this morning? Shall I try banana ice cream with cherry sirup, and some whipped cream and grated chocolate and chopped pecans? And a nice red cherry on top!" Dorothy or Jean piled sweet on sweet in a mountain of ingenious combinations, and the art students left their toast and coffee half finished and fled.

Or Mrs. Belle Brobach came in, the large lady artist whom we had had to evict from our room the first night, and who became one of our solidest (in every sense) customers. Mrs. Brobach ate regularly and well with us and paid her room rent on the dot. She was also useful—as I have said—at pointing out things that were out of order: "Dear Miss Mackenzie"—I would find a note under my door when I staggered to bed at two A.M., written in her big bold hand—"The bulb is out on the porch," or, "There is a constant drip in the bathroom—a new washer, perhaps?" And at least once a week she would breeze into the store at the peak of the breakfast hour and call to me in a lecture-platform voice, "Miss Mackenzie, the cesspool is acting up again and there's a slight odor—" This also was guaranteed to speed the breakfasters, finished or not, on to their art studies.

We were also frequently visited by Miss Hattie Black. Firm in her conviction that the pursuit of art was inseparable from malnutrition, she would station herself inside the doorway, clap her hands for attention, and admonish, "Boys and girls, are you getting your citrus juices? So good for the elimination!"

Mercifully, during the breakfast frenzy the store proper would be fairly quiet, except for a youngster wanting bread or cream his mother needed for breakfast. But deliveries would be coming all the time, and salesmen arrived early and continuously. After the art students left, summer people dropped in for their papers and a quiet cup of coffee, and business at the meats and groceries began to pick up. Along about this time I streaked over to the guesthouse to make up the rooms and put out fresh towels.

At eleven Dorothy was out in the kitchen, mixing the dough

for her cakes and pies and biscuits and the sandwich spreads, hamburgers, and whatever else she planned for the dinner trade. She learned the hard way to give few choices on the menu. Too much choice slowed up the service. People couldn't make up their minds—and they didn't eat any more or enjoy their meals any better for it.

By noon the store trade was booming, and then the art boys and girls came flooding in again. They stopped home to get their mail first, and if the mail was late the dinner hour was late, too. Also they came equipped for their afternoon painting out of doors. The clutter of easels, camp stools, palettes, and paint cases at the doorway, around the fountain, between the restaurant tables, was a proud sight to art lovers but a hazard to storekeepers; customers and staff were in constant danger of breaking a leg.

From noon on there was no letup in the store. Meats and groceries, fruits and vegetables, drugs, newspapers, magazines, were busy without pause. The fountain was under continuous siege. By five in the afternoon we were generating enough steam to drive a locomotive.

We had been adding services all the time; they snowballed, day after day, during the first weeks. People came in and asked, "What do you do with laundry?" "How do I get a suit cleaned?" "Where do I send a telegram?" Or, "I'm going into town for the afternoon and my husband may call from Boston—will you take a message?" So we found ourselves taking laundry and dry cleaning, delivering telegrams, and running a message service.

This meant, of course, more work and more trouble; the minute you began doing one more thing for people you opened the door for more things to go wrong. But, we assured each other, it was good business. People came into the store to leave and pick up their laundry and dry cleaning, to send their telegrams and get their messages: while they were there they had something at the fountain and remembered or saw something they wanted in the store. Also—as I no longer needed Dorothy to point out to me—it was Service; there was no place in Goose Rocks except the store where people could get these chores taken care of.

We had the good sense, besides, to nail down something tangible for the business.

From the laundry we collected a commission and also got the guesthouse linens done, and we brooked no argument from the driver if the guests used a dozen extra towels. We got our dry cleaning done by the cleaners. Meanwhile we hastily built hanging bars out in back where the clean clothes would not be rumpled or spattered and the cleaning-fluid smell wouldn't interfere with appetites at the fountain and in the restaurant. What to do with the soiled laundry bothered me—the sheet or pillowcase it was bundled in was bound to get stained, lying in the passage outside the storeroom—until one morning I found the solution in a big carton I had just emptied of paper towels. With a huge LAUNDRY on it in black marking pencil it did very well. But I never did find a system for keeping laundry slips from getting mixed up.

We were also developing a registry for cleaning women and baby sitters—no charge—and becoming the central disaster headquarters for the beach. Let any dog catch his tail in a door and he was brought to us for first aid or to be hurried to the vet. We summoned the doctor or the plumber, whichever might be needed. And the store and the Casino were the natural depository for all idle children from nursery age upward. On rainy days or days too bleak or chilly for the beach you waded through children waist-deep. They wore grooves in the floor between the comics magazines, the fountain, and the candy counter.

The old woman who lived in a shoe could have taken lessons from Dorothy (and so could most of the mothers on the beach, if truth were told). Speeding about her work, waiting on the trade, talking with the salesmen, making crucial decisions, carrying a thousand details in her head about the store operation, Dorothy still knew at every moment what every child was up to and was on hand to quell feuds, bind wounds, soothe frustrations, and tame incipient delinquents. They all loved Dorothy and they all minded her. She hardly had to speak to any child more than once on any occasion.

Joey was her special care. Joey looked no more than five but he was actually seven and had the cunning of seventy. Because, being Kenny's little brother, he persisted in trailing the bigger boys, he was always being pushed around and always running to Dorothy for justice. Dorothy knew well that any time Joey got pushed he had probably done something to deserve it. She herself was his victim more than once.

There was the day the pinball machines and the jukebox arrived. The bunch steamed in and made for the pinball machines, and Joey screamed, "No, no, I was just going to play them—I was first!" So the kids went to the jukebox. Again Joey was before them: "Wait, I was first, I was just picking my record!" There was an outcry from the boys, and one or two laid hands on Joey. Joey howled. Dorothy went over.

"What's the trouble, Joey?" she asked.

He looked up at her, a heart-wringing image of despair. Joey's hair, sun-streaked yellow, was crew-cut, but there was always the cowlick they didn't seem to catch and it stood straight up in the middle. His face was tear-stained, his shirt-tails hung out, his shorts sagged around his skinny hips, and his little skinny legs were scratched and scarred.

"Oh, Dorothy, I want to play the pinballs and I want to play the jukebox and I don't know which to play." Tears spilled from his round blue eyes down his round baby cheeks. He held up one nickel.

"Well, here, Joey," Dorothy said, and gave him a nickel out of her pocket. "Now you have two nickels, and you can play the pinball and you can play the jukebox too. All right now?"

Joey looked down at the second nickel in his palm and up at Dorothy again. "Thank you very much, but now I don't think I want to play the pinball *or* the jukebox." And he put both hands with the two nickels in his pockets and skipped joyfully out of the store.

17

The Customer Is Always

I was learning about customers. I learned a little, painfully, every day, but Sunday was my all-day cram session.

All across the United States, from coast to coast, people look forward to Sunday. They can get up and go to church or they can sleep late. They can play golf or go picnicking or just loll around the house and read the papers. Anybody can do anything he pleases on Sunday—anybody but the village storekeeper.

Any other day, you knew pretty well when people would be coming in to buy their groceries and have their sodas, how many would have breakfast, dinner, and supper and at what times. Any other day you were on an express train with well-timed, regular stops when people poured in and out and running time in between when you got ready for the next stop. Any other day had a rhythm to it.

But Sunday was an all-day local, starting and stopping. We had the full staff on, but even that wasn't enough. With the late breakfast running into the soda trade; the sudden flurry when the weather changed and people who had planned picnics suddenly had to buy for dinner at home, or vice versa; the golfers coming in early before golf and the fishermen after them coming back from fishing and the tennis players in and out for Cokes and soda pop all day long—and three times as many people anyway because every house had week-end guests and the Biddeford and Cape Porpoise people liked to come down on Sunday for the ride to Goose Rocks and our good sodas—no staff would have been enough. Then there was always someone on the staff wanting time off because her date had come down for the day. Sunday was quite a day.

The Sunday newspapers alone would have made Sunday a special madness for me. They came, as I've mentioned, bundled in sections, and I was the one who put them together. No matter how quickly I got started on them after they arrived, no matter how efficient I thought I was getting to be, people were always standing waiting for their papers and snatching them out of my hands before I was finished assembling them—"Wait, you've forgotten the book review!" And my best friends on the beach berating me, "What do you mean, the drama section never came this week! That's impossible—*The New York Times* can't have made a mistake. Look again, Mac, for heaven's sake!" And I would repeat, like an idiot child, "I've looked—it's not here—probably it got dropped off at the wrong station—" And they would go away grumbling; of course I was to blame.

And there was Mrs. Fox, who would say every Saturday, "Don't forget, you promised to save the Boston *Herald* for me, dear!" And in the Sunday scramble Mrs. Fox's daughter would pick up a *Herald* and walk off without saying anything, and I would stand guard all day over the last remaining copy, losing friends by the dozen, until Mrs. Fox came in for ice cream Sunday night. When I triumphantly held out her paper, all the thanks I got for my pains was, "But, dear, what on earth would I do with two?" Yes, on Sundays I got to know the customers real well.

Mr. Painter was the bright spot on Sunday morning. He was usually the first customer—no, the second. Ham Erdman came first, although it was stretching a point to call Ham a customer. Ham came very early and made the rounds of the jukebox, the pinball machines, and the phone booth, feeling for nickels in the coin-return slots. After Saturday night's business there should have been plenty. We always suspected Ham was laying a nice groundwork for his first million. But he was a close-mouthed boy, and Dorothy and I never knew when he found good pickings.

Then came Mr. Painter. In appearance he was a small W. C. Fields, dapper, his clothes a little tight, with a fedora which he neither creased down the middle nor pork-pied but wore with one diffident dent in it halfway, and the brim down over one eye, giving him a rakish look which went oddly with his dainty, mincing walk. Mr. Painter had never married. This summer we were privileged to see love come to him for the first time.

On Sunday morning, as Mr. Painter always carefully explained, he was just out for a little walk and he would save Miss McAllister the trouble of coming in for her Sunday paper by taking it to her on his way. Mr. Painter also bought one dozen lemons. The lemons he did not explain, but as every kid on the beach knew, only Miss McAllister drank lemon juice in that quantity; it was good for the kidneys, she said. When he went out of the store, Mr. Painter looked to right and left to see if he were observed, and then set off briskly and mincingly in the direction of Miss McAllister's cottage, which was a mile and a half out of his way.

Mr. Painter showed an extraordinary interest when we put in sheet music. He was observed poring over the hit-parade numbers on the rack, and finally he chose one, brought it to the counter and paid for it; it was "Because." He put it under his arm with the paper and the lemons, looked to right and left, and minced cautiously away at great speed with his musical gift of love. Miss McAllister had no piano. Did he sing it to her?

Miss McAllister was a tall, thin, elegant, and rather spid-

ery maiden lady, quick-moving and talkative. When she came
to the store she came, invariably, to me. Dorothy and the girls
were all much nicer to her. They took the trouble to say a few
more words than "Yes?" and "No?" when she stopped for
breath, making it sound less like a monologue and more like
conversation. But if I were anywhere in the store she made
directly for me. I had a magnetic attraction for her.

The European lady, on the other hand, was Dorothy's because after the first few times nobody else would wait on her.
She came always at the busiest time, the noon hour when the
fountain, the restaurant, and all departments in the store
were under attack and we were whirling like tops. She went
first to Dorothy at the meat counter and spoke in a high, thin
voice over the heads of the people waiting to be served.

"I would like please a quarter pound bologna in slices," she
would say. And when she had her little package, "And a loaf
bread, also in slices." Dorothy, busy as she was at meats,
would go and get her the bread. She would pick her way
through the crowded restaurant, over the easels and canvases,
sit down, and order a setting and a glass of water. Then she
would unwrap her little bit of meat, put it between two slices
of bread, and eat slowly and meditatively. She never spoke to
anyone, nor anyone to her. When she had finished she got
up and left, picking her way out again, paying nothing and
leaving no tip. On a bleak day, the kind of day you get on the
coast with a northeast wind and fog or drizzle when the cold
gets into your marrow, she would order a cup of tea.

Tea—that was just too much for Susan, who was waiting
on tables. Susan stomped over to Dorothy.

Dorothy said, "Don't mind, Susan. In Europe people often
bring their own lunch to a restaurant table. And the poor creature is probably living on pennies—if she left a tip she'd have
no supper."

"Why can't she at least order coffee, like everybody else?"
Susan protested.

"You only need to put a tea bag in a cup and some hot
water, Susan!"

"But it's so—so *different*!" Susan sputtered, and went un-
appeased to get the tea.

The people I liked to wait on were the people who bought
things I liked to eat, like Mrs. West, who lived down the
road. Mrs. West's Annie did all the serious shopping for the
family, coming in as many as five times a day for a bit of this
and that which she'd forgotten, and she never let anybody
wait on her but went to the shelves and got what she wanted
herself. But Mrs. West came in and asked. "What have you
got that's good?"

That was all the encouragement I needed. Brandied
peaches, pâté de foie gras and every other kind of pâté, gar-
lic olives and imported honey and shrimps in lobster sauce and
Stilton in port wine—Mrs. West would buy them all, and the
little salted tidbits and crackers to go with them, and then
ask us over to eat them. She gave a huge cocktail party for
us at the end of the summer, saying she was only paying us
back: she had sat on her porch and watched us fly by all summer, and we'd been her best dinner-table story.

There was a man I loathed for no other reason but that he
always bought thirteen bottles of milk. Naturally he brought
back thirteen empties at the same time. Thirteen bottles are
hard to carry, even empty, and thirteen full ones are impossible in one trip. He was a rather fat man, too. Probably he
had many children, but I pictured him sitting at home drinking all thirteen bottles of milk by himself, one after another.

There was a man I fell in love with, although I waited
on him only once, didn't know his name or anything about
him, and never expected to see him again. I loved him at first

sight because at first sight he was standing in front of the
de luxe shelves and when I came up to him all he said was,
"Sell me everything I need for a party for a dozen or so
people."

He nodded to one after another of my favorite expensive
little tins and jars and boxes and my affection for him grew
with every one of them, until out of pure shame at taking so
much of his money I stopped suggesting things. At that point
he invited me to the party.

From the day we had opened the store our friends had been
inviting us to parties. They wouldn't believe the store was
anything more than a lark. "Tennis this afternoon?" they
would ask, or "Swim?" "How about some golf early tomorrow morning?" Or "We're having a beach party and I'll
never forgive you both if you don't come." And when we said,
"The store, you know," they either laughed outright or were
hurt. "Who you kidding?" and "Of course you can get away
if you want to," and "What a ridiculous whim!"

But this man looked around the store and said, "I wish
you could come."

I said, "I wish I could."

He said, "Well, if Mahomet won't come to the mountain,"
picked up his change and his fancy groceries, and went away.
I thought, That's a nice man, and put him right out of my
mind.

But the next morning there was a little package in the refrigerator: Martinis, from the party, in a glass jar. I tried
then to remember what he looked like, but all that came to
me was that he was tall enough to stoop a little, the way tall
thin men often do, and his hair was crew-cut, very short and
nearly red. This wasn't enough description for Dorothy to
identify him, so I put him out of my mind a second time.

People unthinkingly do things to a storekeeper that are
hard to forgive. You've scrubbed the fountain and counted

the cash. You're ready to lock up after a long day—and six in the morning until eleven at night is rather long—and here they come, a whole family with their guests, knocking at the door, buying sodas, buying potato chips, putting in a long-distance call and having to wait to get the call through. And you have to wait, too, standing on one tired foot and then the other. They may be your best customers, perhaps your dearest friends, but at that moment you wish dire calamity on their thoughtless heads.

And there's the customer who comes in frantic for her laundry on Friday when she knows it isn't due back until Monday. She hasn't enough sheets for her week-end guests and Mac, darling, what is she going to do? Well, what? You could say you wish she'd plan her housekeeping a little better. You could say you're busy and you don't care whether her guests sleep in sheets or in their clothes. You have the choice of dropping everything to make a special trip to Biddeford to get her laundry back, provided it's ready, or lending her your sheets. Probably you lend her your sheets.

But the people who shocked me, right down to my sandals, were the shoplifters. Yes, that's right. A woman, one of our very good customers, would be buying twenty dollars' worth of meats and groceries. Her husband, down for the week end, Back Bay accent, English tweeds, wanders around, just looking, and out of the corner of your eye you see him put two peaches into his pockets, one in each. Your fine peaches from Mr. Baumgarten, nine cents apiece! When his wife is at the cash register you wait until he joins her, timing it just right, and you ask, "Anything else? Some fruit, perhaps? The peaches are nice today."

She turns to him and asks, "Would you like me to get some peaches, dear?"

He answers, not batting an eye, "No, dear, not especially," and walks out with his plunder bulging in his English tweed pockets. I wouldn't mind if he'd taken a peach and eaten it, and not offered to pay for it. But this was plain thieving, Back Bay accent notwithstanding.

A woman who has just paid twelve or thirteen dollars for groceries walks past the fancy stuff on the front shelves. A jar of shrimps in creole sauce is just of a size to fit into her handbag. She slips it in and walks out of the store. What do you do? Call after her to come back and pay for it?

There was one couple who had me fascinated. They seemed to be very well off indeed; they ran a big bill every week and paid it regularly. Yet every so often they would come in rather late, near closing but not so near as to make a nuisance of themselves, and use the phone. The phone booth was at the back, near the meats, and on top of the meats was a display of packaged cheeses. While one of them would be in the booth talking, the other would idly study the cheeses, and sooner or later one package would be gone. Though I watched them, I never saw how it was done. I couldn't even be sure whether it was the husband or wife who did it, because they took turns on the phone. But I know a package of cheese disappeared every time they came in to phone, because I counted.

People took magazines by the score. They would pay for the big one folded under the arm that you could see, but not for the smaller one tucked inside it.

All of us saw people take things, Dorothy, I, the girls, even Dorothy's doctor, who came up with his wife for a week end and hung around the store playing detective. He was horrified. "Why don't you speak to them, Dorothy?" But what would you say? They were good customers. They could afford to pay for what they took. Poor people hardly ever took things, and if they did, one would certainly look the other way because they must need what they took. But the others—

we couldn't think what to do about them, and so we did nothing.

The most astonishing discoveries, however, were the ones we made about ourselves. Nothing we had ever done before had even touched our capacity for sheer hard work. Whatever needed to be done, whatever time of day or night, we could do it. Either of us, or both—and if it was really hard, we made it easier by doing it together.

A storekeeper knows, and only a storekeeper knows, how many and what kind of things you can't hire anyone to do. That snow-white vegetable table which must be scrubbed every night after store hours. The sparkling floor, the color of a battleship and as clean as a battleship's deck, which Dorothy mopped every morning at six while I went for the day's fresh produce. Hauling crates. Lifting sacks. Stacking things, sorting things, checking things—we did it if at the moment it had to be done there was nobody else around to do it: and because of the store hours we kept, generally there was nobody around by the time it had to be done. Scrubbing the kitchen and the soda fountain, which had to be kept like a kitchen, and the meat counter and the refrigerator and the ice room. Brother!

I've heard people talk about how their feet hurt. I never say a word. Because only a storekeeper—not a waiter, not a sales clerk, not even a mother of young children, but only a storekeeper—knows how feet can hurt. You walk from the counter to the shelves and back, to the bins and back, to the deep freeze, the refrigerator, and back, and then the customer remembers she needs eggs too and you go to the refrigerator again and back. Sometimes Dorothy and I were sure we had walked fifty miles in the course of the day. The staff had eight hours of it, broken up in shifts, but we started at six in the morning and when the store closed at eleven at night we had an hour or more of work yet to do. It was the heels of our feet that really hurt; no matter what shoes we wore, flats with cushion-soft bottoms, rubber heels, or whatever, all the thousands of tap-tap-taps we had made all day were stored up in our heels to rebuke us at night. We felt our feet were worn off to the ankles and we were walking on stumps.

Some nights, after we had cleaned up and locked up, we walked out of the store with our loafers in our hands, across the road, across the beach, right into the water, and just stood there. But it was odd how our spirits were always ready to revive. Even while the cold Maine water lapped around our feet, mercifully numbing them, one of us observed that it was a marvelous night, that the sky over Maine had more stars and brighter ones than anywhere else. And the other remembered some special piece of idiocy perpetrated during the day by a customer—or by herself—and we walked out of the water and up to the town house, stifling our giggles so as not to wake the whole beach.

In our little Victorian parlor we lit a tiny fire, put the coffee percolator on, and ate the snack Dorothy always remembered to bring from the store, while I added up the day's accounts. We sat with our bare feet, reddened from the cold water, stuck out toward the fire, and as they warmed we got sleepier and sleepier until we could just barely stand up and climb drowsily up the stairs. We muttered our good nights and went into our rooms, asleep before we reached our beds. Those were good times.

✤ 18 ✤

Scotty Rebels

There was a day at the end of July, with half the summer gone, when suddenly and to my own great surprise I rebelled at the life of a Maine storekeeper.

I guess I was pretty tired. We hadn't had a day, not an hour off, in a month. People were horrid. Nobody was honest, nobody was considerate—what was I doing this for?

What happened was that I got my feelings hurt. Dorothy said, hesitantly and as though she had been thinking how to say it for a long time, "Scotty, dear, do you think you could try to be a little less—well—brisk?"

It was early Saturday morning, meat day, and we were cutting up the meat. It wasn't the best time, perhaps, to bring up a delicate matter, but there never was a good time for talking, and this was the rare hour we were together in the store, alone, and not too beat to talk.

I said, bristling immediately, "What do you mean, brisk?"

"Well, it's your New York pace, darling. Sometimes you're a little too quick with a customer, and some customers are touchy."

"I see, you don't mean brisk, you mean *brusque,* don't you?"

"Maybe I do." Dorothy was having a hard time with it. I was being really disagreeable. "Like giving change—sometimes you slap it down on the counter just—well, just too hard. Some of the customers—"

"Some of the customers have spoken to you, I suppose."

"Well, yes, they have." She didn't say who, or what they had said, but my imagination took care of that. All the times I'd been impatient with slow customers, sharp with overbearing ones, rude—or the next thing to it—with rude ones, all this rose up to accuse me.

"I dare say I haven't the temperament to be a storekeeper," I said, on my very high horse. "I'm not meek enough."

"You don't have to be meek. Just slow down a little. There will always be touchy customers, but they aren't many. Everybody likes you tremendously, Scotty."

I doubted that. And of course that was my sore point. For all my grousing, for all my indignations, I wouldn't have been anywhere else, doing anything else, for any amount of money. I knew the disagreeable people were few, the shoplifters were few, the inconsiderate and huffy ones were few. They just stood out more. What really bothered me was, did they like me? Would they ever accept me? It wasn't only the State of Mainers I had to woo. It was the whole darn population, summer people and all. I loved Maine and I wanted Maine to love me. And what Dorothy was saying to me—or what I thought she was saying—was that I was too sharp, too prickly, too New Yorkerish ever to make it.

Dorothy said, "Forget it, Scotty, it's too trivial to bother about." We finished cutting up the meat.

I tried to forget it all morning. Going about my chores, waiting on people, I was soft-spoken and lamblike and never even exchanged a quip. The dinner hour came and went, and then somebody innocently said to me, "Scotty, don't you feel well? You're so subdued."

I said, "I'm fine, thanks," and finished the order, and then I told Liz to tell Dorothy I was going over to the house for a minute. I ran home and fell on the bed and cried.

I got up and washed my face, feeling like a fool, and put

on fresh lipstick and started back to the store. From across the road Frank Carter, Agnes's attractive husband, called to me.

"Mac, come on up and talk to Agnes—she isn't feeling well." When I hesitated he teased, "Aren't Marg and Liz doing all the work anyway? Come on, they can spare you for a few minutes."

I was tempted, and I fell. I went up to Agnes's cool chintzy bedroom, and Frank brought up Manhattan cocktails, and I sat down and put my feet up and took a glass in my hand. When I thought I ought to be getting back, Frank suggested he could send a message over to Dorothy and if she needed me she'd send for me. It was too delicious, sitting there with my feet up. I said all right.

Mike Cary was going by on the road, and this is the message he took to Dorothy: "Mac says to tell you she is at Carters' and you can call her if you want her and please send over some maraschino cherries because they're out of them." Dorothy sent Mike back with the cherries.

When you've had no sleep, very little food, and have sat down for the first time in weeks, two drinks can make you feel very odd when you get up on your feet again. I thanked Agnes and Frank and went over to the store and straight to Dorothy.

She said, "We're getting along all right, Scotty. Why don't you take the rest of the afternoon and get some sleep?"

So—she didn't need me. Probably she was glad to be rid of me. I turned around and went back to the house. On the way, passing the gas pumps, I remembered something: Dorothy and the Gulf man, the day before we opened the store. She'd taken that afternoon off, and the evening, too. Why, I had this coming to me!

Guiltless as a babe—wasn't I only paying Dorothy off for the Gulf man?—I slept. I rose, bathed, and put on a dress, the first thing with a skirt I'd worn since the store opened. I fussed with my make-up and my hair; I'd never realized what a luxury it was to sit and fuss in front of a mirror without a thought of time. When I was good and ready I went down and over to the Casino and walked in at the front door.

Dorothy was in the box office. She looked at me without blinking an eye and said, "How nice you look, Scotty. Have a good time. This is on the house."

And I did. I danced with everybody, I was charming to everybody, I was the belle of the ball. Old Pete Charbon with the fiddle kissed his hand to me. Henry whirled me through the polka. The kids goggled at me and all the husbands cut in. I had a wonderful time.

When the last couple had said good night, and Pete Charbon and his fiddle, always the last to leave, had rattled away down the road in his Chevvy, Dorothy and I were alone. I stood there in my finery, feeling displaced, while Dorothy went around checking the windows. She said, "I'm starved, aren't you?" while she snapped off the lights. She locked the doors and put her arm through mine, and we walked over to the store.

As always by the end of the dance it was locked and dark, the back door bolted from the inside with a great wooden bar. Dorothy unlocked the front door, and we went into the kitchen by flashlight. She foraged in the refrigerator, got out a tempting small jar that I knew must hold something special, took a box of crackers off a shelf, picked a package of my favorite cheese and some chopped chicken liver—her favorite—out of a refrigerator case. I followed her silently with a shopping basket, and she put the things in one by one.

Like most people, I have always been an enthusiastic midnight icebox-raider. But raiding the icebox on such a scale— having a whole store to raid—is a special privilege reserved

only for storekeepers. Getting our snack each night gave me
the same feeling of deep-down warm security that I got out
of the money in the till. I have been told by our psychiatrist
friends that even quite rich people can have an unconscious
fear of somehow waking up one day to find they are without
food or money to buy it—a leftover from infant days, they
say. Raiding our giant icebox, I had the comforting feeling
that as long as we had the store we need never go hungry.

At last Dorothy was satisfied with the contents of the
shopping basket. We put out the light, locked the front door,
and went to our parlor. With our shoes off, we stuck our feet
out toward the little fire and opened our snack on the table.
The inviting jar held shrimps in sauce, a special treat to both
of us. I speared one with a toothpick, put it on a cracker, but
when I got it up to my lips I found I couldn't take a bite. I
put it down.

Dorothy looked at me inquiringly. I said, "I'm sorry about
today."

"There's nothing to be sorry about," Dorothy said. "Do
you realize that you haven't had a day off, not even an hour
to call your own?"

"Neither have you!"

"Oh, but I have—remember the day before we opened the
store?"

The shadow of handsome Jack Riley, which had been
hovering behind me all that day, rose up grinning wickedly
between us. "Come to think of it, it must have been quite a
lunch that gasoline salesman bought you," I remarked; I
was, of course, bursting to know all about that day, but to
ask a direct question was beneath me. I was already feeling
much better, however, and reached for my shrimp on a
cracker.

"Well, we didn't really get any lunch at all," Dorothy
said. "I had some marketing to do in Biddeford."

"Was that when you bought the potatoes and carrots and turnips?"

She nodded. "Then I remembered I wanted to go out to the Clock Farm and some other places, where they grow the best strawberries and blueberries—"

I remembered the luscious strawberries that had appeared like magic in the store without my realizing it was strawberry season—and the biggest blueberries I had ever seen were even then sitting in their baskets in the refrigerator room.

"I wanted to make sure we would get the best, you know, so I saw all those people that day to arrange the concession in advance. I almost didn't get the strawberries—we had to go to several places."

"How did Handsome Jack like going without his lunch?"

"Mr. Riley," Dorothy said, ladylike and prim, "was very nice about it, but I had to promise to have dinner with him. So we went to the opening at Biddeford Pool. You know, they have a buffet supper every year when they open for the season—"

I had had no dinner and had been barking shins and jamming fingers, learning to lift crates, just about the time Dorothy was enjoying her elegant buffet supper with an attractive man, greeting her friends. Then another thought struck me.

"Is that how all the Biddeford Pool people got to know about the store?" They had streamed in on opening day and thereafter and seemed to know an awful lot about the store in advance.

"Why, there were lots of people, and since Mr. Riley insisted on taking me there I thought I might as well use the opportunity," Dorothy admitted, spreading Port du Salut on a cracker for me and chopped chicken liver on another for herself.

I said, feeling guilty again, "So you really were working

for the store all the time, when I thought you were carousing without a thought of me—"

"Oh, I had a lovely time," Dorothy corrected me. "Mr. Riley managed to make it quite a festive occasion." Her enthusiasm, as always, was restrained, but she seemed the least bit pleased with herself, as though she had been at the cooky jar when no one was looking.

The next morning, Sunday, I was up at five-thirty and about my business in the store, happy as a clam at high tide. I'd had my fling, the mystery of Dorothy's day off with Handsome Jack no longer teased me, and everything was in balance again.

That morning we had a letter from Connie. She was coming up to spend her two-weeks' vacation with us.

19

Breakfast at the Colony

Connie Van Ost was the last friend we had seen in New York before we took off for Maine; we had had a farewell lunch at the Colony Restaurant together. In fact, Connie had unknowingly given us the name for the store.

On a day in July the Coca-Cola people came to put up one of those signs on the front and asked us, "What's the name?" That was when we realized that the store was launched and afloat—afloat? Careening like an excursion boat loaded to the rails—without ever having been christened. We were still using Herb's old bill forms with a rubber-stamped "D. B. Mignault, G. Mackenzie" over his name.

A card had come from Connie that morning: "What goes on, you two? When do we lunch at the Colony again?" Dorothy and I laughed. The Colony? New York? Never heard of them.

So when the men came and asked, "What name?" it rolled off our tongues together: "The Colony!" We knew at once it was perfect. To Goose Rocks it meant, of course, the summer colony. To us it had meanings within meanings. We wrote a card back to Connie right away: "You'll have to come to Maine for it!" and drew a picture of the new sign with the name on it.

We never dreamed she'd take us up. The last thing in the world we could use was guests. Even Connie.

Connie was not Madison Avenue or even Park or Fifth. All that was *nouveau.* Connie was Murray Hill transplanted to Westchester. The Van Osts were residents of Manhattan before Peter Stuyvesant; half the island had belonged to them at one time or another. As for Connie, she was purest New York. Her life followed an immutable pattern. She bought her summer clothes in January, her furs in August. Henri did her hair and Marthe did her manicure as they had since before her coming-out at Pierre's, and her lipstick and nail paint were the right color, always. Connie had done all the correct charity chores a good little debutante must do, and now she had a job, also correct. She worked on one of the leading fashion magazines and she took a two-weeks' vacation, like a good little debutante with a job. Her world was perfect, orderly, and not subject to change, and within it Connie was the most flighty, scatterbrained bit of fluff you can imagine. Or so we believed.

The State of Maine Express delivered Connie at 6:13 A.M. I picked her up at the Kennebunk station. Her face and hair and dark little summer suit had the mat-finish perfection of a fashion photograph. She began—as Connie invariably did—by announcing enthusiastically, "I'm afraid I'm going to throw up! How are you, Scotty darling?" she continued without a pause. "I just can't wait to go to sleep in the sun! What a barbarous time to get up in the morning! How could you *bear* it?"

Of course it was practically mid-day for us, but I didn't try to explain that to Connie. I bundled her and her three large and handsome pieces of luggage into the truck; she sat with me and the dogs in front, and her bags were in back with the produce and the meat we picked up before turning home to Goose Rocks. It was Saturday, unfortunately for Connie, but she didn't know how unfortunate that was. I tried to tell her about the store as we bowled along, but she

couldn't listen. The combined fragrance of onions and rasp-
berries from the back of the truck gave her peculiar sensa-
tions, and when a whiff of lobster bait reached us, as it frequently did, she turned pea green.

She stepped down unsteadily at the store, and Dorothy
was on the loading platform to greet her, but all Connie
got was a quick peck. The meat and produce had to be unloaded before the sun got any higher. We did that and took
her into the store. Dorothy said, "We haven't had time to
make up your room, darling, but we'll give you breakfast in
a minute. Meanwhile—"

"Meanwhile," I interrupted, "we've got to get this fruit
sorted out"—I was bringing the boxes out of the ice room
where they were stored overnight—"and throw out the
spoiled before we can put in the fresh that I've just brought.
Connie, why don't you tackle the oranges while you're waiting for breakfast?"

Connie obediently tackled the oranges; the first one she
picked up had a soft spot, and her long beautiful red nail
went all the way in with a *squush*. I said callously, "Just
throw the soft ones in this barrel, Con," and went on with
the crate I was lugging. I didn't dare look at her face.

She stuck to it. We got the vegetables hosed and trimmed.
When, having survived the ordeal by oranges, she came over
to ask, "What can I do next?" we were about to start on the
meat. She looked at the quarter of raw beef, at Dorothy with
the cleaver and me with the knife, at our butcher aprons—
and said, "I'll just go and sit down a minute and wait for
you."

Dorothy weakened. "Scotty, for heaven's sake, give her
some coffee. I'll get started here."

"She can get her own coffee. It's right there in the Silex.
She'll have to get used to this if she's going to stay."

It was rough, but Dorothy had to admit that we couldn't

baby anybody; we hadn't time. And Connie had better know what she was in for. We couldn't be hostesses. We loved Connie dearly but we had not a spare moment when we could look after her comfort.

We finished cutting up the meat, took off our gory aprons, washed up, and went over to the fountain. Connie was still there and, what's more, she was on her feet. She was behind the fountain, pushing down spigots, experimenting with making Coca-Cola with sirup and fizz. She had even discovered the shaved ice.

"I've had three cups of coffee and two Cokes, one lemon, one cherry. The cherry was a bit sweet. Can I give you some coffee now?" She poured us each a cup, and when she handed Dorothy hers she looked at Dorothy and began to giggle. "Your hair, darling! When I last saw you in that other Colony—! I thought I'd die, just now when we said hello. But do you know, I like it!"

When we'd finished our coffee and I said, "Come on, I'll get you settled and you can change and go to the beach," she shook her head.

"Don't be silly. I'll change and come back here."

"I thought all you wanted was to go to sleep in the sun."

"Whatever gave you that idea? I'm going to work for you in the store."

We were willing enough to try her. No matter how many we had in staff we were always shorthanded. The question was, where to put her? Neither Dorothy nor I could think of anything she could really *do*.

Connie, of course, wanted to stay on the fountain. When she had changed into shorts she gravitated back there. She was there when the breakfast rush came in, and there she stayed. She was not wholly an asset. Jean and Susan were awfully nice about it, but she was in their way. Also, the only thing she knew how to make was Cokes; when people asked for scrambled eggs and bacon Connie asked sweetly, "Can't I get you a Coke instead?" Long afterward, in fact the day after she went back to New York, one of our steady breakfast customers came in.

"Has that girl gone, the one with the beautiful hands and the hair-do?"

"Connie? Yes, she left yesterday."

"She did?" The customer sighed. "Then can I have an egg for breakfast? I've been having corn flakes every morning because she said eggs made her sick!"

Connie had always seemed to me a girl with no business sense whatever. But in the store, surprisingly, though she looked and sounded just as impractical as ever, she never pulled a boner. There was not one crisis, while she was there, which could be laid at Connie's door. After a week Dorothy and I relaxed about her.

I must confess that Connie taught me something about myself. Unlike as she and I are, her strangeness in the store in my eyes was not unlike my strangeness to the Goose Rocks people. That sounds farfetched, if you know Connie. She is slow and full of pretty prattle, while I'm fast and spend neither time, gestures, nor words on anything but the business in hand. We haven't one characteristic in common. But I saw that I expected her to do everything wrong, just because she was so unlikely in that setting. And to the Maine people I was just as unlikely in that setting. (Dorothy couldn't be unlikely in any setting, and besides they knew Dorothy.) Connie gave me perspective on my life-and-death struggle to coax a kind word from the State of Maine.

Looking for something Connie could do, Dorothy put her on the One-Day Specials. This was something we had developed, a gimmick. That was the Schmoo year—do you remember Schmoos? A salesman came in, and Dorothy bought some. We had one big showcase four or four and a half feet high, and on that Dorothy put a display of Schmoos. We sold a hundred, maybe a hundred and fifty, of them in one day. So we looked for more gimmicks: a dollar pen for eighty-nine cents, a tie-in of bath soap and toilet water, late in the summer a special on sun oil, and all kinds of silly toys and gadgets that salesmen kept coming around with. We'd put them up on the showcase for one day, sell a hundred or so, and take them down. Dorothy let Connie set them up, and from then on she took a proprietary interest in pushing their sales.

I showed her how to set up my produce gimmicks, the sales tricks and eye-catchers I picked up every now and then in Mr. Baumgarten's store, like the peaches in the baskets. When peaches went out we had pears. We made displays of berries in season. And one I was very proud of: the cellophane lettuce. This was before cellophane packages of washed greens for salad were everywhere; it was my very own idea. One day when the lettuce looked especially good to me I chose a couple of dozen of the best, trimmed them in two strokes as I'd seen the market men do, washed and shook them, wrapped them in squares of cellophane, and snapped on a bright red rubber band. I carried them out to the front of the store and asked Dorothy, "How much more than the regular can I get for these?"

"How nice they look!" she said first and then, more cautiously, "Maybe three cents extra."

I was so pleased with them I would have upped the price ten cents, so I averaged Dorothy's caution and my recklessness and made it five cents additional on each head. It was robbery, sure, but it was still only a couple of pennies more than Baumgarten charged in his retail store without cellophane.

People looked at them, first eagerly, then suspiciously— what were we hiding?—but they bought them. When they got them home they found there was nothing hidden under the fancy wrapping. It was first-quality lettuce all the way through. It was also washed, and because of the wrapping it kept fresher than the regular lettuce; even the outer leaves were not wilted. So they kept buying them, and I boasted to Dorothy, "See? Five cents more a head!" She asked, "What would you be saying if they hadn't sold?" I refrained from answering that one.

Connie learned to wrap the cellophane lettuce and set up the fancy fruit displays, and she took an interest in pushing those, too. There at the front of the store where she began to spend most of her time, she was near the drug counter, and that was how we discovered Connie's hidden talent. One of our most sensible matrons would stop for a tube of tooth paste, and Connie would sell it to her. Then Connie would pick up a jar of night cream and, turning it idly in her pretty hands, would ask innocently, "Have you ever tried this?"

Just to be polite, the customer would say, "No, is it good?" That was all Connie needed. She would hold the matron spellbound with her description of what that stuff could do for the skin. "Especially in the summer, you know." The customers listened and looked at her beautiful, cared-for skin, and darned if they didn't buy it.

She never used the stuff herself. Connie was a soap-and-water girl; Pear's soap, cakes and cakes of it precisely stacked in her bath cupboard, was part of her New York upbringing. But then, she didn't say she used it. She just said what it might do. Connie's performance with the cosmetics confirmed us in our idea of taking a beauty-selling course at one of the salons for next summer.

No matter what she undertook, Connie really worked at it. Now and then she worked too hard. From the front of the store she often watched me pump gas. Came a day when we were all busy at something else and a car drove up to the pumps and Connie ran out to take care of it.

There isn't much to pumping gas. Once you've seen it done you know how. As in everything, there are a few tricks you learn with experience. For instance, one of our strawberry farmers, who drove an ancient jalopy, showed me that if you jump on the bumper of an old car you can get more gas into the tank. Say the customer wants five gallons, and at 4.8 gallons the gas is at the top of the tank. You jump on the bumper, the gas runs down into the car, and you can get the last two-tenths in. The customer knows his tank is really full, and you've sold an even five gallons.

Connie ran out to serve a chauffeur-driven limousine. She appeared smoking a cigarette in her long cigarette holder, which caused the chauffeur to blink. Even after she had stamped out her cigarette, the chauffeur continued to stand amazed at this long-legged girl in shorts and a cashmere sweater, looking like something straight out of *Vogue*, who was serving him gas. She pumped the gas all right, but then she got up on his rear bumper and began to jump up and down, jostling his passengers.

"Here!" he yelled. "What are you doing?"

"I don't know," Connie yelled back, "It's part of the service!"

But it was something else entirely that endeared Connie to us forever. We were having terrible trouble with the dishwashing. We had boys come in, one after another, as dishwashers, and even a couple of girls, but when they found they were hired for that, needed for that, and weren't going to graduate in a few days to the fountain, they quit. Nobody wanted to do dishes. I couldn't blame them. You were stuck away in the kitchen where you saw nobody and—what was worse—nobody saw you.

But we were serving food all day, and all day the dishes piled up. The staff was good about it. All of them, even stepping out for a cigarette, stepped out into the kitchen and washed dishes while they smoked. Luckily Herb had (as I have said) left us a monumental supply of dishes—he must have had dishwashing trouble too—or we would have gone out of our minds.

We never asked Connie to wash dishes. With her beautiful manicure and soft smooth hands, it would have been pure vandalism. Dorothy and I were doing dishes every minute we could snatch from something else, sometimes at two in the morning.

So the moment when our love for Connie overflowed all previous bounds was the moment we looked around for her one night after closing and found her in the kitchen, doing the dishes. For Connie that was the supreme sacrifice.

Suddenly on a Sunday night Dorothy exclaimed, "Connie! Aren't you due back on your job tomorrow morning? You've been here two weeks!"

Connie said, "My job? In the store? Oh, on the magazine—I wrote them ages ago. I like my new job better." She stayed right on to the end of the summer.

Mrs. Van Ost, however, came up at that point to see where her daughter had disappeared to in Maine.

Connie was one thing but Mrs. Van Ost was quite another. The thought of her walking into the store seeking her child gave us shivers up the spine. With her hat and gloves and pocketbook—woman's club president, Gray Lady in the hospitals, her name on every correct charity or fund-raising letterhead—Mrs. Van Ost could do no wrong, say no wrong, or ever be in the wrong place at the wrong time. She was always superbly underdressed, like the English, in tweeds imported from London and sweaters from Scotland.

She wrote Connie that she would stay at The Beeches, a small, exclusive hotel away down on the beach by itself, and that we were not to take any trouble about her at all. She came into the store, walked in unannounced, and although we had been anticipating her coming that day, we were more shaken than by a fanfare of trumpets. We didn't know what to expect.

She looked around everywhere, and without a change of expression she said, "I just can't wait to be part of what you wonderful girls are doing!"

Nor did she. Half an hour later she was selling penny candy to the kids at the candy counter, her elegant pocketbook under her arm, her well-pinned hat on her head, only her gloves laid aside. She came up from her hotel every day, and before a week was out she knew every child by name, and anybody who had Family she out-familied two to one. I caught on at last to what she was doing. She was giving us quality.

And the quality showed. Every night after the store closed, while Dorothy and I were cleaning up, there she was out in the kitchen with Connie, doing the dishes.

20

Birthday Party

There was a day when we nearly lost Connie, and I was to blame. The one particular piece of negligence I could not tolerate in the store was leaving the door of the refrigerator room unlatched. With all our meats in there, and with the expense of keeping the room down to temperature, I could not see why the staff wouldn't learn to push down the bolt on the outside of the door whenever they fetched something out of there. On the subject of the refrigerator door I automatically went right through the roof.

It was August fifteenth, my birthday. Most people do whatever they normally do, on their birthdays, going to work if they have a job, pretending that it isn't really a special day but hoping someone will find out and make a fuss. I have always despised such transparent deception. I don't expect anybody else to make a fuss about my birthday. I make my own fuss. No matter what my job or who my boss may be, I take the day off. It seems to me that having survived another year all in one piece is worth celebrating. I celebrate by spending that one day in the year doing just what I please.

So on that morning Dorothy stole past my door at five-thirty in her sock feet, carrying her loafers. I heard her. Waking at five-thirty was automatic by now, but it was all the more delicious to flop over and go back to sleep, knowing I was privileged to do it. When all the art students had gone and the breakfast clatter at the store quieted down, I got up, ran myself a steaming tub and soaked in it. I fixed myself some coffee in the parlor and sat over it as long as I felt like. Then I strolled down to the beach with a couple of favorite books under my arm, lay down in the sun—and promptly fell asleep again. I had thought I might go into Kennebunkport in the morning and go shopping, or borrow a boat and go sailing, or get out my clubs and shoot some golf. I certainly thought I would swim. It turned out all I really wanted to do was sleep.

I woke near noon and found I was out of cigarettes. That, at least, was my excuse. What really got me on my feet was that I missed the store! Dorothy had said, "Come in about one-thirty, after the dinner-hour rush, and I'll give you a nice sit-down lunch." But I couldn't wait. I went up across the beach and across the road, telling myself all I wanted was a pack of cigarettes.

Of course I didn't know, and didn't guess, that the lunch I would be given at one-thirty was to be a party, planned by the staff for days, and that Dorothy had been baking a cake all morning. I say all morning, not because it normally takes Dorothy that long to bake a cake, but this one took considerable doing, on an ordinary store day and with one staff member absent, meaning myself. She began mixing the batter right after the breakfast rush. She had no sooner got started than she saw through the kitchen doorway old Mrs. Barnes with her kerosene can.

Mrs. Barnes was little and frail and gentle. She always wore a starched flowered housedress and, exactly centered on top of her neat, faded hair, a regulation Navy gob hat, spotlessly white. She was the widow of Jacob Barnes, who had been a sort of lay minister of Goose Rocks years before. In a black string tie and a big black hat and a rusty black frock coat, he would exhort all the residents to come to serv-

ices in the Casino on Sunday morning, and after the sermon
he would pass his big, black hat. Everybody thought, naturally, that Jacob's collection was for the Lord's sake in the
sense that it supported the Lord's servant, Jacob, and Mrs.
Barnes. By accident of being the village storekeepers who
come to know everything about everybody, Dorothy and I
were the ones to discover how the community had misjudged
Jacob.

We were well acquainted with Mrs. Barnes principally
because of her kerosene stove. Every few days, it seemed,
she came with her five-gallon oil can to be refilled. Now,
filling the kerosene can for a customer was one of the meanest
chores in the store. There was a two-hundred-and-fifty-gallon
kerosene tank in about the most inconvenient and inaccessi-
ble place you could think of; why Herb had put it way at the
back of the big storeroom, where cases and cases were bound
to be stacked in front of it, nobody could ever figure out. To
fill a can you had to climb onto the cases, lean precariously
down behind them, and hold the can with one hand by its wire
handle all the time it was filling. Have you any idea how
heavy five gallons of kerosene can get? And how a wire handle can cut into your palm? Mrs. Barnes, it is true, would
pay for it out of her worn little change purse, pick it up with
her knuckle-swollen fingers wrapped around the handle, and
swing away out of the store with it as though it weighed
nothing at all, frail as she was. She made us, young and
muscular, feel ashamed. But the sad fact was that nobody
wanted to fill Mrs. Barnes' oil can.

She was perfectly willing to wait. She stood quietly until
someone came up to take the can from her, and then she said
wasn't it a pleasant day or, if it wasn't, hadn't it been a
pleasant day yesterday. Because she was so patient and willing to wait, Dorothy and I of course couldn't bear to keep
her waiting. Our young and insouciant staff, I must reluc-

tantly note, used to duck out somewhere, to the ice room or the refrigerator room, or else they were very busy at the shelves with their backs turned when Mrs. Barnes and her oil can appeared. It was always up to Dorothy or me.

So when Dorothy caught sight of Mrs. Barnes through the kitchen doorway she quickly wiped the flour off her hands and hurried to fill the can. She went back, scrubbed the kerosene smell off her hands, and continued mixing her batter. She got a few more ingredients in, and then a car honked, and again Dorothy wiped her hands and went out, this time to pump gas. She scrubbed her hands, got something more into the batter—and there was a salesman to see her. The fourth time she was called, she no longer had any idea what was in the cake and decided it was then or never. She put the layers into the oven.

Somehow, in the same discontinuous fashion, she got the layers out at the right time, put the cake together, and decorated it. When it was finished—and it was beautiful— Connie exuberantly took it up and carried it into the store to show everybody. And just at that moment they spied me coming across the road toward the door.

"Mac's coming! Connie, hide it, for heaven's sake!" everybody shrieked. Connie vanished, cake and all.

I, of course, knew nothing of all this. I came in at the back door, past the stockroom, past the ice room, past the refrigerator room—and the refrigerator door was unlatched. I might have expected it. The minute my back was turned they relapsed into their old carelessness. No doubt I should have had a more tolerant spirit that day, it being my birthday, but I slammed the door shut with all my strength and jammed the bolt down. That would fix them. They'd be lucky to get it open again when they needed something out of there. And I stomped self-righteously into the store, took a pack of cigarettes out of the showcase, and stomped out again without saying a word to anybody. They all seemed to be very busy anyway.

By one-thirty I was starved—and sorry, too, that I'd been too cross to speak to them all before. I turned up for lunch full of love and good will.

They had been shooing customers out as fast as they could. The minute I appeared, a sign went up in the window: CLOSED UNTIL 3:30 IN HONOR OF MAC'S BIRTHDAY. Henry, stationed inside the door, bowed the last customer out—a half-eaten sandwich still in his hand—and locked the door.

The big table in the restaurant was set with fancy napkins and paper hats. Dorothy came out of the kitchen with a big platter in her hands, Jean behind her with a salad bowl. I was soundly kissed all around, and we sat down to my birthday luncheon. There were presents piled at my place, and as I opened them I was really touched. The kids had decided that it would be no fun for a storekeeper to get birthday presents out of her own store, so they had planned and clubbed together and gone to Kennebunkport to shop for them.

Dorothy had brought a bottle of wine over from home. She, Henry, and I drank a toast. Henry, who never drank, was so inspired by one glass of wine that he rose and spoke a poem in my honor, one of his own about Maine. Halfway through the poem I saw Dorothy looking around apprehensively, and I noticed an empty chair. I looked at all the faces, and when Henry sat down and we had finished applauding, I asked, "What's become of Connie?"

"That's what I was wondering," Dorothy said.

"And the cake!" Liz let out a muffled scream and clapped her hands over her mouth.

We all stood up in a state of alarm. Connie was such an unpredictable character, flitting here, flitting there, none of them had realized until that moment that they hadn't seen her since they had shooed her out with the cake, at least two hours before. I couldn't be sure, but it seemed to me they were all more anxious about the cake than about Connie.

We flew around calling, "Connie! Connie!" and at last we heard her answer faintly, "In here!" Henry got the bolt up on the refrigerator door, and there she was with the cake, blue with cold. I myself had locked her in.

We got poor Connie thawed out and went on with the party. If there was any gas or kerosene or other unfamiliar ingredient in the cake, or anything missing from it, we never noticed. It looked magnificent and tasted divine. After lunch we sat in the windows with our paper hats on, listening to more of Henry's poetry as the spirit moved him to recite, and when people came to the door we waved them off, shouting, "Go away, it's Mac's birthday!"

It was a wonderful birthday, and the funny part of it was that I stayed in the store the rest of the day, birthday or no. When Dorothy looked at me quizzically I said, chip on shoulder, "On my birthday I can do just as I please, and I'm doing it!"

🌿 *21* 🌿

The Man with Nearly Red Hair

I hadn't remembered what he looked like, nor ever expected to see him again, but the minute I saw him I knew him: the man who had sent me the Martinis from his party. I knew him even before he turned around, because he was standing in the same place looking at the same de luxe groceries.

"Giving another party?" I asked.

"No—I just figured that if I stood on the same spot again eventually you'd come over. But I'll give another party if you can come to it this time."

"I still can't come." He had sun-bleached shaggy eyebrows with a quizzical upturn that made you think he was laughing at you, although his face was dead-pan.

"Doesn't your boss give you any time off?"

"I don't have any boss."

"Oh. Well, you're not Dorothy, so you must be the other one."

Liz was at my elbow. "Miss Mackenzie, they're out of black raspberry."

I nodded to Liz. "I'll order some right away."

The nearly redheaded man said, "You're busy. I'll take—I'll take a can of beans."

I sold him the beans and he went away.

He came back in the afternoon when I was taking cash, stood around a while, and bought a magazine.

He came back in the evening when Dorothy was on the fountain, and I saw them shaking hands.

When he came the next morning—for come he did—I knew more about him. He was originally from Bangor and had stayed with his great-aunt in Goose Rocks a couple of summers when he and Dorothy were children. She remembered him as a redheaded, freckled, gangling kid. The great-aunt died and the house was sold, and he had never come back, until that week end in the middle of summer when he stopped off to visit some people out near Fran Sergeant's. His name was Bill Gordon and he was—of all things—in advertising in New York. Dorothy had met him in business, and I had heard his name around. Now he was back for ten days, staying at a little guesthouse down the beach.

He came in early while I was setting out the cellophane lettuce. I said good morning and what could I do for him and went on setting out the lettuce.

He glanced over to the fountain where the Sunday breakfast rush had not yet begun, and said, "I'll have a cup of coffee until you're free."

When he came back after his coffee the papers had arrived and I was busy again, assembling the sections. He squatted down and began to assemble them too.

"How big an order do I have to buy," he asked, "to be waited on by the junior boss lady again?"

"You mean me? Why, I'll sell you anything you need, big or little, a package of razor blades if that's what you want."

"All right, sell me some blades, but don't hurry." He went on putting papers together in a leisurely fashion. I was jumping around, busy as a grasshopper, knowing that the whole beach population would come storming in at any moment demanding their papers. And they came, as usual, be-

fore we had finished putting the papers together. He got out
of the way barely in time to avoid being trampled and stood
leaning on the drug counter, watching with his poker face
and amused eyebrows.

In a lull I went to get him his blades. He didn't know what
kind and didn't much care; I suspected he used an electric
shaver and didn't need the blades at all. But a second wave
of the Sunday-paper attack began, and I couldn't stop to find
out. He hung around a while, and then he went away.

He took to coming in five or six times a day. He'd buy a
paper or have a soda and wait until I was through whatever
I was doing. Then he'd corner me and ask for some obscure
item. All summer long I had turned cold every time I heard
a customer say to Dorothy, "Have you got . . . ?" or "Don't
you carry . . . ?" or "I'd hate to go to Biddeford for . . . ,"
because Dorothy would order it, whatever it was.

So I said to Bill Gordon, finally, "If we had a pineapple
slicer, whatever that may be, would you really buy it?"

"Naturally. Why would I ask for one otherwise?"

"I haven't a notion why you'd ask for one, or what you'd
do with it if one existed and we got it for you—"

"I'd slice my pineapples with it, of course!"

"I didn't know anybody sliced pineapples, except maybe
Del Monte. But listen, promise me one thing. Don't ever
ask Dorothy for one of these curious items you seem to need
in your life, because she'll go right out and order them if
they're to be had. Dorothy believes in service. Can I sell
you some medicated dandruff-dissolving shampoo? The man
who asked for a bottle had gone back to town when the case
came, and we've got twenty-four bottles which nobody wants.
I could name you half a dozen things like that. So please,
don't let Dorothy hear you."

He promised. The next morning at six, as I was rolling
along in the truck on my way to market, with a pink mist ris-

ing from a pearly sea and the pines glittering with diamonds along the roadside, I turned the corner and there was a man in a raincoat with his thumb out. It was Bill Gordon. I stopped and moved the dogs over and he got in.

Was he going fishing? No. It was too early in the morning for golf, tennis, sailing, going to the bank, or shopping or anything I could think of, except one thing which I couldn't, in all modesty, ask him. I said, "It's none of my affair, but what business can you possibly do at this hour of the morning?"

"I've just attended to my business," he said. "I came out to discover who wakes me up at six every morning, driving by at eighty miles an hour in a contraption with every possible noisemaking device."

"You lie. Our top speed is only forty. We rattle, but not that much, and certainly not enough to wake you way down there on the beach."

"All right. It's Mahomet coming to the mountain, all over again. How else is a man going to see a girl if the girl happens to be the village storekeeper?"

So he drove to market with me and back, every morning that week. He went around with me on my market calls, keeping quiet and out of the way except to haul and lift and carry things. He came back to the store and unloaded the truck and helped me hose down and set out the produce, and we had breakfast together. On Saturday morning, his next-to-last day, he stood transfixed with wonder and admiration while Dorothy and I cut up carcasses into steaks and chops. I had been moderate in my first estimate of him: Bill was an extremely nice man to have around.

Driving to Kennebunkport and back, we talked. He knew every cove of Goose Rocks, every rocky point, every inlet and salt marsh and sandspit. He knew where the clams were and the mussels, and where the fishing was good. He knew the shore birds, their nesting places and their calls and their habits. Getting up at six to thumb a ride with me was not quite so flattering a sacrifice as I liked to suppose. He had been the kind of kid who gets up with the sun for fear of missing a minute of daylight and roams and explores in happy solitude for hours while everybody else is still abed. He'd had two wonderful summers on that beach and he loved it. It was why he had come down that week end. Why he had come back again for ten days at the end of the summer, he didn't say and I didn't ask. But when he talked about the beach and the early-morning wanderings, the clamming and the quiet hours with a fishing line in a small boat just off shore where the water was still, fishing along with the birds who were doing their breakfast fishing too, then I longed as I hadn't longed all summer for time, just time. I had given up tennis and golf and beach-sitting and the life of the summer colony with hardly a pang. But this was something else again.

"I feel really deprived," I told him.

"You're underprivileged," he said. "But I guess you're making lots of money."

"That's the funny part of it—we don't know. We won't know until after the store is closed."

"How did you two girls get into this?"

I told him. "And we're not really deprived. We want to make money, but a thing like this gets hold of you, too. And we're free of New York. That's worth something. Also, we're in Maine."

He said, "You can fall in love with Maine."

"Yes, people from everywhere love Maine. But Maine people don't love anybody!"

And we were off. It was a running argument that went on through the rest of his stay and afterward. He was a State of Mainer who had chosen to work in New York; I was a New Yorker who had chosen Maine. We were well met.

I said, "New York is supposed to be unfriendly, but if you trip and fall in the street a dozen people gather round to help you up, pick up your packages, your purse. In Maine you can drop dead and nobody cares. You can break your neck to do a favor for someone, but if you didn't do it *today* he doesn't remember it. And it never occurs to him to return it. If you ask for information they look at you as at an idiot child because you don't know something they know. Just because you speak differently, dress differently, they treat you as if you're subhuman—"

"Hey, wait a minute! How long have you been in Maine? Two months, two and a half? What makes you think you know all about Maine in one summer?"

And another time he said, "We Maine people suffer from one big mass inferiority feeling. Everywhere else, people travel, go places, see the world, get rich. Maine people stay in Maine—"

"You left."

"How many others do you know, besides me? Maine people fish in their cold water and scratch in their stony soil and struggle through a long winter. And then the lovely summer comes—and everybody else is out playing on their beaches and swimming in their ocean while they work to make a living in two months that will last them the other ten."

"That's not true. There's lots of Maine that doesn't live by waiting on the summer people."

"Oh, sure. But you never see the other Maine. The summer-season Maine is the only one you know. And that's the one you're complaining about."

And still another time Bill said, "Wait until you've spent a winter in Maine. Then I'll listen to you."

That was the day he was leaving. He also said, "Are you girls serious about this store? Do you mean to stay with it?"

Dorothy was there too, saying good-by to Bill. She looked at me and I looked at her. We had never discussed this.

She said, "I'm game if you are."

I said, "I'm game."

Bill laughed. "Well, I'll be seeing you." And he drove away, back to New York.

🌰 22 🌰

Summer's End

The end of summer came with a rush. We roared along at top speed almost up to Labor Day, and then—sudden death. During the last week people bought less and less. With a choice of carting groceries back to town or leaving a fortune in foodstuffs for the cleaning women, housewives took inventory of their pantries and used up what they had. They came to the store less to buy and more to beg—a box this size, a piece of twine so long. We were packing for every family on the beach.

Dorothy and I shared the feeling of the year-round residents of a summer town the world over—tired of the summer people, tired of running our feet off for them, wishing they'd go and leave us in peace. By the afternoon of Labor Day, with half of them gone, we could hardly wait for the next day when the exodus would be complete. Tomorrow night, we said—by tomorrow night we'd have ourselves to ourselves again. Goose Rocks would be heavenly quiet and next summer would be a million light-years away.

Early in the morning the last of the laden cars drove off. Dorothy and I stood by the gas pumps waving good-by.

We went back into the store. Suddenly the store was cold. It must have been cold the day before, and the day before that, because in Maine you feel the chilly hand of winter even before August is gone; but we hadn't noticed it. Not a de-

livery truck drove up to our door all morning; not a salesman made his cheery entrance. When a lone car stopped for
gas we both ran out to the pumps. Noon came, lunch hour,
and no art students piled in, tangling canvases and easels in
the doorway. We sat down side by side, alone at the fountain,
and ate in solemn silence.

The afternoon wore on. We stood in the show window together watching the sky and the sea turn orange and ver-
milion and rose and finally purple, and when the early evening closed in we looked up and down the beach. Not a light
went on. Not a door opened and banged shut. Not a child,
not a dog, appeared on the long stretch of sand or on the
road as far as we could see.

Dorothy murmured, "It's quiet."

"It's awful!" I exploded. "Please, God, send them back,
and I'll never be rude to a customer, I'll never say no to a
customer again, I'll run errands for them all day long from
one end of the store to the other on my little stumps—only
send them back!"

Dorothy laughed. "Heavens, Scotty—that's how I've
been feeling all day, and I didn't dare say so! I thought you
were so glad to see them go!"

"So did I."

We had, of course, a mountain of work to do. Not only
did we have to clean up and clear out the debris of the summer and take inventory of our stock, we also had to move
everything out of the store or it would freeze up solid over
the winter.

We had decided to keep the little accommodation store
going all winter in Herb's kitchen as he had done. The local
people had begged us to—"Don't know what we'll do without a store, girls," they said. We had engaged the Barkers,
a young husband and wife with two little children, to live in
the town house and run the store in return for their expenses,

a discount on their food, and a small weekly salary. It seemed like a good business arrangement which would give the community a store, give us our freedom, give the young Barkers a home—and it would all pay for itself. Or so we figured.

There was one task to be done which I half looked forward to and half dreaded: the bookkeeping. We had paid our July bills and had money left in the bank, but there were all the rest of the summer's bills for us to pay and all our charge-account bills to be collected. We couldn't yet tell, we couldn't even guess, whether we owed money, had made money, or had broken even on the summer.

We attacked the job of unstocking the store. What was not needed in the winter store we stowed where we could; under any bed in the house on the Point you could find enough canned goods to live on though you were marooned for weeks. I found, to my great joy, that anything we didn't want to keep in stock (such as Herb's original canned goods with the stained labels) I could part with to Pete Charbon in his little store on the Biddeford Pool road; he would take it at a fair price, and glad to.

We got the screens off every building, including the Casino with its giant floor-to-ceiling windows, and tabbed and stored them all. We laid tar paper over the bowling alleys against unforeseen leaks and drips. We aired and vacuum-cleaned the guesthouse's twenty sets of bedding and moth-proofed the blankets and wrapped the mattresses in newspapers against the red squirrels who would move in as soon as we moved out. We had Abby Peace to help with the cleaning and Will to help with the heavy work, but we didn't know how much money we could afford to spend for more help so we did most of it ourselves. And at every step of the way we got hung up on little decisions. Should the screens be painted before they were stored or when they were taken out in the spring? Should we leave all the electricity turned on in the

store or none, and if some, which? Should we give away the
Lost and Found now or keep it until next season when people came back again? And somebody's laundry and somebody
else's suit from the cleaner kept arriving after the people had
left and had to be sent after them. We got it all done at last
and moved back to the house on the Point.

On the day I sat down to the bookkeeping, the sea beyond
my window was a crystalline blue, the sun golden with the
honeyed gold of Indian summer. This surely was the loveliest
time of year, after the sinister line storms, when the Maine
coast took its last sighing farewell of summer before steeling
itself against the gales and sleet and lashing seas to come.

But I had something more engrossing than nature's mood
to attend to. The first figure I was after was our total gross
business for the summer. I had columns and columns of digits,
each entry representing that moment at the end of a day
when I added up the contents of the cash drawer, deducted
my kitty of forty-three dollars, and wrote down the day's
take. I went over and over my sums until I got the same answer three times, and still I couldn't believe it: fifty-two thousand dollars had passed through our hands in the ten weeks
we had been open! In a business that's done in pennies!

Now the other side of the story. Dorothy had told me
many times, "If we come out even or only a little under we
ought to consider it a very good first year." Still, the pencil
shook in my hand. And this was more complicated: check
stubs to compare with bank statements, unpaid bills to take
account of.

There were bills for stock we had ordered the last of
August and the first week of September, because people still
needed things, and we had to keep essentials on the shelves
until the very hour they left. I had vouchers, on which we
could never read the writing, and anyway vouchers didn't
show prices, because one of us would have settled the price

with the salesman and we never had time to keep a record. As a matter of course we trusted the salesmen. It never occurred to us that anybody would take advantage of our inexperience, and it hasn't occurred to us since. The salesmen were on our side. They wanted us to do well and stay in business. They explained, advised, encouraged—and when they made a price with us they held to it. The American salesman is a professional man, with professional ethics. He is also a traveling information bureau about his own product and a great many related products as well.

Some of the bills I had to reckon were for the whole summer's operation. The Biddeford Hardware, where Dorothy's family had bought for twenty years, never sent her a bill until after the end of summer. They did the same now, but the store bill was something quite different from a family bill; we had bought hundreds of dollars' worth of paint, shellac, turpentine, paint remover, brushes, tools. The same with the cooking gas and fuel oil.

Of these bills I had some and could estimate others. But there were also bills we didn't expect for things we had long forgotten. Will had repaired the big refrigerator—in July? August? It was October when he got around to sending the bill for fifty-two fifty. Andrew Austin had sent a plumber in midsummer to fix faucets in the guesthouse. We paid the man for his labor on the spot, but months later there was a bill for the hardware he had needed. The little old gentleman came down from Portland to turn off the soda fountain, and we paid him his time and wished him a good winter, and in October we received a bill from Portland for special wrenches and special wires to go into certain pipes. We never saw the wrenches or the wire any more than we saw the pipes, but one pays such bills without question. And suddenly there was a water bill for a hundred and twenty dollars.

Bills like these were likely to be coming right up to the first of the year. When I added up my estimates they were not overwhelming, but all the same the figure for profit that I was looking for at this moment would be more a figure of speech than a final sum of money. Still, I couldn't wait. I had to know whether we had a profit or a loss. I had to know whether, when I had written checks for all the bills I knew about, there would be any money left in the bank.

Finally I got it, a round number. I ran down to Dorothy.

She was stowing our winter meat in the deep freeze. We had bought—at wholesale, of course—and cut up enough meat to last ourselves and the Barkers and the accommodation store. It's a very snug feeling to know you have food in the house for the winter.

I shrieked, "Dorothy! We made a profit! Maybe as much as ten thousand dollars!"

She was holding a porterhouse steak in her hands. She flipped the steak into the air and we fell into each other's arms.

When we stopped shrieking, Dorothy looked over the figures with me. She said, "That's right. And that. And that's near enough," to my estimates of bills still to come. Finally she said, "You made one mistake. You forgot to deduct for our salaries."

I felt silly. Heaven knew we had earned them! But it was a technical mistake. Our salaries, deducted or not, would still be part of the money in the bank. And the money in the bank was all we really cared about. Ten thousand!

"We'll celebrate," Dorothy said. "We'll have this steak for dinner." She retrieved it from where it hung precariously over the edge of the freezer.

"It's big enough for ten people, Dorothy!"

"Then we'll have guests. Look out the window. The guests are just down the beach."

All the time I had been working on the accounting, I had

been aware of voices somewhere near. My window, however, faced the sea and Timber Island, and I was too absorbed in my columns of figures to go to another window. Now I did.

Over at Mr. Woodbridge's, three men were building an extension to the studio. They were, as I might have guessed, Albion, Chris, and Roy Kinney from Biddeford, a genial fellow, who worked with Chris and Albion now and then. He was given to high spirits on occasion, when he would drive along the beach at top speed with one hand on the wheel and a .22 braced against his shoulder, popping at flying crows and never missing. I opened the window and yelled, my voice echoing in that clear rarefied air, "Hi! Come in when you're through—there's a pot of coffee on the stove." They waved and nodded that they would. When it was time to quit for the day they put up their tools and came in, and all three cheerfully accepted our invitation to share the steak.

One thing our ten thousand was going to buy us for sure was a fireplace. We had had architects and builders in, but the best plan any of them could suggest still cut up the rooms into pretzels. Dorothy, I knew, had great faith in the native ingenuity of the local men and their skill with materials, especially of the three who were our dinner guests. So I was not greatly surprised when she said after dinner, "Where do you think we can put a fireplace in this house? Everybody says it can't be done."

They had been sitting at their ease, each in his characteristic way. Albion, with his natural dignity, needed only tweeds and a pipe to look like an English country gentleman. Chris was being decorative without trying, his long legs stretched out with their handworked cowhide boots, his sleeves rolled up, and hands clasped behind his fine, white-crowned head, showing the Indian bangle on his muscled brown arm; Chris, of course, was doing all the talking. And Roy—Roy just sat, his eyes half closed, replete and sleepy. Here were three

Maine men who had been born and lived all their lives within a few miles of each other, all of the same age, working—and not working—at the same trades, enjoying the same opportunities and education or the lack of them. And yet in essential personality they were as different from each other as three men could be who had met here from the farthest part of the earth. Who says there's a Maine type?

At Dorothy's challenge the three came to their feet and began to walk around, measuring with their eyes, figuring in their heads, talking that doubletalk of skilled workmen which now I understand a little but which then was as clear to me as Sanskrit. They went down into the cellar, up into the bedrooms, even into the attic.

In the end it was Roy, now thoroughly awake and functioning, who came up with the answer that would put not one but two fireplaces in the right spots—one in the living room, one in the sunroom—and cut only a few feet off one of the bedrooms upstairs. The others looked for bugs in the plan and found none. And Dorothy said to Roy, "All right, when can you start?"

Whatever the date was that we set that night, Roy and his tools and helpers and the mason from Biddeford didn't get around to starting until after the pleasant weather had broken. When November gales whipped the sea and roared icily across the land, they roared also through a hole in the house which went from cellar to attic and right through the roof. We brought mattresses downstairs, and we and the shivering dogs lived, ate, and slept huddled in the kitchen for three and a half weeks that seemed like a six-months' polar winter. Then the chimney was finished, and we had two fireplaces wide and deep enough to sleep in, dogs and all.

🦋 23 🦋

Maine Winter

Bill had said, "Wait until you've spent a winter in Maine." I hadn't long to wait.

The change came with the first snowstorm. It began on a gray afternoon and snowed through the night. The wind kept me awake, shrieking like a horde of demons. All at once it stopped, and in an absolute stillness in which the snow kept silently falling and falling, I went to sleep.

Very early the sound of a car on the road woke me. Sounds travel in that sharp clear air, and I recognized the cough and rattle of our neighbor Phil Smith's 1940 Chevrolet. The sky was clear, the sun shining. I threw up my window and put my head out over snow inches deep on the sill. Across an ice-blue sea the rollers marched in regular rows toward the beach, carrying white crests so dazzling that the tears started to my eyes. The beach was deep in snow above the tide line. The air was still but it seemed to shimmer with the dry cold, and my face stung like sunburn from it. I closed the window and ran to another to look out on the village. Snow lay on the branches of trees, on the roofs and porches of all the shuttered, boarded-up houses. It was drifted against the doors; drifts blocked the driveways. I looked down at our own driveway and saw that we were effectually snowed in. But the road must have been plowed, or Phil couldn't have driven by.

Dorothy called to me. Dorothy was down with a bad throat

which had turned into flu. She had been running high temperatures for two days. Hearing her, I ran into her room. She looked better but she had hardly any voice.

"Have they plowed the drive?" she whispered.

"The road is plowed. Are they supposed to plow the drive, too?"

"Yes, with the small plow. Poor Scotty—you're getting a big dose of Maine winter, all at once."

I said, "Don't give it a thought. I'll get breakfast."

I had washed up the breakfast dishes, got a big fire going in the wonderful fireplace, and got the dogs dried off after their run in the snow, and still the plow hadn't come. It worried me. I had prescriptions to fill for Dorothy in Biddeford, and we were out of several grocery items. But mostly I was worried about Dorothy's medicines.

Over the crackling of the fire I heard what sounded like an automobile motor sputtering. I looked out, and there was Phil's Chevvy, about halfway up the drive, and Phil himself with a snow shovel, shoveling his way to our kitchen door. He had come back, apparently, to dig us out!

I ran to the door and called to him. "Phil! What are you doing there?"

"Morning, Mac. Pretty cool this morning," said Phil.

"Come in and have coffee with me," I said.

"Glad to. Be through here in a little while."

He came in, stamping and blowing on his hands; his face was beet red. He nursed his hot coffee, and I asked, "What a kind thing to do, Phil, but why did you?"

"Plow broke down outside Biddeford," he said. "I noticed when I went by you girls couldn't get out. And Dor'thy sick, too."

"That's really good of you, to do this for Dorothy. I'll tell her."

He looked at me out of eyes still red-rimmed with the cold.

"I wasn't just thinkin' of Dor'thy. A girl all alone, nursin' her sick friend— Coffee's good and hot, Mac."

He bent again to his coffee, which I had kept scalding for him, and I felt a warm sensation go through me as though I and not he were drinking the hot coffee. Phil Smith owed me nothing except perhaps a neighborly good morning if he chose to give it, and many times through the summer he hadn't even returned my greeting. But he had thought of me, seeing our drive unplowed, seeing the plow disabled. He had thought to save me the struggle of digging out this morning in case I needed to get out for something. It was the beginning of what Bill had hinted it, one of the rewards of a winter in Maine.

There were others.

I got to know our neighbors. Dorothy took me up the hill to the Chilton farm, where as a child she had often gone with her mother to get fresh milk right from the cow. Mrs. Sarah Chilton had come often to the store in the summer. She was by now a very old lady, nobody knew how old, but busy and spry, though her memory often led her far afield and she told the same stories over and over. She brought chickens for us to sell, and Dorothy took them and paid her for them, though she never offered them for sale. They were not the plump birds our customers would buy, but Dorothy would not hurt old Mrs. Chilton's feelings by refusing them. She used them for soups and salads or creamed chicken at the fountain.

Rawl and Lucy Gooden were Mrs. Chilton's next-door neighbors. Rawl still drove the first car he had ever bought, a 1912 Model T Ford. Lucy did beautiful laundry, and she collected china animals. Dorothy remembered, as a child, standing beside Lucy's ironing board with the clean smell of starched, freshly ironed clothes in her nostrils while Lucy ironed and told her about each one of the animals in the china closet as Dorothy pointed to them.

Even during Prohibition these gentle people remained untouched and unaware, although the world and the underworld brushed very close. From her family's house on the Point, on a wakeful night, Dorothy as a little girl used to watch a mysterious drama enacted; it was a childhood secret which she never asked her parents to explain and which she never understood until much later. At one or two o'clock in the morning there would be a signal light out at sea; if she looked hard she could see a man rowing out to sea toward the signal. From then on the dory went back and forth until about five. Then she heard a truck starting and saw the flash of its headlights as it drove down the Old King's Highway and was gone. For a moment in history, mobsters and racketeers had exploited the serenity of this sheltered spot, where a fast cutter could deliver its cargo of liquor unobserved.

Lucy had never been farther than Biddeford, where she went to sell her eggs—rather, to barter them. She had never ridden in a plane, a train, or even a bus. The only horseless vehicle in her experience was the 1912 Ford.

But Lucy knew everything that happened on the beach, because old Mrs. Chilton told her. Old Mrs. Chilton's happiest hours were those she spent sitting at the kitchen window on the Chilton hill, "taking the glass to it" whenever she saw movement anywhere on the beach. Her next happiest hours were at the telephone, listening to every conversation on the party line and contributing her own tidbits to the community pool of news.

All the people on that line knew that Sarah Chilton would be listening and tried to mask their conversations. She had a grandfather's clock with a powerful, assertive tick, and you could hear it all the time you were talking. Once when Chris and I were discussing the cost of lumber for a record cabinet for the big house—what people paid for things was always of great interest to Sarah—the grandfather's clock suddenly began to strike. It struck one, two, all the way up to eight, and when it stopped there was a moment of dead silence punctuated only by the tick. Then Chris said, "Sarah Chilton, that old clock of yours is ten minutes slow!"

"Is it!" exclaimed Sarah, and promptly hung up, no doubt to go at once and set it right. But if Chris had intended to rebuke her, she was not at all discouraged from her favorite pastime. The old clock continued to tick through every conversation on Sarah Chilton's line.

That was old Maine. I got to know young Maine, too, in Bob and Majorie Wilkins and their little boy Stevie who lived in a small trim house on the beach. Marjorie and Bob had both been away to college, and Bob had an executive job in a Biddeford mill. If you surprised Marjorie at six in the morning the beds would have their ruffled spreads on and no dust under them, and Marjorie would have on a pretty cotton dress and fresh lipstick. Marjorie didn't seem to mind at all her isolation through the winter. She relied for her knowledge of the world mainly on the thick, meaty women's magazines which came every month, bringing her the latest advices in homemaking and child-rearing. We had dinner with the Wilkinses and they with us; we listened to music and played Canasta and talked. Marjorie, I thought, was as brisk and well informed as any young wife and mother in a Long Island or Westchester suburb.

Dorothy and I discovered mail-order Christmas shopping. In New York I had come to resent Christmas more each year: the pushing, scrambling brawls in the stores, in the streets; the transparent come-ons of competitive merchandising making a fast dollar out of Christmas giving, making a burdensome obligation out of what should be a warm voluntary gesture. I remembered especially those last hours of shopping when you wildly paid twenty-five dollars for a present for someone who was down on your list for, maybe, a five-dollar gift, and that for some people unless the package came wrapped in the well-recognized wrapping of certain Fifth Avenue shops, neither the gift nor the giver would be much valued.

All these things Dorothy and I could laugh at, sitting before our fire of driftwood sparkling with green and blue lights, studying our catalogues and choosing gifts we really wanted to buy for people we really cared about. We sent our checks in November and wrapped and tagged and mailed our packages before the first week of December was gone.

Even mailing them was joyful. You drove over to Cape Porpoise, to the little white house where the Misses Mayberry ran the post office like their own well-kept house. You parked your car with plenty of space to park, walked up a shoveled path between neat little snow-decked evergreens, and opened a white front door. Miss Birdie or Miss Helen would take your packages, chatting while she weighed them, about the weather, about somebody gone up to Boston for the winter—"Aren't they foolish?" she would say, her wrinkled cheeks pink with healthy color, and to your surprise you would agree heartily and sincerely. Anybody was foolish who voluntarily gave up the privilege of wintering in Maine.

We had no country winter clothes; we bought those by mail too, from the beautiful pictures in the catalogues. We ordered from Abercrombie and Fitch, a store we knew well, but also from L. L. Bean in Maine, who outfit the really serious hunters and sportsmen of New England.

We gave each other presents we could not possibly have imagined in our other life: an electric heater, half a fireplace. And we discovered a surprising fact: storekeepers get no business loot! In the advertising and public-relations business everyone you deal with, from the clients down to the printer who prints your stationery—and especially every last salesman of every variety of product or service—loads you with gifts. On Christmas Eve you had to take a taxi to carry all the gaudy packages home—perfume, leather address books with your name stamped in gold, monogrammed cigarette lighters, luggage, handbags, belts. But now that we were storekeepers, though salesmen besought us all summer long, nary an item of Christmas plunder came at Christmas time.

We gave business presents, though. During the fall, already thinking about the next summer, we had written to S. S. Pierce in Boston to say that we wanted to carry that famous New England brand of fine canned goods. This turned out to be no light matter. The reply came in the form of a courteous but exhaustive request, not only for bank and business references, but also for personal ones. We found that in the pleasantest way and with the most impeccable manners everything about us was carefully scrutinized: our relations with customers, with workmen, with local businessmen and tradesmen, our prestige in the community, and whom we knew in Boston. In late fall a call came to us in the house on the Point from a high-up official of the company. He was coming down to Maine and would like to stop by if we found it convenient. We found it convenient and asked him to lunch.

He came, and for the first time I understood what made the cultivated Boston businessman so special. He had charm without glibness, was affable and yet reserved, and through the pleasant social conversation at lunch he was quietly learning a great deal about us. We took him to see the store, chilly and bare but clean, and at his request showed him the shelves we were so proud of, where we would display his celebrated labels. He had already looked around Goose Rocks and indicated that he regarded the community with favor.

His friendly reserve turned to astonishment and then to enthusiasm when he realized the many-ringed circus we had kept going—store, restaurant, guesthouse, bowling alleys, dances—all summer and all at once. He spent the afternoon and left us with our hands full of catalogues and the feeling that we had gained a good business friend.

In one of the catalogues we found a Christmas special, fine glazed fruits festively packaged. We ordered thirty-some, and before Christmas Dorothy and I presented one to every family in Goose Rocks, signing the cards "The Colony" so that there would be no mistaken feeling that they were obliged to give us presents in return.

We gave a Christmas party for the Goose Rocks children. To play Santa Claus, nobody but Albion would do. Albion also put up the tree. Dorothy baked and baked, I fetched and ordered, and together we ransacked the store stock for toys and presents. We wrapped little packages of candy for the guests to take home, and fruit and gingerbread men and candy-speckled gingerbread trees and Christmas cookies. The preparations went on for days. There were nineteen children, from age two to age thirteen.

I was nervous, but my nervousness was nothing to compare with Albion's. Nineteen children, and six of them were his! I spirited him upstairs and helped him into the Santa Claus suit over his clean dungarees and two pairs of overalls. He sat in a chair while I put on his white wig and whiskers and red-tasseled cap, and he shook like a bride dressing for her wedding.

"Would you like a drink to steady you?" I asked.

He was shocked. What would the children think! I rouged his cheeks—he was Santa Claus in bronze, and I thought he could do with a little ruddy color. He said, "What will I say to all the children?"

"I'll talk to them," I said reassuringly. I who hadn't been able to say a word to them in the hour since they had come trooping in, scrubbed and starched and with shiny shoes under their galoshes. But neither had they been able to say a word to me. They knew me in the store well enough, but in a house I was strange and fearsome. Dorothy had taken over altogether; I was no help at all.

I went down, leaving Albion to shiver and shake alone. At

the proper moment there was a great stamping and banging upstairs, and Albion-Santa Claus came thumping across the landing and down the stairs, carrying his pack, brushing the front of his red suit as though it had soot on it from the chimney.

"Well, hello, children!" he roared. They stood mute; even the faces of his own six showed utter belief. He turned his pack out on the floor and handed out the presents. One of the little ones climbed on his knee and touched his face. "You're cold, Santa Claus!" she exclaimed. And that wasn't imagination. Albion had stuck his head out of the window upstairs to be revived for his ordeal, innocently strengthening the illusion that he had just come in from outdoors.

He picked up his empty pack. "Got to go see some children in Zululand, now," he said. "Merry Christmas!" He stumped up the stairs again, banged a window up and down, and was still. Suddenly Albion's youngest boy shouted, "There's Dancer! There's Vixen!" and pointed out of the window, out over the ocean to Timber Island.

Out there against the crystal-blue sky, over the blue ocean frosted with white, the island rose glistening in the winter sun, white-iced. It was a pastry mirage, a confection of fantasy, in which perspective and reality had no part. Without half trying, I could see Dancer and Vixen, too, drawing the sleigh up and over the blindingly bright horizon. I had dressed Albion in his white whiskers and red suit, but winter in Maine would end by making me believe in Santa Claus.

The party was breaking up, but the children and Dorothy —and even I—were reluctant to part. The next day was Christmas Eve. "Would you like to go carol singing?" Dorothy asked them. There was no doubt about their enthusiastic answer.

So we went carol singing with the children, too. We tramped through the snow from house to house, holding the littlest ones by the hands. Everyone asked us in to get warm and gave us apples, candy, cookies, walnuts; Marjorie Wilkins gave us hot chocolate, the thoughtful girl.

Albion had made us promise never to tell that he had played Santa Claus, and we never did. But somehow, by Christmas Eve, everyone in Goose Rocks knew. He'd been so pleased with himself he hadn't been able to keep his own secret.

Bill flew down for Christmas. I told him the danger in which I stood, how winter in Maine was melting my New York crust and getting down to the softie in me, including believing in Santa Claus. He looked amused and pleased. He said, "I wouldn't worry about the Santa Claus part—I doubt if it's permanent." And he suggested, "How about coming down to New York to see the plays and have a few Maine laughs at the way the cityfolk live?"

Bill discovered my fear of mice, and he went around the house nailing metal plates over all the openings through which mice might take a notion to come calling. He measured and cut panes of glass for cracked windows and puttied them in. He saw the damage the summer tenants' children had done to Dorothy's lovely old furniture, and one day when we drove into Biddeford he spent a long time in the hardware store. When we got back he showed me how to repair and French-finish furniture. He had nice long-fingered hands, and they were very skillful.

When I was driving him to his plane he said, "You've done what I've always dreamed of doing. I've been wanting to come back to Maine. Now I think I'm going to."

I laughed outright. "You think you are. Dorothy and I didn't think. We just did it."

He said, "But a step like that takes thinking."

"You're a Maine character," I taunted him. "You'll think about it for ten years and then you won't do it."

"Wait and see," he told me.

24

Farewell to New York

The day after New Year's we bundled ourselves and the dogs into the car and drove down to New York. Not because Bill had suggested it—although I found I was remembering things Bill had said, which was no great feat of memory because he was, after all, a Maine man and not given to many words. We had thought of going sometime during the winter, but we were spurred into going almost immediately by a telephone call for Dorothy from New York. Her great friend Eric had returned from foreign parts, his military service ended.

Eric was one of several fellow law students who had wanted to marry Dorothy, and he hadn't given up trying. Dorothy had been getting letters from him all summer. She was fond of him; she said he was fun to be with. When he telephoned, just before New Year's, and said he was back at last and wanted to get the next plane to Portland, Dorothy told him joyfully, "Hold on—we'll celebrate your homecoming in town!"

This was going to be fun. Here were two nice men to whom we felt close, ready to squire us around, and we could attend to our business in New York at the same time as we enjoyed a bit of city gaiety. We had already made up our minds to collect our belongings—mine were stored around with this friend and that—and move them to Goose Rocks. Maine hereafter would be our year-round home. And in the back of both our minds there was the feeling that maybe we ought to take one more look at New York, at the shops and theaters and friends we were giving up, and be sure of what we were doing. We couldn't know whether the store was going to support us in style, although Dorothy felt certain it would make us a living. We couldn't know whether we could ever again afford to whizz off to New York for a big-city binge. As for our friends, Maine is far away in the winter and people get involved. If you're not a few blocks off on East Sixty-fifth Street or in an office around Madison in the Fifties, you might as well be in Alaska.

We spent a week. We collected and packed books and records, sorted and gave away most of our city wardrobes, and arranged with movers to deliver our possessions to Goose Rocks. We bought our summer work clothes in the winter cruise shops; the saleswomen thought we were more than half mad because we bought no bathing suits, no tennis dresses, no golf clothes, only quantities of shorts and shirts and jeans. Remembering the wear and tear on our feet, we experimented with all kinds of footgear.

It was the first time in my life that I was aware of spending money. When I had a job and a weekly salary, if I had a hundred or so dollars I would spend it on clothes or anything I liked without a second thought—what was I going to do, rough it? And for what? But this money we were spending might be money we would need for the guesthouse septic tanks!

I saw Bill every day, for lunch if not for dinner and the theater. I was talking over all our plans with him by now. Some of our lunches were for four. Often Eric whisked Dorothy away for an afternoon or evening alone with her. Dorothy told me he was pressing her for a decision. He had come back to an advance in position in his law firm and wanted her to marry him now.

The last evening we four spent together: dinner, the theater, supper afterward, doormen blowing whistles, taxis swooping to the curb. It was the New York I had always known, the only life I had thought possible until Maine showed me otherwise. I hardly realized that I might be leaving it forever; I think I hardly suffered a pang. If Bill hadn't been with me I would have been content to enjoy the play— I always loved the theater—and go quietly home to bed. The high surface shine of a New York evening was no longer the gleam of precious metal; it was merely chromium finish. Taxis were transportation; dinner was food, however good, and the importance of the evening lay only in whom I was with.

Eric was at pains to give us his best, and Eric at his best was the most delightful companion imaginable. Bill was content to let him shine, Dorothy was quiet for her own reasons, so Eric and I tossed the conversational shuttlecock back and forth between us. He gave his own zany version of the lush living of a soldier on occupation duty, and in return I sketched him a picture of the village storekeeper's life. Somewhere along the way I realized he was talking about his own future, and very ambitiously. He intended to be a rich and successful New York lawyer.

Eric found a moment to say to me, alone, "Dorothy tells me you are moving up there altogether—I can't believe it. Burying yourselves, giving up all this, actually going on with that mad venture—it isn't true, Scotty, is it?"

"Yes, Eric, it is. That's what we came to New York for, to gather our belongings—"

His face took on a black look and for a moment he had no words. "You can't! She can't do that! It's no life for her!" he burst out at last.

Temper was no stranger to me. I said, as soothingly as I could, "It's her life. She's got to live it her way. I know it hurts her to hurt you—"

"Hurt me? Ridiculous." He pulled himself up as Bill came and took my arm.

Driving back to Maine, Dorothy told me Eric had looked at a place in Connecticut. To please him, she had spent one of her precious days in New York driving out with him to see it. "He had it all planned. We would marry in June."

"In June! We'll be opening the store in June!"

"I told him that."

"Did you like the Connecticut place?"

"It's beautiful, a perfect little jewel. Even under snow I could see— But I don't want it, Scotty. I don't want to be the smart suburban wife of a smart New York lawyer. Except for the fun of shopping, honestly, Scotty, I've hated this week. I could have gone back after three days. Maine is my home."

"Did you tell Eric that, finally and completely?"

She nodded. "He wouldn't listen. He never will. He'll just have to wait and find out that I mean it."

So Dorothy was glad to get back, and so was I.

Except for Fran our Maine friends did not seem especially glad to have us back. Running out with the dogs in the freezing morning, I saw Phil Smith getting into his car. "Hi, Phil!" I called, jubilant.

He looked over at me sourly. "You're back, are you?" and got into his car. But now I could laugh at a greeting which would have had me close to tears a few months ago. Because when we had opened the door to the house at one-thirty that morning, stiff and cold after our long drive, we had found the light on over the back porch and, inside, the Florence heater in the fireplace shedding warmth through the living room. Phil had known we were coming back that night. We had wired him to let in the moving men if they got there before we did, and that we were mailing him the check to pay them. We hadn't asked him to leave a light or turn up the heater. Of course the note he left said only, "You need this heater cleaned before summer."

Everyone else knew we were coming, too. Sarah Chilton had taken care of that. She had listened in when our wire to Phil was delivered by phone, and had "taken the glass" to the van when it arrived and watched every piece that was unloaded and carried in. It must have been a real triumph for her when she called one after another of the local people and announced, "Girls are comin' back!" They had been betting that we had fled the Maine winter and wouldn't be back until spring. With her usual thoroughness she had added, "Cost them three hundred and sixty-five dollars, movin' down from New York. Don't know what for—wasn't anything worth that much in the whole lot!"

So our Maine friends drifted in to greet us, each in his own way, that first morning we were back. Albion came and said, "Where the devil you been?" It was more like vituperation than greeting. But I knew Albion's reverse English by now. He was telling us he had missed us.

Chris shook hands with Dorothy, but he gave me the business. "So you been to New York! Been racing around in taxicabs, riding in subways, putting a coin in a slot, having yourself a time! Buying boots at Abercrombie and Fitch to go clammin' in! New Yorkers!"

I burned. Here I had come back for good, foreswearing New York, breaking all ties—and this was his welcome. I said nothing to Chris, but that night I asked Dorothy, "Do I have to stand Chris's nonsense all the rest of my life? He's going to drive me either crazy or back to New York."

Dorothy said, "Why don't you tell him off?"

"He's an old friend of yours, a family friend—how can I?"

"That needn't stop you. Go ahead—tell him what you think."

My chance was dumped in my lap almost the next day. It was one of those freakish days you get in the dead of winter, a promise that warm sun and gentle air are not gone forever. The day was so still and clear that its brightness stung the eyeballs. The sea lay flat and silky under a sky with a depth like infinity. The sunlight was yellow and the white beach was yellow with it. In sheltered sunny places snow was actually melting. It was so warm that we got deck chairs out of the garage and sat out.

We could see for miles, and we noticed that at the end of the sand point, two miles away at the far end of our cove, there was a car. We got the glasses and saw that it was a jeep, and there were people. It was dead low tide; at high tide that point was under water.

When it got chilly and we went in the jeep was still there, though the tide was coming in by then. Fran, whose house was just on the other side of that point on the second cove of the beach, phoned during the afternoon. The people were at her house. Their jeep, which they had been trying out on the sand with its four-wheel drive, was stuck, and they were trying to get help before the tide swept over it. "Do you know where everybody is? I've tried to find Chris or Albion."

We hadn't seen either of them, we told her. "Shall we come over and help?" we asked.

"No, this foolish boy, Jack Donoghue, is getting some of his friends from Biddeford to come over and pull him out."

That evening Chris and Albion dropped in with some firewood.

"Gawd, it's cold out," Chris said. That called for a drink, and I got out a bottle and glasses.

Dorothy said, "Did you hear about the jeep that was stuck out on the sand point?"

"No, we've been over at the Port all day," Albion said.

Chris hooted. "Probably some damn-fool New Yorkers! They get stuck out there every summer."

I was holding the bottle, about to pour him a drink. I said, "This isn't summer, Chris, and that was no New Yorker. That was Sam Donoghue's boy from Biddeford with his new jeep."

"Was it? Well, now, did he get off all right?"

"So you care! What if it had been a New Yorker? Would you care if he got off? New Yorkers are people, too."

Chris protested, "Why, Mac, I'm always gettin' New Yorkers out of one mess or another all summer!"

I ran on, not giving him time to defend himself. "New Yorkers don't know everything you know, but they know a lot of things you don't. Just because someone is in trouble New Yorkers don't call him a damn-fool. Why, you get your bumper tangled with someone else on a New York street, and six people hurrying by will stop and help you lift it off. You Maine people have no more heart in you than—than a lobster!"

"Why, sure, now, Mac—"

Dorothy was silent. From the corner where Albion was sitting I thought I heard a low rumble, Albion's chuckle, like distant thunder. But I wasn't through.

"And let me tell you something else, Chris—I won't take any more of this damn-fool New Yorker talk. I don't think I look funny in my Abercrombie and Fitch clothes—"

He was shocked. "Gawd, Mac, I never said you looked funny!"

"No, you didn't, but that's beside the point. Where I come from and where I buy my clothes is my affair. I happen to live in Maine. My business is in Maine. I have as good a right to be here, no matter how I dress, as you or anybody who merely happens to have been born here. Even if I do come from New York! And I think it's indecent to make fun of people because of where they come from or how they dress!"

He didn't say a word. It was the first time—and the last— that I've known Chris to be without an answer. Maybe it was because I was still holding the bottle, and if he answered I would answer back and he'd have to wait that much longer for a drink.

I relented and said, "Would you like a drink, Chris?"

"Why, thanks, Mac, I would," he said, and I think he was as relieved as I that that issue was closed.

There was no more talk about New Yorkers, although Chris found other things to tease me about, on which I was not so sensitive. When they were leaving that night, Albion said at the door, "Good goin', Mac!"

🌿 25 🌿

Midwinter Accounting

We were really snowed in. After our spell of mild weather winter shut down again. From then on winter was a close gray wall of furious winds and fierce cold and now and again a soft smothering fall of snow, deceptively gentle until we tried to get about in it, or a driving, howling blizzard against which we locked and bolted the door. We wouldn't see our nearest neighbor for days unless we happened to be shoveling drifts from our doors at the same time.

But I could read all the books I had always wanted to read, listen to all the records I had had no time to hear. I had always been one of those people who feel guilty if they pick up a book or a magazine during the day—daytime hours are meant for work. But now, righteous in the knowledge of how hard I had worked all summer, and abetted by the weather, I learned for the first time to enjoy leisure. If I wanted to spend a whole day refinishing a table I could do it. I didn't have to fly to Saks to buy a dress I didn't really like for a dinner party I didn't really want to go to. Bill had taught me a good deal about staining and polishing, the few days he was with us, and I got books and manuals and wrote him questions and learned still more. I discovered a whole new source of happiness and absorption, working with my hands.

Fran Sergeant was with us almost every day, or we with

her. We would have been together anyway, loving her company so, but we had discovered Fran was afraid, not of being
alone, but of the sea. When the first line storms began to beat
against the beach in September she would call us at six in the
morning, sometimes earlier.

"Dears, the tide won't be high for two hours yet, and the
waves are already beating over the sea wall."

We'd say, "We'll be right down," and tear into our clothes,
grab the dogs, and drive down through the beating, slashing
wind. In places the tide rose a couple of feet over the road,
and we would leave the car and walk through people's gardens and climb over their fences to get to Fran's house.

In summer Fran's house had the most beautiful setting
on the beach (except the big house we were in, on the Point,
which I really loved best). Her lawn sloped down to a sea
wall, and beyond that was the beach, and the ocean. Sitting
down in Fran's big living room, you looked right out on
water; you might be on a boat instead of in a house. But when
it stormed, or when the high tides and violent seas of winter
came, the waves hit against the sea wall and washed over it
and across the lawn and up against the house, throwing all
the debris of the sea upon the lawn with dreadful frightening
noises: logs, beams, some of them big enough, I thought, to
have been the masts of clipper ships wrecked long ago. Spray
that was heavy enough to knock a man down lashed the windows and poured down, leaving them coated with brine.
Many times we were certain the windows would shatter and
the sea come pouring in. Miraculously, it never did. Although the windows on the sun porch did crack once, they
didn't give, and the house stayed dry. One had a new respect
for the elements, after a winter in Maine. It was humbling,
but it was magnificent and challenging too.

Most of the time we were snug. Fran and Dorothy knitted
by the hour while I read aloud. I learned to cook; between

two such cooks I could scarcely avoid learning, supposing I had wanted to. I loved bundling up and going out in below-zero air, romping with the dogs in the snow. I had never known such heart-lifting days.

When Dorothy and I had settled down after our New York fling, we did an accounting. It was not an altogether cheerful session. Our glittering ten thousand, which had looked as big as a million, had all but melted away.

We had paid for the fireplaces. We had paid for septic tanks to replace the cesspools which dear Mrs. Brobach had noticed so tactfully at breakfast time during the summer: five hundred dollars to dig the trenches, and the job cost sixteen hundred. We couldn't judge whether or not it was a fair price. How do you know whether you're getting rooked on a septic tank? We asked Albion. He said, "Why, Gawd knows, it would get a good price, a job like that!" Negotiating with the contractor, Dorothy would be quiet and balky, and I would blow my top: "Good Lord! I could buy plumbing for Rockefeller Center with that kind of money!" Between the two of us we got the price down a little and a little, and probably we didn't overpay—much.

We had paid for repairs to all the buildings on the store property, roofs and window frames and doors, floors that had sagged. And plumbing. We boast about American plumbing, but when you have to pay for repairing it you wish you lived in a little Italian village on a hillside where the plumbing is *à la nature*.

Then there was the winter store. The Barkers did the best they could. They ran a neat, efficient store and were friends with all the residents. But the store was purely an accommodation. For all their protests that, "Gawd, we couldn't be without a store all winter!" the local people never bought anything there if they could go to Biddeford for it. And the Barkers, however hard they tried to economize, were expensive to keep in a house without winter heating. Herb and Clara Atwood had lived in their parlor, close to the cooking range. They never went upstairs all winter except to fix a leak. To keep from freezing to death with their two little children, the Barkers had to have electric heaters all over the house. The bill for electricity alone was sixty-two dollars a month.

We had believed, naïvely, that the winter store would pay for itself. We were shocked when we estimated that, barring any more serious expenses than we had already had, the winter store would end by *costing* us well over a thousand dollars.

I said, "Lord, Dorothy, how did Herb do it? Everybody knows Herb took a tidy bank balance with him from Goose Rocks. And we're going broke!"

Dorothy said, "I guess that's what they mean by a family business. Herb never hired anybody to run the store for him. He, Clara, the two children, their husbands when they married, Henry, and some cousins, all came down in the summer to help in the big store. They worked for their keep, I suppose, and there were enough of them to take turns so nobody stayed at it too long at a time, except maybe Henry. And all winter Herb and Clara ran the little store alone. Herb said it didn't pay in the winter."

He had said that. I remembered.

"They never spent a dime, either—"

"Well, their needs were modest. They were never tempted by Saks Fifth Avenue." She smiled; we both love good clothes.

"And Herb never repaired anything," I pointed out. "Look at our repair bills!"

"That's not fair. Property always needs repairs. Herb had the advantage of being able to do most of it with his own hands."

Anyway, there it was: We were on the way to being broke. Dorothy said, "I can always get a mortage on this house."

I bridled. "I won't have you jeopardizing your house! And what was all that talk last June when we were counting up how much money we could raise to buy the store? All that about 'keeping one thing free and clear'?"

"Of course!" Dorothy said. "So you can raise money on it when you have to! Like right now!"

But I wouldn't hear of it—not her house! Dorothy had a property owner's objectivity about it. She loved the house; her family, her childhood, everything permanent and good and happy was embraced within its four walls. But she could mortgage it if she had to (and then work like a fool to pay off the mortgage as fast as possible, yes, indeed). But to me, who had never owned anything of my own except my weekly salary and what I bought with it, a house was the last bulwark against disaster. As long as you had a roof over your head nothing dreadful could happen to you.

"You're making it a symbol of security," Dorothy told me. "It's nice to own a house, but it's still only a house. Your security is something inside yourself."

"Then I guess I don't have it inside myself," I said. "A house is something I can see and touch and be safe in. It keeps the rain out. It keeps me warm."

"Only moderately warm, if you're talking about this one," Dorothy reminded me. We were wearing our heaviest sweaters and ski pants and sitting practically in the fire. It was a particularly bitter day with a high mean wind and sleet. Wind made the house cold, even though the windows and doors were tight, with storm sashes besides. It beat against the house, now from one side, now the other, and no house however sound could keep out its probing cold.

"You're not mortgaging the house, not yet," I said. "And what's more, I'd feel better if we paid the taxes and the mort-

gage payments on the store all the way to June, right now.
Then we'll see."

Dorothy said, "All right, if it makes you happier."

I had a sudden frightening thought. "But Dorothy, what
about the improvements to the store! We can't afford any
of those now!"

We had been dreaming and planning since the day we
turned the key in the door of the store for the winter. Beautiful display counters, self-service shelves, the vegetable bins
we had wanted and had had no time to put in last summer.
And a cosmetic bar—we were to have gone to Boston in the
early spring to take the beauty course. And a practical item:
the store really needed a coat of paint. We had wanted to
paint the town house too; another summer of that bilious
green and gory red was too much.

Dorothy said cheerfully, "Oh, no, there'll be no trouble
about that. The store will pay for the improvements."

"Isn't that a little—well—rash?"

"Why, no, it's business."

I was silenced. I knew, and I mentioned at the very start
of this chronicle, that for all her gentlewoman's ways Dorothy had a good business head. But even I hadn't guessed
how much business wisdom that head contained. Because it
all worked out as she foresaw, every bit of it.

Well, almost every bit. If I had been willing to do it her
way, by raising a mortgage on the house, that little bit would
have worked out too. But I was stubborn, and she saw no real
harm in giving in to me. I conscientiously paid all our Maine
bills as they came. But the New York bills, the frills and
frivolities—ah, those were hard. I said to myself, "They
won't mind—they can wait until next month," and hoarded
the bank balance against I hardly knew what emergency. I
knew that many of my Park Avenue friends let their bills
with the Fifth Avenue stores run on and on, but I never had.

I didn't talk about those bills to Dorothy. It was my fault that I was uncomfortable about paying them. But I confided in Fran. Fran said, "Only poor people like us pay their bills promptly, child. People who have more money than they need will let a bill run until it's grown to a good size, and then they pay it. They can't bother with little stuff like that stuff you're worrying about."

I was only partly reassured. The bills were not so big or so old, but there they lay, neatly stacked on the corner of the mantel, and every time I looked at them they accused me. One evening, while Dorothy was in the kitchen and I was alone with those bills, I did a dreadful thing. I threw them on the fire and burned them. For a moment I felt simply wonderful.

Dorothy came in, and in a little while she asked, very casually, "Where are the bills?"

I shuddered. "I've temporarily disposed of them," I answered.

But I'm sure I looked as guilty as I felt because when we were going up to our chilly bedrooms Dorothy said, "Darling, you won't go to jail. The stores will all send the same bills again next month."

🌿 *26* 🌿

Spring, and a New Store Budding

April came, full of rain and melting snow and plans. We went to Boston—yes, despite my fears, the bank account was still sturdy enough, even after paying those New York bills, to take us to Boston and back again. We took our beauty course; we learned how to give those beauty demonstrations we had talked about, and especially we learned how to recommend the right cosmetics for the right skin. We ordered cases of a sun-tan lotion which contained the only insect repellent the Maine mosquito had any respect for. The art students, male and female, even if they couldn't afford more than a ham sandwich for lunch, would plunk down a dollar sixty-five for this; it was as necessary as paint and brushes when they worked out of doors.

We went to Boston's annual Gift Fair and ordered that tempting stock of gifts and toys we wanted to put into our big show windows. We called on our Boston wholesalers and discussed our policy of a village store that would sell staples at competitive prices and also luxury goods; we could show that it worked, even on our first try. We were going into it whole hog this summer.

In May the store began to get its new look. Gone were the mahogany counters in a square which had filled the center of the floor. Down the center now ran two sets of open self-service shelves, pyramid-shaped, and there would be shopping carts. Across the back were the vegetable bins. The drug counter swelled into a cosmetic bar.

The show windows became a show in themselves. Inside them we now had curved glass shelves on which one could compose a display with style. On the right inside the door we had our big semicircular check-out counter with the cash register on it. You went through a swinging half-door to sit on the high stool and take cash. This was now a perfect vantage point and the most entertaining spot in the store. From it you could see clear to the back of the store, along the whole length of the soda fountain, and into the farthest corner of the restaurant. You could look outdoors, keeping an eye on the gas pumps, seeing everyone on the beach or passing on the road. Taking cash was going to be more fun than ever.

The order came from S. S. Pierce, and Dorothy and I gleefully opened the cases and stocked the shelves. With their crimson and blue labels, the cans made a solid wall of color striped with the white edges of the shelves, a handsome sight. The fanciest items we put nearest the front, where one of us would be sitting on the high stool at the cash register. Right off I made my bid to take the late-afternoon shift on the cash register. Those were the heaviest shopping hours, and I knew from last summer that during those hours, especially on Fridays when people came to buy for the week end, you couldn't get me out of that corner of the store. From three-thirty until closing that's where you'd find me, selling the goose-liver pâté and the shrimp under glass—to the men.

And now that I had the tobacco and gift items there, any man would be fair game for me and the table delicacies. While his wife was buying the meat and potatoes for his dinner, sooner or later he would wander over to my corner, look-

ing at the tobacco, exchanging the time of day. I would say
how nice to be down for the week end, and how the weather
looked, and presently I'd suggest, "If you'd like something
really good to have with your cocktail tonight, look at this."
And at this, and this—his mouth would be watering in no
time. Even the first summer, I had had men go out with
five to fifteen dollars' worth of tins and jars, of which I could
never sell a woman more than one at a time or maybe two
(excepting only Mrs. West, who bought quantities). I was
already looking forward to that moment of opening the
drawer at midnight, especially on Fridays, and seeing all that
money that hadn't been there in the morning! Most of it, of
course, came from the regular stock—people have to eat, no
matter what—but the extra dollars from our de luxe corner
were my special delight.

In the S. S. Pierce shipment was the first of a series of split
cases containing a variety of delicacies. These were usually
new items sent for us to try out. Dorothy tried them in the
restaurant, and when there was just one jar or tin of something really special she and I had it at night for a particularly
festive snack.

Chris did a complete outside paint job; the store, the town
house, and the guesthouse were newly white. And while the
first summer we had barely managed to keep the grass cut,
now the lawns, the gas pumps, and the drive back to the Casino were cheerful with flower borders.

We had had the truck repaired. Since Ham had started it,
it had run like a dream, but there was no doubt about the
noise it made. The Irish have some kind of conveyance they
call a jaunting car, and I'm not certain what it is except that
it can look nothing like a 1932 Ford half-ton pickup truck.
But our little truck was a jaunting car in spirit. Its clanks
and rattles were not complaints. They were sounds of sheer
exuberance as it ran through the freshness of a Maine sum-

mer morning. Still there was the danger that some part might bounce clear off in its enthusiasm, so we'd had it fixed and, alas, silenced. (How would I wake Bill now, supposing he were to come up and stay at that place on the beach again?) We wanted to have it painted, too, but that we dismissed as an extravagance.

It was in May that Dorothy made a journey to a sanitarium, not for her nerves—hers are sturdier than most— but for the final clue in a piece of detective work she had been pursuing all winter. Herb had left us some pictures of Goose Rocks houses for post cards. But many were missing, and Dorothy was determined to open the store with a complete set.

"I like to see our house on a post card—why shouldn't everyone else?" she asked reasonably.

She would not be balked, even when she found that the photographer had moved from Portland to another town, and another, that he was out of business—and finally that he was out of health. Whether from photographing unlovely people or their houses, he was in a sanitarium. Dorothy sought him there, found him not too ill to see her, ascertained that the negatives were in a relative's attic, and bought them outright from the relative, who had charge of his affairs. She returned triumphant, minus five hundred dollars but bearing a complete set of Goose Rocks houses in a box.

The end of May brought the school picnic. Herb used to throw open the store for the three hundred or so school children of the township, aged six to sixteen. We would do no less. It was a dress rehearsal for the store opening: we stocked ice cream, soda pop, candy. Dorothy took the counters and I was behind the soda fountain.

From the morning on there were never fewer than a hundred children in the store—what is there to do on the beach in May? It's too cold to swim in Maine even in late June, except for polar-bear types. The children played a little soft-ball, then came flocking to the store. From two o'clock on we had all three hundred with us. They spilled out the windows and the door, drinking pop, eating ice cream, buying candy. Have you ever stood behind a counter while a child makes up his mind which candy he's going to spend his penny on? Dorothy stood and stood and smiled and smiled and took their pennies one by one.

We thought we knew all the tricks of a kid with a deposit bottle, but these country youngsters showed us one more. Two of them, a tall skinny one and a short fat one, kept coming to Dorothy with five, six, ten bottles at a time, getting the deposits and spending the money on candy and ice cream. Finally Dorothy came over to me at the fountain.

"Where do you imagine they're getting all those bottles from?"

I said, "The little devils. There aren't that many bottles anywhere except in our own—"

Looking through the window behind me, Dorothy exclaimed, "That's right!" and ran out. She had caught sight of them skittering around the store to the back. Those boys had discovered a gold mine: cases and cases of empty bottles —in our own stockroom!

It was a rough day all around, but it paid off in good will. All summer, local people came from every part of the township to see us in the store and stayed to buy something: "You girls gave the children such a good time at the school picnic!"

We spent June polishing off the improvements, ordering stock—and scheming: this summer, no crises! Everything was in our favor. We had the experience to avoid mistakes, the time to prepare for eventualities. We would unravel every snarl in advance.

We had been harried by licenses. Every time we put our hand to something we had found we needed a license or a tax sticker to do it: a cigarette license, a margarine license, a milk license; licenses to run the restaurant and the guest-house; tax stickers for the jukebox, the pinballs, the bowling alleys, and a special license to serve lobsters. Some licenses were permanent, others had to be renewed. We went down the list with a fine-tooth comb and attended to them all.

We looked for ways to save labor. The self-service shelves were one saving. We thought of another: we had served sodas in Herb's tall soda glasses, an added washing chore and a broken-glass hazard. We bought paper cups and in-stalled dispensers. (And of course some old customers pro-tested: "So much nicer, a soda in a tall frosty glass!" So much more work, too.)

We were ashamed of the way we had handled money the summer before—dripping out of our pockets, being carried in unspecified amounts from one cash register to the other, and every morning Henry sweeping up silver, sometimes folding money. And the cigar boxes spilling over on our bed-room bureaus. There would be no more of that. I discovered moneybags at the bank and marked them plainly with the denominations each would contain. We determined on one cash register for the store, and tabs to be punched for the fountain and restaurant. We bought blocks of them marked up to two dollars—a single check was almost never more than that—and ticket punches such as the conductors use on trains. The waitresses and the soda-fountain clerks hung them on their belts. This delighted me especially, irked as I had been from the beginning that I could not tell how much each department was earning. (I was somewhat less de-lighted when at the end of each long day I had endless col-umns of five-, ten-, and twenty-five-cent fountain checks to add up.)

We figured out how to control the Saturday night dance crowd better and make more money out of Saturday night at the same time. We had sold soda pop right in the Casino the first summer. Now we would keep the pop in the store and lengthen the intermission from fifteen to forty-five minutes.

The first summer, the young people had often asked why we couldn't have swing music some of the time; they didn't want to dance square all evening. But the only music except square that Pete Charbon and his boys could play was "Humoresque." Nevertheless, they were in great demand, the year round, and there was even some doubt whether we could get them regularly for the summer again. Meanwhile we had been hearing from the local youngsters about this or that Rotary or Lions' dance, and they always ended, "Say, that was a great dance band!" We found the dance band. Its leader was a girl with a corn-fed look who might have been a farmer's wife with a bouncy brood growing up around her, and her eight men looked like respectable businessmen. But she and they played the brightest, most danceable swing music we'd heard. No wonder her band had people following them wherever they played in Maine. We hired them— and then began to figure how much we would have to charge in order to come out.

We had all six of our girls back: Jean and Susan in their crisp white; Marg and Liz, Sally and Carol in the new beige uniforms with blue collars and blue trim. We had Henry back.

But this time we were going to hire enough people *in advance*. Especially we would hire people for those burdensome chores, the mopping, the dishwashing, the cooking. On the subject of the cooking I was very firm. However brilliantly she tossed it off, Dorothy was not to be exploited again. The business could support a cook.

We hired Willie to wash dishes. Willie was a charmer; during his occasional stint at the fountain he drew girls as bees to honey. But he understood that he was hired to wash dishes and he vowed he would stick to it.

We had a foretaste of Willie's imperfections before the store opened. There was a great deal of preliminary work to do in the kitchen, and when Willie was twenty minutes overdue on his first morning I drove down to the end of the beach where he lived to fetch him. Dorothy pointed out that this would prove a fatal mistake. Why should he get up early and walk to work when he could sleep late and ride? She was right as usual. I was fetching Willie to work all summer.

At the end of that day, after Willie had gone, we were checking up in the kitchen. Dorothy noticed something on a high shelf that should not have been there and climbed on the ladder to see. She found four pans and six milk bottles unwashed. This was another cross we had to bear with Willie. He could cheerfully wash his way through mountains of dishes and silver and glassware, but he had an unconquerable aversion to milk bottles, pots, and pans. We wrestled with this, too, all summer, pleading, cajoling, threatening. Willie promised each time. (And the last day of summer, after Willie had departed—paid in full and dismissed a day early so he could get a ride to the city, and with pledges of undying devotion to Goose Rocks, the store, and ourselves—that night we found pots and pans and milk bottles on the top shelf, unwashed, a parting token of his affection. But the fact remained that Willie had stayed and washed dishes all summer, as none before him had done.)

We hired Mel to keep the store clean. Mel was a chubby man, and his cap, too small and perched on the top of his head, gave him a comic look. The first morning after opening I found Mel tinkering with a door hinge—useful work, but then he didn't get to mopping until the breakfast crowd was climbing on the fountain stools and filling the restaurant.

He went poking around and under the customers: "Move your foot—push your chair back—get up a minute here—" As mopping it was useless, but as nuisance it was tops. I mentioned the advisability of mopping first and tinkering afterward. I coaxed. At last he said, "Mopping—that's women's work." I could not convince him otherwise. Mopping, to Mel, was and forever would be woman's work, and if he couldn't stall his way out of it he'd as soon quit. We parted, and Henry cheerfully took over the mopping chore again.

We had been so happy with our teen-age summer-girl clerks that we decided to snatch up any likely boys who wanted to work for us. And we made a discovery which teachers, psychologists, and notably parents would probably consider routine. Every one of them, without exception, started out by being wonderful, a dream of a soda clerk or stockroom boy or whatever we had hired him for. And every one of them collapsed sooner or later into pranks and teen-age horsing around before he quit.

We came to recognize the signs. There would be a sudden epidemic of sodas upsetting over girls' dresses. Or customers would complain that their coffee tasted funny or there was something in the hamburgers. Dorothy would dip her finger in the sugar bowl, or shake a salt shaker into her hand, and taste, and we knew that our latest boy was switching the salt and sugar and would shortly leave us. But it was all in a spirit of fun, and they came back all summer, bringing their high spirits and also their nuisance value to the fountain, ordering great huge sundaes with half a dozen flavors, doing their best to confuse the pal who had taken the job they had left.

All of them attracted the girls to the fountain while they worked there, and now and then one of them did a job somewhere in the store that was a monument to youthful ceative energy. There was the one who tackled the stockrooms. These two rooms were in a chronic state of disorder that had me constantly in a tizzy. Cases piled up and nobody had time to straighten them out. You would take half a dozen cans of something to replenish a shelf, and the opened, half-empty case would go into the stockroom. Then when you needed a can, say, of green beans, you had to lift all the other half-empty cases off the one you wanted, which somehow was always at the bottom.

One of our youths named Boyd accordingly went at the stockrooms. He opened the cases at the ends so you could reach in for what you wanted, and stacked them in tiers. He combined like with like, cutting down waste space. Out of a piece of dirty work everyone had been avoiding, he created a functional masterpiece which we had no trouble keeping in order even after, like all the rest, Boyd began spilling things and mixing up orders, and finally left us.

Two days before we opened we still had no cook. We had left orders with employment agencies all over Maine, in Boston, in New York. We had almost given up hope when a letter came from a GI who had learned to cook in the Army and had stayed on in Paris to go to cooking school on the GI Bill. No experience, no references, but a GI rated a chance. We wired: "Come ahead. You have job."

Ken Harrison arrived the next day. He was no movie hero for looks, but he had a rugged open face and he looked healthy and very, very clean. He was a natural-born cook. There was nothing he couldn't cook, but his lobster Thermidor was a gourmet's dream. (Early in the summer the word spread, and people were coming to the restaurant from miles around.) We had to admit the Army trained them— he was a good executive in the kitchen, too. He cracked the

whip at the girls, and Willie did not skip a pot or a bottle
when Ken was on duty. By opening day we knew he was a
find.

We had put our telephone and telegraph message service
on a business basis. Both companies were going to charge the
sender twenty-five cents for message delivery and remit the
fee to us. We had found that we and the girls and whatever
boys we had had, the summer before, had been losing a great
deal of time looking for people, and although the service was
a courtesy for which we were not paid, we rarely got thanks
and always got complaints when a message went astray. We
had tried having the youngsters who delivered a telegram
collect a delivery fee of a quarter, but the people minded
paying, and if they paid the quarter they didn't tip the lad.
Our girls, called from waiting on a customer to answer the
phone, would neglect to write the message down. Liz would
call to Walter, who was delivering groceries, "Stop and tell
Mrs. Jones her brother is calling from Detroit." Walter
would go off without anything in writing, and if he remembered to stop by the Jones's he would probably say only that
she had a phone call at the store. By the time Mrs. Jones got
to the store after giving her youngsters lunch and getting
them off to the beach, Liz would have gone off duty and nobody knew who called Mrs. Jones from where or what she
was to do about it. When there was a fee everything went
more efficiently. We put telephone pads in the phone booth,
hung a pencil on a string, and although people were always
absent-mindedly walking off with the pad in a pocket, mostly
the staff remembered to write messages down. We had an extension of our own phone—the one that was also at the "town
house" next door—hooked up at the big new check-out counter and kept telegraph blanks there so that whoever was taking cash could also take incoming and outgoing telegrams.
And since the fee was paid by the sender, people cheerfully

tipped our boys. The one thing that bothered us about taking telegrams was that some of them brought bad news.

We had added one more new service. We were already an agency for cleaning women; now we became renting agents as well, also at no charge. Through part of May and all of June we tramped the chilly beach with prospective tenants, showing houses for our friends and customers who stayed snug at home in their steam-heated mansions in Boston or New York or wherever. We rented the houses, had them cleaned, even got them repaired. We put up a keyboard behind the cash register; we already had a guest book where newcomers registered so we would know where to deliver their messages and direct their guests. The renting was time-consuming, and we became the landlord-vs.-tenant complaint-and-grievance department along with everything else. But each new family on the beach was a potential customer.

We rented Dorothy's big house again. The cottage, River-view, was reserved this summer for her two maiden aunts. We also rented the tower room in the town house, to a writer who had taken a house on the beach for his family. He saw the tower and begged for the room, to write in. It was hot and cramped, but up there he would be as safe from intrusion as in a jail cell, and he had a view to inspire another *Hamlet*, if *Hamlets* are written on scenic inspiration.

27

Open Season on Storekeepers

We opened the store that morning like a pair of veteran stage managers who knew the script by heart, had seen that every actor and every prop was ready, and were prepared for every cue. We had foreseen everything. There were to be no crises.

We laughed at our innocence of the summer before. Imagine, forgetting lettuce! Imagine, no paper bags!

Came noon, half the families arriving, everybody pouring into the store hungry after the journey and in a hurry to stock their pantries—and a majestic woman strode into the store, calling, "Dorothy! Where is Dorothy?"

"Aunt Alice!" Dorothy came running from the meat counter, wiping her hands on her apron. I had heard of Dorothy's two maiden aunts, and now I saw Edie emerge from behind Alice, a small meek shadow. "You weren't due until tomorrow!"

"I decided we would come today," Alice boomed. "Pay the taxi, please."

I said, "I'll take care of the taxi." I discovered the taxi had brought them all the way from Lowell, Massachusetts, and the fare was staggering. I groaned, and paid.

Dorothy came out with the aunts. They were to stay in Riverview, but the water wasn't turned on, the gas tanks weren't in, and Abby Peace was only going to clean the place the next morning. However, the rooms in the guesthouse had just been put in shipshape order for the art students who would begin arriving that day and the next.

Dorothy said, "We'll put you next door in the guesthouse overnight, Aunt Alice. You'll be comfortable there."

To avoid argument—I knew Aunt Alice by reputation—I took two bags and started for the town house. The taxi driver brought the trunk, which had been strapped on the back, and left it on the porch.

Aunt Alice said, walking through the parlor, "Hmph. Cold in this house. Why don't you have a fire?"

Obediently I put down the bags, threw newspaper and kindling in and a log on top, and lit the newspaper. We proceeded down the passage to the guesthouse.

When I came back, I heard an unmistakable *grumph, grumph,* in the chimney. Mel was bringing in the trunk. I said, "Mel, what's that noise?"

"Nothin', just the draft. Chimney's cold." He went on to the guesthouse with the trunk.

Mel was to have cleaned out the chimney. I'd told him to, but I hadn't checked whether he had done it. I thought in alarm, Can a fire start in a chimney? Halfway to the store I looked back. Not only smoke and sparks, but wads of burning stuff were shooting up. I ran into the store.

"Dorothy, I think there's a fire starting in the house."

Dorothy was buying candles from a candle salesman. She said, "Well, call the fire engine," and went on buying candles.

I called the firehouse. Flames were coming out of the chimney by the time the engine arrived. The volunteers—all our winter neighbors—drove up in their cars. I had routed the aunts out of the house, but Aunt Alice was making quite a to-do about her trunk.

The volunteers stood around. In Maine everyone has his own opinion of how anything is to be done. A town meeting precedes any group action, including fire fighting.

Someone opened the discussion. "I say, let 'er burn. She'll burn herself out."

"Let 'er burn, and in two minutes the house is a goner!"

"The trees," I put in feebly. We had magnificent pines and oaks overhanging the roof. I think I cared more for them than for the house.

Two men were pulling the hose out of the truck. "Don't let 'em in with the hose, Mac. They'll do more damage than the fire," said Chris.

Albion shouted, "On the roof!" A ladder went up, and Albion and someone else clambered up on the roof with the hose. They got the hose into the chimney. "Water, you idiots! Where's the water?"

The timing was off. Before the water could get up into the hose, the hose burned right off in Albion's hands.

Suddenly and with horror I remembered and screamed to Albion, "The writer! The writer in the belfry!"

I'm sure I sounded as though I had bats in my own. Albion shouted back, "Who? Where?" I pointed to the tower.

At that moment a head came out of the tower window. It was the writer, smoking his pipe. And there he stayed, smoking and watching the fire from his private box seat. Possibly writers are professionally equipped with a fatalistic philosophy. I know I wouldn't stay in the top of a wooden house if there was a fire burning in any part of it.

Albion stayed on the roof with the amputated hose. Once the water gushed up to him he put his hand over the stump and kept spraying the roof and the trees, quenching the great lumps of flaming stuff which flew out of the chimney. In the end, as someone had predicted, the fire burned itself out. If not for Albion on the roof, it also would have burned the house down.

When the excitement was over I once again installed the aunts in their room in the guesthouse. Smoke and soot had made a mess of our freshly painted walls. We would just have to do them over again. "There are chairs on the porch," I suggested, and made my escape before Aunt Alice could find fault. Edie, poor thing, had not said a word since their arrival.

And so, without further incident, the store was opened. The next red-letter day was the Fourth.

We had decided to sell fireworks for the Fourth. It was a question with two sides to it: you had to take out extra insurance, and no matter how much you stocked you were likely to be wrong. If you had too much you were stuck with it and if you had too little people would be mad at you.

"But there are children who grew up during the war who never saw fireworks," Dorothy said feelingly, and that clinched it. We would do it for the children.

According to the law, you could display fireworks but you couldn't sell them until July third. The kids, however, were in a fever; they had to be sure of their fireworks. So Dorothy took their orders, wrapped their purchases and marked them in big, black crayon with their names, and stowed the packages under the counter until the third. They went away content.

You can plainly see that we began this season full of love and tenderness for the kids. All of last summer's mischief was forgiven; the slate was clean. And in return we got what all grownups deserve who get sentimental about children. We got it in the neck.

We opened the Casino for the season on July second with a gala première: movies! It had taken some doing. Movies, for the younger set, had to begin in broad daylight, at seven-thirty. The Casino's windows, from floor to ceiling, had to be covered. Fortunately we found Herb's black-out shades left over from the war. The windows were opened for air and the shades fastened down over the sills.

Mike and Ham and Georgie and the gang went to work on the blackout shades. Everybody else paid his quarter and went in like ladies and gentlemen through the front door, but these three made it a point of honor to see the movies without paying admission. They attacked window after window, and each window was left with a rent through which light poured. Finally they had the effrontery to attack the entrance-door shades, almost within arm's reach of me in the box office.

I joined Henry in the chase, but we were no match for them in a foot race. I ran over to Dorothy in the store.

"Those hellions!" I stormed, and told her what they were up to this time. "After all the trouble we took about fire-works—for the children! We're a pair of softhearted suckers!"

Dorothy, who knew children better than I and knew better than to expect gratitude from them, said, "It's a lucky thing we have those fireworks. Let them go. Just tell me who they are."

The next morning—the third—every kid on the beach came for his fireworks, and the wild bunch were of course at the head of the line.

"I'm sorry, Mike, I have no fireworks for you," Dorothy said. And as he opened his mouth to protest, "I think you know why."

Mike stepped aside without a word. Ham, who was next, came out punching. "You have to give them to us! We paid for them!"

"That's right, but you did more damage at the movies last night than your fireworks are worth."

Joey's cowlick stuck up above the edge of the counter—he hadn't grown much in ten months—and Joey's big blue eyes swam with tears. The little phony, I thought. Dorothy would never resist him.

Dorothy said, "You, too, Joey. You let them boost you up to tear the shades where they couldn't reach."

George came next, waving his big paws in the air and screaming, "I'll get my father!"

"Get him," Dorothy said. "That goes for all of you. I'll be glad to explain to your parents why you can't be trusted with fireworks."

The gang melted away. The rest of the children got their fireworks in due course. But the beach was buzzing.

Georgie's mother came with him. "Georgie really wasn't to blame, were you, darlin'? Didn't you tell me, darlin', that Mike—?"

"Sure, Mike, and Ham, and Kenny and Red and Bib—and they boosted Joey up, like you said. I didn't do anything. I just went along and watched."

"You see, Dorothy? You want to be fair, don't you, honey?"

Dorothy put Georgie's fireworks into her hands. "You'll have to be responsible for these, Carrie," she said.

Ham came with his father. "I don't get it, Dorothy," he said irritably. He had been on his way to golf. "The boys paid for their stuff, didn't they? And my kid wasn't the ringleader. Ham will tell you the names. Here"—he threw a couple of dollar bills on the counter—"that ought to pay for your paper shades."

Dorothy handed over the fireworks to Mr. Erdman without a word.

Mrs. Cary did not come in until afternoon, and then she came to do her shopping. Mike was with her, pushing the shopping cart. Red, Bib, Kenny, and little Joey were ostensibly playing the pinballs. Actually they were watching to see what was going to happen to Mike.

Mrs. Cary came to the check-out counter where Dorothy was taking cash. Dead-pan, she said, "Dorothy, Mike gets twenty-five cents a week allowance. I'm sure the damage he did was many times the price of the fireworks, but I imagine by Christmas time he will have paid up the difference."

Mike rubbed the back of his hand across his nose but said not a word.

Dorothy said, "I'm sure Mike is sorry, and really I think he could have his fireworks—"

Mrs. Cary interrupted her. "Excuse me, Dorothy, but Mike realizes he doesn't deserve his fireworks. Do you think you ought to have them, Mike?"

"No," Mike answered in a choked voice.

Dorothy by this time was ready to cry too. Mike had not only owned up and was taking his punishment, but he was the only one who hadn't accused others in order to absolve himself. Dorothy said firmly, "It won't be necessary for Mike to do any more. Emily, if you'll give your permission, I would like to give Mike his fireworks. I'll trust him with them."

Emily Cary didn't smile. She said, "That will be between you and Mike, then. I won't object, but Mike will have to be responsible to you."

Mike gravely took his package. Kenny and Joey, Red, and Bib, hovering, had heard it all, but they waited for Dorothy to call them over. Not only Joey, but even Kenny and Bib were red-eyed. Red was bigger and wouldn't cry, but all of them looked much chastened.

Dorothy beckoned them. "What do you say, you three? Can I trust you with these fireworks? Can I count on you to help Mike take care of things? You were very helpful last summer, you know."

They made solemn promises. What's more, they kept them. Ham did as Mike told him. Except for Georgie Randolph, who now and then broke out from the sheer desperate need to prove his manliness, there was no really serious trouble from the gang for the rest of that summer.

The Fourth went off in style, fireworks, beach parties, and all, and from the beach the whole population poured into the store. Unlike last year, we were ready for them, having instructed the staff to come back to work.

When I added up the books that night, the figure for the Fourth of July take was $894.

An unexpected bonus from our big Fourth of July was Marian, who came to ask us for a job the next day. She was a beautiful kid, a natural blonde with a feather cut, legs like Grable and other features to match. She came of a nice New England family, went to a good school in the winter, and had made up her mind to strike out for independence this summer. She had come to Kennebunkport with friends and taken a job in a sports-clothes shop there. Her friends had brought her over for a Fourth of July picnic on Goose Rocks Beach, and she had fallen in love with the beach, the store, and Goose Rocks altogether. She was irked by her daytime job and by the distance from Kennebunkport to the beach there. She wanted to sun and swim and play tennis in the daytime and work, if she could, in the evening. We were charmed with her and hired her on the spot to work on the fountain every evening from six until closing. Her friends helped her find a room down the beach.

The moment our chef laid eyes on her he was a gone goose. And from the first time Ken barked at her Army-fashion, Marian began to melt. They asked, separately, for that Saturday night off to go to the dance. From then on when we thought of Ken or Marian we thought of them together.

By the time the first dance night arrived, the Saturday after the Fourth, Dorothy and I were feeling very pleased with ourselves. Every department was running in high gear. We loved the hum and bustle of the store, loved to be working in it again, and besides we were about to unveil our new and improved version of the Saturday Night Dance. We had figured and figured: with our increased expenses we had decided that we could still let the children in for fifty cents if we raised admission for those over sixteen to a dollar. Some of the art students painted big splashy posters for us. We put up signs in the store.

Our lady maestro, who played the piano, understood that for the first hour and a half of every dance the crowd would be principally age twelve and under. She was happy to play square dances and polkas for them, and to keep the country atmosphere that we all liked in the Casino she would give us square dances intermittently through the evening. Her saxophonist, she said, was a good caller.

Now that we were graduating from just square dancing we had decided we needed lighting. We had bought spotlights with blue and gold gelatins—to throw patches of alternate bright and soft light on the dance floor—and a baby spot for the band leader and anyone who was taking a solo. The band had lighted music stands, and they brought with them their own master switch, microphones, and amplifying system. Henry and I and faithful Will spent a couple of hours that afternoon with the band leader and two of her men, setting up and testing.

We opened the Casino doors at eight o'clock, expecting the kids to come pouring in all slicked up. The lady maestro looked to me in the box office for a signal and struck up "Dig for the Oysters." It sounded just fine. The saxophonist tried out a few calls on the microphone to the empty floor and he sounded fine, too. I waited.

Five minutes and two choruses went by. The box office seemed somehow hot. I went out on the porch. There, hanging around below the steps, were a lot of the kids, but they weren't dressed for the dance. They were wearing their dirtiest, fishiest jeans and blouses and sneakers, their hair was rumpled as though they hadn't combed it since the day before, and their hands and faces were extra grimy.

I said, "What's up, all of you? Aren't you coming to the dance?"

No answer, just funny looks. I addressed the nearest little girl by name. "Katie, you're not even dressed the way you used to be. What's going on?"

Katie said, "It costs too much."

"Why, it doesn't, Katie. It's fifty cents for each of you just the way it always was."

"Our parents say a dollar for grownups is too much, and so we can't come."

I went back into the box office. Could the child possibly be right?

The band struck up "Mountain Gal." Three choruses of that and we were still waiting. Some Biddeford people came in, looked at the stark bare floor, said, "Dance not started yet?" and went away.

Dorothy came in, looked around, and turned pale. I got out of the box office a second time, said something hypo-critically reassuring to the band leader, and Dorothy and I went back without a word to the store.

The store was jammed full. People were having sodas, buying magazines, buying fruit and candy and everything in sight. But they weren't, apparently, planning to come to the dance. I burned.

"Dorothy, for two cents I'd close the Casino right now," I said.

Dorothy said, "It's awful. You'd think they would have spoken to us, instead of just staying away. But you know, most of them are new people, this early in the season. They don't really know us."

It was true, our closest friends, among those that came regularly to the dances, weren't down yet, or someone would have told us what was up. Fran would have mentioned something, or Mrs. West, or the Carters, but they didn't usually come to the dances and so, no doubt, had heard nothing. Even our own staff hadn't known our dance was going to be boycotted.

One of the teen-age boys whom we knew ambled by as though he would like to speak to us but didn't quite dare, and Dorothy called him over.

"Do you know about all this, Jack?" she asked.

He nodded. "They think the price is too high," he said, and blushed.

"Do you? Do the young people think it is?"

"Well—two bucks—time you take a girl, buy her a soda and all—it adds up," he said, jingling the coins in his pocket.

"But we've got a big expensive band! Don't you realize . . . ?" I began, still furious.

"Oh, sure, Miss Mackenzie," he said placatingly. "Listen, could you—I mean—well, I think they'd pay seventy-five cents admission."

Dorothy and I looked at each other, remembering our figures. We wouldn't make a dime, but if the place was full, really full, we ought to break even.

Dorothy said, "We could do it, Jack, only if everybody came. Otherwise we'll have to give up the dances."

Jack said, "Gee, Miss Mignault, don't do that! We'll get them—gee, that swell band—"

He ran to spread the news, first to his own crowd, then to others. People disappeared like magic; in five minutes the store was empty and our staff was standing there goggle-eyed. Then they, too, sped off to get ready for the dance.

In the box office fifteen minutes later I was selling admissions as fast as my hands could move, seventy-five cents for grownups and fifty cents for kids, and all of them were slicked up and dressed for dancing. The dance that night was a smashing success. The dance band went over big. But I felt badly bruised. It seemed such a cruel way to tell us they didn't like our price. Didn't they understand what things cost—dance band, lights? Where could they go to a dance like that for less than a dollar?

Dorothy said, "You never know, do you, when you're selling things to people. There's always a surprise waiting for you." Just when you feel you have the combination, apparently, that's when it hits you. We still had a lot to learn.

One thing more happened that night. As I mentioned, we had decided not to sell pop in the Casino, but to lengthen the intermission from fifteen to forty-five minutes so people could, if they liked, come into the store for ice cream. The change was so successful it nearly proved the death of us. Partly because the dance had got going so late, and partly because it was her habit to give the customers all the dancing they could handle, our band leader didn't take any breaks to speak of, between dance numbers. Also, out of some spirit of showing us, perhaps, that they really wanted the dance in spite of the demonstration, nobody seemed to sit out any dances—everybody danced all the time. As a result the crowd swarmed into the store as dry as though they had walked across the Sahara.

The fountain was besieged. So were the fruits, the groceries, and every other part of the store. Mothers of families finished the marketing for Sunday that they had begun before the dance. Fathers wandered around buying paper books, magazines, tobacco, gadgets, and my favorite delicacies.

Of course we had let the staff go, once the dance started. To keep our girls working on dance night would have been inhuman as well as impossible. Ken and Marian, too, were off by special permission. So there we were with twice or three times any ordinary daytime rush—and no staff! We had never anticipated anything like this when we planned the long intermission.

Marg came in with her date for a soda, took one look around, left the lad flat, and began waiting on the trade. A minute later Liz joined her. Marian and Ken ducked behind the soda fountain and dished up sodas and sundaes, radiating happiness. Every dance night for the rest of the summer the intermission was the same wild stampede, and always Liz and Marg, sometimes the others, slipped aprons over their dance dresses and went to work. Nor would they take any pay for those forty-five minutes of frantic work.

The intermission business—and the staff's generous loyalty—made up somewhat for the hard lesson our first big dance taught us. But I don't think we ever again made the mistake of forgetting that serving the public is a hazardous business, and good will rolls over dead before a price a few cents higher than people feel like paying.

⅏ 28 ⅏

What Price Efficiency?

Our slogan, No More Crises, had acquired a plaintive tone. It did not seem to matter how clever we were or how forehanded. As the summer rolled on, so did the emergencies, the situations, the crises.

By now we had so many well-wishers among the men with whom we did business that we felt free to turn to any of them for advice. Gordon Wells, a vice-president of one of our biggest canned-goods suppliers, and Mrs. Wells came down for a week end. They had entertained Dorothy and me when we were in Boston. We asked Gordon to point out our mistakes, show us how to run a more rational business.

We asked wistfully, "Please, what's wrong with the way we run this place? Everybody else in business must have an occasional peaceful moment. Why can't we?"

Gordon came in early on Saturday morning, stayed around all day until closing, and did the same on Sunday. He went over the books with me. By the time the four of us sat down to Sunday night supper in the restaurant, he was exhausted—from the effort of keeping a straight face.

Yet nothing unusual had happened.

On Saturday, one of our teen-age fountain clerks upset a banana split in Miss McAllister's lap while trying to attract some girl's attention. It was a brand-new white sharkskin dress, and she was wearing it for the first time, having a lemon ice and a cosy tête-à-tête with Mr. Painter. Susan mopped her off and Dorothy assured her we would have the dress cleaned. Miss McAllister was not comforted. She turned faint with the shock and distress of it all, had to be revived with smelling salts hurriedly brought from the first-aid cabinet, and recovered sufficiently to make a statement, audible throughout the place, to the effect that the store's encouragement of young hoodlums and delinquents was a disgrace to Goose Rocks and she would see that we were dealt with by the proper authorities. She was then tenderly escorted from the premises by Mr. Painter. The unfortunate fountain clerk's trick knee promptly and psychosomatically went out of joint, and he had to leave us in the middle of a hot Saturday afternoon rush at the fountain.

Willie, recruited from dishwashing to take the youth's place, came to the cash register while I was momentarily occupied somewhere else, helped himself to a fistful of nickels, and fed them to the jukebox. Willie liked music and thought it helped business to keep the jukebox going. It made the store gay and festive, a perpetual carnival. We didn't mind the noise. After the first few days we heard it only when it stopped and we knew we weren't making our fifty per cent. But I had explained to Willie until I was hoarse just how we lost five cents out of every nickel he took from the cash register: the jukebox company got half of that nickel, and we failed to make the two and one-half cents out of a nickel a customer might have put in the slot instead. And besides, it made a shambles out of my accounts.

I caught Willie red-handed, but before I could stop him the phone rang. It was Georgie Randolph's mother: "You'll have to do something about those dreadful people, those people trespassin' on our beach and doin' I don't know what mischief and I don't want them around here offerin' bad companionship to my darlin'—"

Some Biddeford families, apparently, were picnicking too close to Carrie's. "I'll watch for the policeman, Mrs. Randolph," I told her.

"Why, no, that won't do at all, you'll just have to go and get him and get these dreadful people—" and she was off again. Customers were waiting to pay for and take their groceries. I tucked the phone under my ear and made change, saying, "Yes, Mrs. Randolph, yes, I'll try, yes, yes—" until she hung up.

But Willie had escaped me, and the jukebox was blasting away at our expense.

All this was routine. So were the customer whose laundry hadn't come back (because she had forgotten to send it), the long-distance calls for which people had to be summoned from wherever they were, the inquirers for guest rooms, the visitors asking for directions, the last-minute pleas for baby-sitters for dance night, the one night when positively no baby-sitters were to be had.

It was routine to discover that we were suddenly out of some favorite flavor of ice cream—chocolate chip, I think it was that day—and that neither Jean nor Susan, nor of course Willie, had remembered to warn us. This meant a special call to Hood's, to plead for a rush delivery, and a quick check to add some extra containers of other flavors to give the plea more weight.

Routine also was Jean's rebellion at the art-student customer who came in regularly for afternoon coffee and got into an argument about surrealism—or was it existentialism? —while his coffee cooled, and then raised the dickens in a loud voice because he had been served cold coffee.

Jean said stoutly, "The coffee was hot when I poured it, and I poured him two cups of coffee yesterday and three the day before and I just won't pour any more hot coffee for him."

Dorothy soothed Jean, poured a hot cup of coffee on the principle that the customer is always right, and went back to the kitchen.

And why was Dorothy in the kitchen? Didn't we have a cook? Indeed we had. And there had been no suggestion when Ken was hired that he would have Saturdays off—the week end? impossible!—until Dorothy caught a glimpse of Marian hovering behind him, big-eyed, and decided that anything was worth doing to keep Ken happy.

"I have to cook one day a week anyway—Ken must have a day off," she appeased me.

So Ken—and of course Marian too—got Saturdays off, and Dorothy went ahead with a Saturday menu she had planned long before, of Boston baked beans with frankfurters, just that one item, nothing else. It was a hit. No matter how many pots of beans she baked she never had enough to satisfy the demand.

That's why Dorothy was in the kitchen that Saturday afternoon, as I explained to Gordon. And then there was Hedi.

Our friends from New York were dropping in on us all that summer. It became the thing to work at the Colony in Goose Rocks. Hedi was one of them, and Hedi was easily the prize. She was a ravishing tawny brunette with a Mittel-Europa accent which I always suspected her of carefully cultivating. She wore a kerchief tied gypsy style, big circle earrings like curtain rings, and on her shoulder her marmoset, Cheechee. Hedi was a clever, free-lance advertising artist. She was also something of an intellectual with psychoanalytical overtones. She had arrived the previous Friday, and when she saw us cutting up the meat the next morning she had a comment.

"You know, of course, with thees meat chopping is the way of how you are expressing the aggressions."

She had something there. It was better to use the cleaver on a quarter of beef than on a customer.

So Hedi, too, came under Gordon Wells' observation. On Saturday night Dorothy brought Gordon and Mrs. Wells over to the dance, leaving Hedi momentarily alone in charge of the store. I came out of the box office, and we four stood chatting. Suddenly I caught sight of a tawny head whirling down one of the sets—Hedi! I waded in and grabbed her wrist.

"For heaven's sake, Hedi, who's looking after the store?"

"Nobody." She shrugged. "I became tired." She went on clapping her hands and tapping her foot to the music.

All, you see, perfectly routine. Gordon also got a full dose of Sunday, from the Sunday newspaper rush on. It happened also that Ken and Marian had one of their blowups that day, just as we four were sitting down to supper and a conference.

This was not the first explosion in the kitchen. Marian turned out to be a very good waitress as well as an efficient counter hand at the fountain, but she was just too attractive. The swish of her crisp uniform around those Grable-type legs, as she passed between the tables with her tray, was more than the art students, male, could stand, and they wouldn't let her alone. Ken, stuck in the kitchen, wanting to do a first-rate job as a chef, couldn't be unaware of the byplay in the restaurant. Marian was, after all, only a kid. She was in love with Ken but she couldn't help responding to the flattering attentions of the uninhibited and really amusing lads. Her laughter bubbled up in spite of herself; Ken, his ears tuned to her voice, heard her above the hum of the store. Like many good-natured men, Ken had a low boiling point. Being neither rich nor handsome nor—by his standards— socially in a class with Marian's family, he also felt unsure. July was only halfway gone when Dorothy, sniffing something wrong, went out into the kitchen. She found Marian there in tears and Ken's apron and cap in a heap on the floor. Dorothy picked them up and put them on and supper was served as usual.

That was the first one. By now Dorothy had the explosions pretty well timed. So this evening, coming back from the house in her fresh dress, ready for supper and a good talk with Gordon, she was not surprised when Marg whispered to her that there was trouble in the kitchen again. She went out and put Ken's apron over her dress and took over the cooking for the rest of the evening. But since it was Sunday and Jean and Susan were off, she insisted that Marian come back and wait on table. Marian obediently mopped her eyes, powdered her nose, and brought us the lobster Thermidor which Ken, luckily, had finished preparing before he erupted.

It was at this point, when Dorothy departed to cook instead of sitting down to eat in civilized fashion with her guests, that Gordon finally let go with the laughter he had been struggling to suppress all week end.

"No fair," I protested. "You haven't been standing around here for two days just for laughs. You could have been on the beach or playing golf. You're supposed to tell us how to manage better."

"I can't," he said, wiping his eyes. "I don't believe anybody could. This business doesn't fit any of the rules. You buy wisely, your sales ideas are bright and lively, your layout is handsome—"

"What about customer relations?" I demanded. "What about personnel?"

"With customers like yours, I'd say your customer relations are being handled with great skill. What more could anyone do with a Miss McAllister?"

"We know her exact counterpart in Boston," Mrs. Wells put in.

"As for personnel: well, your cook is temperamental, but a great cook has a right to temperament and he's a great cook." Gordon was enjoying his lobster Thermidor. "The girls are lovely—those summer kids make perfect summer-store clerks. The waitresses are good waitresses. This is their second year with you, all seven girls?"

"All except Marian." I nodded, indicating her shining head bent over a near-by table.

"Six of them, then," Gordon went on. "And you're complaining about personnel! As for your French import—"

"Hedi's Hungarian," I told him.

"Import, anyway. She makes difficulties, no doubt about that, but I've watched her with the customers. They're crazy about her, Mac, especially the local people."

I had noticed that. The local men made calf eyes at her, and when I saw her good manners with Mrs. Keene and Mrs. Cobb, with Albion's gentle wife Edith and with old Mrs. Barnes, I forgave Hedi everything.

Customers who knew Gordon and Mrs. Wells in Boston came over to say hello and stayed to talk. One of them said, "These girls won't be real Maine storekeepers until they start sending us winter bills to help pay for fixing their roofs."

"What are winter bills?" I asked innocently.

The man laughed. "In ——"—he mentioned another summer town—"where we used to have a house before we discovered Goose Rocks, the storekeeper used to send us bills all winter, long after we had paid our accounts and thrown away the slips. Little bills, but we'd get two or three in the course of the winter. We always suspected we were helping to put a new roof on the store."

His wife said, "Where my family had a house our storekeeper used to count out twelve ears of corn and throw in a thirteenth for good luck, as he said—and then charge five cents extra for the thirteenth ear."

"Ours had another trick," someone else said. "Most of the families didn't have cars in those days, and our storekeeper used to mail letters and do errands when he went to market in town. He was a genial soul and usually invited us kids to go along for the ride. On the bill next month would be an item: Taxi to City, $3."

I was amazed. They seemed to regard such doings as merely atmosphere.

Dorothy came out of the kitchen. "Gordon is a disappointment," I told her. "He just laughs at us."

"Like everybody else," she said. "Haven't you any advice for us at all?"

"Not a thing I can suggest. You're running a very personal enterprise here, Dorothy. This place is a creation of your two selves and this community. There aren't any rules."

"But we don't know if we're making money or going broke," I protested.

"You're making money," he said. He had seen things I couldn't see, in my books. He had pointed out the steady rise in the daily take all through the summer, and that August 1, which marks the influx of a new population for half the beach, almost equaled the peak on July Fourth. "You'll make a lot of money here."

"If you keep your health," Mrs. Wells said. "Gordon, the girls work too hard."

"They're finding their way out of that, too. It takes time. Dorothy, how much insurance do you carry?"

"If you mean all kinds—public liability, fire, theft, storm damage, compensation, and all that—it's well over a hundred thousand this summer," Dorothy said.

He shook his head. "It's too little."

"Too little!" I exclaimed. "It sounds positively megalomaniac!"

"With the plant you have here, the improvements—so

many operations going on, so many people going through, so much greater risk of fire, theft, and especially liability—oh, no. People sue for as much as they think you're worth. Double that figure, Dorothy. Do it right away."

"Double it!"

"Yes. You need that protection," Gordon said.

Dorothy acted upon Gordon's advice the next day.

🐾 *29* 🐾

Storekeepers Tell No Tales

The village storekeepers hear everything about everybody, past, present, and probably future.

One day a minister came to Goose Rocks and called, inevitably, at the store. He had come, he told us, to see about church services. There had been services, we said, and Dorothy told him about Jacob Barnes, long ago.

He knew about Jacob Barnes. But since Jacob had gone to his rest he had not been replaced. Perhaps he could be replaced now. As the storekeepers, who knew the community better than anyone else, what did we think?

At that point I felt moved to express an opinion. People at a summer resort didn't like to go to church because churchgoing was surrounded with too much fuss. Why must people dress in a certain way for church? What had their clothes to do with their religious feeling? Why not a summer church, to which they could come in their sports clothes and go on from the service to golf or sailing or whatever they had planned? Why not a summer minister, in an open sport shirt and slacks? If they were not obliged to fuss with special churchgoing clothes I was certain that many people would go to church who had never gone to church in the summertime before.

The minister thought this was a reasonable suggestion. "Will you help me make it known to the community that there will be services this Sunday, the kind of summer services you propose?"

Dorothy, who thought of practical things as well as spiritual, said, "You will need some money to start with, won't you?"

"Oh, no, that's taken care of," he said. "There is a fund."

And that was how we learned the end of the story of Jacob Barnes. Jacob, the Lord's servant in the big black hat—which he passed after the sermon—had left a will: "To establish church services in Goose Rocks, $285."

So on Sunday morning the Casino once more became a church, as it had been in Jacob's time. Mrs. Barnes listened to the sermon and sang the hymns with a peaceful face, as no doubt she had done when Jacob was the preacher. It was like her to have said nothing through the years about Jacob's will; such matters, like Jacob himself, could be left to the One who saw even a sparrow fall.

Storekeepers get involved in domestic discord. One customer made our week-end mornings agreeable that summer by coming in the first thing to play the pinball machines. He was a big pleasant man who wore his expensive clothes as though he had lived in them for months. Through our message service we had learned how businessmen on vacation protect their leisure time by having no phones in their summer homes and being hard to find when their secretaries are trying frantically to reach them—but *this* man stayed on the phone to his office most of Saturday morning and hadn't taken a vacation, his wife told us, in fifteen years.

One Friday afternoon she came into the store and beckoned Dorothy and me. "I told Jay last week end that if he didn't take the next two weeks off I wouldn't be here when he came today. Will you two hide me until my train goes?"

Things were running smoothly that day at the store. Dorothy and I, feeling like conspirators, took off early and we three went in to Kennebunkport to dinner; then Dorothy and I put Elsie on the train home. When we got back, there,

of course, was Jay. He cornered us. Where was Elsie? Had
we seen her? Had she left any word where she was going?"

"She hasn't left any message for you with us," Dorothy
told him with strict truthfulness.

He got into his car and drove the hundred miles or so
to his home. There, of course, was Elsie. He took his vacation.

Friends dropped in to see and stayed to join the staff for
a week or two or three, some with animals. An actress friend
brought her highly bred Persian cat, Duse. Duse was a problem to me only because I did not always remember to bring
her special kind of fish when I went to market. Duse took a
philosophical attitude, as cats do, but her mistress and I were
distressed.

An artist friend brought an Irish terrier, who fortunately
was on excellent terms with Spike and Imp. This friend heard
me complain that the canned baby foods and dog foods
weren't moving off the shelves. Together we worked out and
she designed a package, a cardboard dollhouse to hold six
cans of baby food (and a larger size for twelve). I consulted
a pediatrician about a week's balanced diet for a baby and
filled the dollhouse accordingly. For the dog food we did the
same, substituting a doghouse. They were perky little eye-
catchers on the Specials counter, they were practical toy
houses—and they doubled our baby-food and dog-food sales.

While our friends pitched in at the store, they and their
animals managed not to become involved with our neighbors
and customers. All except Hedi.

The big story that summer was the way Don Burke had
fallen for a young newcomer to the beach—and what was
Mary Burke going to do about it? Mary, as everyone on the
beach assumed, had been supporting Don for years while he
wrote stories and novels which didn't sell.

The Burkes lived down the beach some distance from the

store. Don was tall and thin and very attractive in an unhappy boyish kind of way, with thin, young-looking wrists that seemed to be still growing out of his sleeves. Even his walk was a prep-school lope. His clothes, which must have had excellent beginnings, had been washed and worn to a softness only good clothes can achieve in their old age. Every woman who met Don wanted to mother him.

All summer Don's typewriter had been gathering dust while Don hovered around Bab Sears on the beach. Bab was a pretty and vivacious blonde, but Fran Sergeant said Don was really paying more attention to everybody's children than to Bab. Children gathered around him wherever he was, and he spent hours telling them stories.

"He's like a starved spinster looking for someone's children to love. The poor man just wants a family!" Fran said. She was alone in this sympathetic opinion. The rest of Goose Rocks talked about how shameless Don was, hanging around Bab, taking her to the dances, flaunting her before "poor Mary."

On this particular Saturday night I did not see Don at the dance, although Bab was there for a while. Once during the evening, standing on the Casino porch getting a breath, I heard Hedi's Cheechee chattering somewhere near. Hedi was with Dorothy in the store, but the hot rhythms of our swing band must have stirred the little monkey's jungle blood. She had apparently escaped from her mistress and stationed herself in a tree from which she could hear and see the drummer through the high Casino windows. Even from the box office I could hear her jabbering excitedly up there during lulls in the music.

Suddenly there was a rifle shot, and then another. The window splintered above the bandstand and glass fell on the drum, missing the drummer's hands but tearing a gash in the skin of the drum. I ran out, just in time to see Hedi—and hear

her—run screaming toward Don, who stood beside his car
swaying, with his .22 in his hands.

"I've fired two shots over that damn monkey's head," he
yelled, "and the next time will be fatal!"

"Murderer! Storm Trooper!" shrieked Hedi. Dorothy
walked up to Don and quietly took the gun out of his hands.
Don looked at her, at all of us converging on him. Dorothy
handed me the gun, pushed Don into his car, got in after him,
and drove him home.

Hedi coaxed Cheechee down from the tree. The monkey,
I think, was the calmest member of the crowd. She was voluble, but I had an idea she was only protesting because the
music had stopped.

"For these thing I call the police!" Hedi announced and
rushed into the store with Cheechee, unhurt, clasped in her
arms.

Dorothy came back from taking Don home. The State
Police came, and Dorothy persuaded them and Hedi not to
take action.

"He's an unhappy man, Hedi dear. And he didn't hurt
Cheechee, after all."

"To be unhappy, yes, who is not? But thees is no excuse
to express the aggressions on poor innocent little creature.
Thees thing I will positively discuss with him."

"Some other time, Hedi. He's gone to sleep," Dorothy
said.

The police took the rifle for safekeeping, the crowd went
back to the dance floor, Henry swept up the glass, and the
dancing resumed, with the drummer cheerfully beating out
the rhythm on his traps. I found a moment to ask Dorothy
what was eating Don.

"He'd been drinking—you saw. He said Cheechee was
making fun of him. The trouble is Mary won't give him a
divorce."

"That's his problem," I said callously. "What about the drum and the broken window?"

"He said he'd pay for them."

"With Mary's money, I suppose!"

Dorothy said, "He's so unhappy, Scotty." And of course that excused everything. I was inclined to agree with Hedi.

As it turned out, the drum was adequately insured and the drummer was a nice guy. Don came over the next day to apologize and promise again that he would pay for the window. We said we'd have it fixed after the season, and the money could wait.

And so the second summer rolled to a close. Aunt Alice and Aunt Edie went home to Massachusetts. The last week we did a rousing business with sales. We had learned, the summer before, why storekeepers would rather sell at a loss than carry their stock. But we didn't lose money on the sales, although with a twenty per cent cut we were selling some items below wholesale. We made up the difference on the fancy groceries, which made us a profit even at twenty per cent off. People, knowing they had to stock their kitchens in town as soon as they got there, loaded cases of quality canned goods right into their cars.

To our surprise, Hedi stayed on. She professed to be working on some textile designs, and she collected odd pieces of driftwood to sketch. I had a notion she was working on something less abstract—any available man, for example, whom she could persuade to be her guide on driftwood expeditions. "He is so kind to carry for me, no?" Hedi would explain.

Again, as the first summer, we were doing the packing for the whole beach. "Have you got a box this size for the cat?" "Would you have a little bit of twine? I'd hate to buy a whole ball for just that much!" And finally they were gone. As before, we couldn't wait to see the end of them, and no sooner was the last car out of sight around the bend than we were tearfully wishing them back.

We turned to go into the store again—and there was Ken. Ken on the job had not survived the summer. The week before the end he had had his worst blowup and simply disappeared.

Marian had stayed on in the store, waiting, working at her job, by turns furious and forlorn. On the last day, Dorothy had had a talk with her and advised her to go home to her family. She had wept but she hadn't made any preparations for going. And now here was Ken, back again after ten days.

He looked terrible. He had tried everywhere in Maine to get a winter job, without success, and had hitchhiked back to save what money he could for fare to New York.

"I'll get a job," he said, "but I'm not going anywhere until Marian and I get straightened out." And he said, his tired face reddening, "I'm sorry I was so much trouble to you." We told him to forget it, and he went away.

Three weeks later both Ken and Marian were still there. Marian continued living with the same nice family down the beach; apparently her parents were willing to let her rest in the post-season quiet of Goose Rocks until time to go back to school. Ken kept his room over the store. He helped us move the stock and close up for the winter. We were glad to have his help, and he was glad to have the pay. When that was finished he lived off the land, hunting, fishing, clamming. He often brought us part of his catch, and we often had him and Marian eat with us.

One morning Ken drove into Biddeford with me. I was going to New York for a few days, rather proudly, to pay back the last of the loans I had raised to help buy the store, and also to see Bill, who was going West on business and would be gone some time. There was some buying, too, to do for next season.

"How are you kids doing?" I asked Ken.

"I wish I knew," he said dispiritedly. "It's hard on Marian, being in love with a guy without any dough."

"You've got a talent!" I exclaimed. "You crazy kid, don't you know that's as good as money—better than money?"

"Oh, sure, I like to cook. But maybe being a cook's wife isn't what Marian wants."

Thinking of Bill, who still talked about coming to live in Maine, I said, "Maybe you could find work to keep you in Goose Rocks over the winter. You can live cheap enough if you're willing to rough it. And you know you can have a job with us next summer."

"Thanks, I—" he began eagerly, and then, "No, I guess it would be too lonesome for her. She's used to better things. And besides, she's still just a kid." He sighed.

He waited, walking around with me, while the car was being greased. At the auto-parts store, where we went to buy me a new jack, they were having a sale. Whenever Dorothy or I went into town we brought back a Biddeford present. It might be some bright or silly gadget for the kitchen or some ivy in a pot or a tool like a set of different-sized screw drivers fitted to one handle. This time my eye lighted on a big forty-pound pressure fire extinguisher reduced from fifty-nine fifty to thirty dollars. I asked if it would put out a grease or slick fire, and the man showed me on the metal disk that it said it would. He also told me I only had to take it to the firehouse every six months to check the pressure; it was always ready for use. I bought it.

I walked into the house, lugging this thing, saying, "I have a very interesting present which I hope will be forever totally useless."

Dorothy was pleased. She said, "We'll put it up right now and we won't think about it again." We hung it by the cellar stairs.

I drove off to New York early the next morning. Three days later the fire began.

30

Holocaust

It was a beautiful day in New York. I was up early, Maine fashion, and phoned Dorothy to report and also to enjoy the warm feeling of talking to home. I asked, "What's the weather in Goose Rocks?"

"Hot and dry," Dorothy answered. "The dogs were barking all night. There was a glow in the sky over Biddeford—it's still there, faintly. It was quite beautiful."

"Could it be northern lights?"

"Mm," Dorothy said, noncommittally. "Ken and Marian are here with clams."

"Yummy. Save me some."

I would get an early start the next morning, I told her, and be there well in time for dinner.

I did everything I still had to do, that day, and spent the evening with Bill. I drove him out to the airport and waited until his plane took off. I drove back thinking how pleasant it would be if Bill, so congenial, so solid, would only make up his cautious Yankee mind and come to Goose Rocks to live.

The world was very nearly perfect, just as it was. We'd had a tremendous summer. We had very little cash, but we had paid off all the improvements, and what improvements! Next summer would be a breeze. We'd learned how to be Maine storekeepers and also live a little. We had the whole beautiful leisurely Maine winter ahead of us. And tomorrow morning I would be going home again. I had a home to go to, at last.

Back at my hotel, I packed, laid out my things for the morning, and went to bed.

At six I lifted my head and flicked the radio dial to get the weather. The news was on, and to save time I went to run a bath. When I came back I got the tail end: ". . . sweeping across southern Maine. The entire township of Kennebunk, including Biddeford, Biddeford Pool, Goose Neck Beach—"

They always get the name wrong! I fretted.

"—and parts of Kennebunkport have already been wiped out in what threatens to become the biggest fire—"

Fire!

I jiggled the phone. "Long distance. Person-to-person in Maine. The number is—" The operator in Kennebunkport always knew where people were. She might find Dorothy.

Long distance took forever. At last she came back. "Wires are down. We can't get through."

I called *The New York Times.* "Where are the survivors?" I asked.

"I have nothing on that, Miss," the man said.

I called the Time-Life office, where I knew people. Someone passed me along to someone else. Yes, he agreed, it might be a big story. "It's already big," I said. "You really ought to fly your photographers and crew right up." I was selling hard. If I could get them to send a plane, maybe they'd take me. "By the way, I live there now—"

The man said, "I believe we'll cover the story from Boston."

I put down the phone. Why did I want to go to Goose Rocks? Dorothy couldn't still be there. Or maybe she was. Nightmare images began to rise up. I had never seen a forest fire but I had seen pictures of people burned.

I grabbed the phone again just as it rang. Dorothy? No, a

friend who had heard the news. I cut her off abruptly and dialed the Red Cross. I had a good friend there.

"Where do they take survivors?" I asked her.

"To the nearest place that's not burning, generally," she said. She got hold of department heads, one after another—department of devastation, department of explosions. They were kind and told me how these things were managed. I said thank you and good-by. I still didn't know where Dorothy might be.

Biddeford was a mill town, bricks and stones and pavement. Would that burn? I tried long distance again. No, she couldn't get through to Biddeford.

I called Western Union. I'd send Dorothy a wire. But where? And who would deliver it? At the store we had delivered the wires. I hung up.

By now every time I put the phone down it rang. Friends calling. I cut them short. The next time I got long distance I called the manager of the New England Telephone Company in Boston. I didn't know him but I got him. I pulled the business about being a storeowner and asked to talk to whoever knew anything about the situation in southern Maine. I talked and listened and waited. And then, miraculously, there was the familiar voice of the Biddeford operator!

"Your store has burned—the big house is still standing but it has been burning—no, I don't know if anybody's there —I do know that the Red Cross was trying to get through to the big house during the night. There are some Goose Rocks people at the Narragansett Inn—want to talk to them?"

She put me through to the inn. A man answered. I didn't know him, but he knew Dorothy Mignault.

"No, she isn't here. No, no cocker spaniels. No, I'm sorry, I don't know where she might be, but they're saying—" he hesitated.

"What are they saying?"

"It's no comfort to you, but they're saying that all the Goose Rocks people that got out of Goose Rocks are here."

I hung up and began dressing frantically. The phone rang again almost at once. It was Eric.

"Couldn't sleep, so I tuned in the news," he said. "Scotty, I'm going down there."

We debated whether to go in one car or two, and decided two. Cars would be needed. He said, "Meet you at the Waldorf in an hour."

"Dear God, why wait an hour?"

"I'll get some things. They'll need lots of things." He hung up.

I drove to the Waldorf, parked, tipped the doorman to let me stay there, and went in to get coffee and a paper.

It was an hour and a half before Eric finally pulled in to the curb. He was full of apologies. He had battered down the doors at Abercrombie and Fitch, and his car was full of packages: tins of food, Sterno, thermos bottles, a mountain of first-aid supplies, flashlights and extra batteries and a couple of electric lanterns, warm clothing, fire axes, a gun. And soap that lathers in salt water!

While waiting for Eric I had phoned back to my own hotel for any messages. There was a wire from Biddeford: "I am safe, Dorothy."

As the miles between me and Maine went by under my wheels I pondered that telegram. From Biddeford—then Goose Rocks must be completely gone. And that message couldn't be from Dorothy. She would have said, "We are safe." She would have tried to tell me something about Fran, about the dogs. I imagined them all lost, and Dorothy lying in a first-aid station, barely alive enough to give someone my name and address in the city. By the time I got there she would be dead, too.

The pall of smoke was our first sign that we were getting

to the fire. It met us miles before, blinding, choking, slowing our speed to forty, thirty, finally fifteen and ten and five miles an hour. We took turns leading; even following Eric's taillight was getting difficult.

Through the smoke we saw the people, all going the other way, driving cows and horses ahead of them, pushing wheelbarrows and baby carriages—all going down Route 1, blocking it from edge to edge, glazed and reddened eyes in grimy faces staring at us as they made room for us who were going into the fire.

Outside Wells the State Police had a road block and were turning cars off the road and directing them up to the barracks. We got out of our cars, stiff, and went into the main room. At one end were troopers with headphones and one marking the fire's progress on a map. "Mousam Bridge is going. ... A woman and child are trapped in a car off Route 9 . . . ," one of the men with the headphones was saying as we came in, in that even-toned voice without exictement but not without feeling.

I identified myself to the trooper whose job it was to check people going into the fire. He knew Dorothy, and he knew there were two of us in the store. He didn't know where Dorothy was.

"The fire's out of hand," he told us. "I don't advise you to go through. Some of the wooden bridges are out—there are looters and arsonists around—"

I could understand looters, but arsonists!

"Oh, yes, they come swarming from out of state, even, to help the fire along—"

I shook my head. I wanted to say that it didn't matter about the bridges and the arsonists, but the words stuck. It came over me that almost everything and everybody that meant anything to me was in Goose Rocks.

He helped me. He said, "I know. You own property and

you live there and I can't stop you from going in if you in-
sist." He added, "They'll stop you at the Clock Farm and
hold you for a deputy to identify."

From Wells Barracks I led because I knew the road. We
hadn't seen the daylight go; in the smoke it had been black
night for hours, but now by the clock in my car I saw that it
was just eleven. It was terribly cold.

My headlight picked up a man wearing a mask, standing
in the road, waving two flashlights. When I stopped he came
to my window and flashed one of the lights in my face. It was
the chief of police of Kennebunkport. "Take care—bridges
are out all along—" He waved both of us on.

Kennebunkport wasn't burning. It was a sleeping village,
dark, peaceful—except for the smoke that stung your eyes,
the smell that filled your nostrils, and the cold. Downhill for
two blocks, the winding narrow main street, turn right a
straight piece the length of a long city block, then left. I was
on Route 9.

Route 9, the cowpath of a road to Goose Rocks, the twisting thin ribbon of black macadam between thick walls of pine,
maples, and elms whose branches met overhead, deliciously
cool and fragrant tunnel of shade through which I had driven
every day, sometimes three or four times a day, always on
an errand, always in a tearing hurry at top speed.

I tried second gear, then slowed and went into first. Even
in a fog my headlights would pick up the white line in the
center or the edge of the road on the right. But the white
line was black and the trees at the road's edge were charred
black. I couldn't put my head out to see where I was going. I
couldn't roll my window down; even with the windows shut
tight my throat ached with the smoke. There was a constant
roaring sound, and in the distance the sky glowed, but that
was the only light.

Branches and trees were down in the road. Each time I

edged out to go around them my headlights met a black abyss, and there was nothing to tell me whether I was going into a culvert. Suddenly I would know, and turn my wheel sharply, and then I would be safely back on the road again. I knew every foot of that road, not only with my mind and my eyes, but with my muscles.

Down a hill, a turn. There was a bridge at the bottom. I blinked my brake lights for Eric and stopped, wrapped a scarf around my mouth and nose, and got out with a flashlight. I crept along the road, bent almost double, following the road with my flashlight to see if the bridge was there. It was. But as I stood there, suddenly with a *hrumph hrumph* the icehouse fifty feet away from me, packed with sawdust, went up, knocking the breath out of me for a moment.

I ran back to Eric. "Take this bridge fast," I told him.

I sped ahead, Eric was right on my heels. Behind him half the bridge fell in. We crawled another mile, and I knew we were at the Clock Farm before I saw the men waving us down with flashlights.

They brought the deputy up in a police car to identify us. A gaunt youth, soot-covered, red-eyed, he was a stranger to me until he smiled and said, "Hello, Mac!" and I recognized one of our teen-age soda clerks who had been such joys and such nuisances to us. He had come down from Andover. All the summer boys who could had come when they heard— from the schools, from Cambridge and Hanover and Amherst and New Haven—to fight the fire for the place they loved.

He said, "Watch the culverts. Albion's bridge is shaky," and waved us on. What about Albion and his wife, their children, their house? No time to ask.

Albion's bridge held. I couldn't see whether his house was standing. Beyond, something off the road was burning as we passed; could it be the guesthouse where Bill had stayed?

Photographs

The store at Goose Rocks Beach shown in a postcard dating from the mid-1940s, before Dorothy and I bought the store and the house next door. (AUTHOR'S COLLECTION)

My friend Beata Gray took this photograph of me sanding the headboard of a bed in the house next to the store. We used this as my author photo on the jacket of the first edition of *My Love Affair with the State of Maine*. (AUTHOR'S COLLECTION)

After the devastating fire, Dorothy's was one of very few houses left standing. It is the one in the upper right of this photo.
(EDWARD D. HIPPLE PHOTO, AUTHOR'S COLLECTION)

Only the signpost and gas pumps remained to mark the location of our store. (PORTLAND PRESS HERALD)

A July 1955 autographing party at the Community Hall to promote
My Love Affair with the State of Maine included two of the Goose Rocks
Beach citizens who appeared in the book. Left to right: Dorothy
Mignault with Spike, Fred Smith ("Chris"), Scotty MacKenzie with
Imp, Ruth Goode, Archie Smith ("Albion"). (AUTHOR'S COLLECTION)

Author of "My Love Affair with Maine" Feted at Kennebunkport Autograph Tea

KENNEBUNKPORT, July 4—

. . . A clambake and lobster feed wound up a Scotty Mackenzie Weekend at the beach resort yesterday that was sponsored by the Goose Rocks Beach Association, Inc. . . .

An autograph party for *My Love Affair with the State of Maine* was held at the Community Hall of the association, where many of the characters in the book had a chance to meet the [author]. They also found out who "Albion" and "Chris Marble," two local characters in the book really are.

Archie and Fred Smith were the men the authors used for the characterizations. Both helped Miss Mackenzie when she started a summer hotel here several years ago. They are not related.

The book, released on May 6, already has gone into the third printing at Simon and Schuster Inc., publishing house. Its effect on the quiet summer colony has been felt throughout this section as tourists stop at stores and restaurants to inquire about the beach location.

Miss Dorothy Mignault, one of Miss Mackenzie's many friends named in the book, said today that many persons have moved to the beach this summer "just because they read about it in the book."

Meanwhile, sales of the book throughout the nation are beginning to climb and well-known bookstores in New York are featuring the volume in window displays. Local stores report the book has been sold out, with orders piling up for more copies.

How the publication of a book about a summer resort affects its subjects can best be summed up by Archie Smith, a native of the beach area and one of the book's principals: "People keep slowin' down as they pass my place and try wavin' at me," he noted dryly.

Some residents at the beach have picked up the book and made it a necessary part of their homes. A popular game that started a few weeks ago is trying to connect correctly the book's characters (who all have fictitious names) with real persons in the colony.

Many of their guesses were backed up by Miss Mackenzie during the autographing tea. It was Miss Mackenzie's first public appearance here since the book's publication, and everyone at the tea, in the book or not, was excited about it.

"The people here love it," she says, "and I guess I wouldn't have fallen in love with them if they weren't the kind of people they are. Seeing them here today was like lighting the torch again."

Excerpted from an article published in the Kennebunk Star (York County Coast Star) *in July 1955.*

I turned left, though there was nothing to show me where to turn; for all I could see I might have driven right into the ocean. But I knew where I was.

I blinked my lights at Eric and stopped. Glass crunched under my feet. With my flashlight I picked out the stumps of the gas pumps. I lifted the flash and there, swinging pallidly in the wind, its bright red horse scorched black, was our Mobilgas sign.

I couldn't see anything beyond it. Store, town house, guest-house, Casino—all were either gone or invisible in the smoky pall. I got back into the car and crawled on along the main road, heading toward the big house on the Point.

I found the entrance to our drive. I followed the drive by feel, and when I thought I had come to where the house was I stopped. Eric stopped behind me.

A shadow loomed up: the truck. It was burned, the rear wheels melted to the ground; shreds of fur and clothing fluttered near the front end. The cab was charred. I thought. I should look in the cab, but I was afraid I might find what I was looking for.

I groped on toward where the house should be. My hand touched the stair rail; it was hot enough to make me jump away. I heard barking: one dog, or both? I climbed the steps to the door, still not sure there was a house behind the door, and opened it.

There was a lighted candle on the fireplace mantel. The room was almost as smoky as outdoors. I heard coughing and then Fran's voice.

"Dorothy, we have company!" And both dogs jumped into my arms.

Dorothy was lying on the sofa in a posture of utter exhaustion. "We're all here, Scotty," she said, getting up. Her shirt was torn and burned in spots, her dungarees were torn, and she was streaked with soot from head to feet.

There were fourteen of them in the house, all very, very tired and very, very dirty. Even immaculate Fran. No water, of course, to wash with; no electricity to run the pump. It was freezing in the house, but no one could bear to light a fire.

Almost all of Goose Rocks Beach was gone, they told us, but this house had escaped. How Dorothy saved the house is part of her story.

I said, "You filthy people. Eric has brought you soap you can wash with in salt water."

✤ 31 ✤

Dorothy's Story

I have to piece together Dorothy's story because in the terrible days that were still before us she told it to me in bits. While the fire still burned, there was no rest, day or night. The house on the Point was headquarters. The fire fighters came in shifts to eat and rest, and Dorothy fed them, emptying our deep freeze, thanking heaven for the forethought that had stocked it for the winter. And we had to watch over the house day and night. The same capricious wind which had shifted away long enough for it to be saved might shift again, carrying burning brands to set it afire once more.

At first we were both stunned to realize that I had called on the telephone from New York—only the morning before! It was such a peaceful morning, cloudless. The sky had seemed overcast with rather more than an Indian summer haze, and there was still the pinkish glow Dorothy had seen during the night, very thin and elusive now in the daylight, so that she wasn't sure she actually saw it.

It was the season for fires in Maine, and there had been an open winter and a dry summer, so people were watchful. Small fires had been breaking out here and there. Every now and then a siren went somewhere. In Maine when the siren goes everyone stops talking or whatever he's doing and counts—*wu-u-up wu-u-up, wup wup wup wup wup,* two long and five short, means twenty-five, and that's Goose Rocks.

Ken and Marian were washing the muck off the clams they had brought, and when they finished the three of them had some coffee in the sunroom. Dorothy left them there talking and went upstairs. Dressing, making her bed, going every now and then to a window to look at the faint pink glow, she found herself thinking of the foolish things people try to save in a fire. She thought, what would she really want to save if she had to?

Not taking herself very seriously, she went around the upstairs rooms in a leisurely fashion, thinking, "I'd take this, and this, and this," and presently she began picking things up and putting them together in a pile in her room. The silver from downstairs, of course, she was thinking, as she gathered some family pictures and our two jewel cases. Our city clothes—we would need them and they would be expensive to replace. Our elegant summer work clothes were not here. We had stored them in the town house, neatly laid in the bureau drawers between folds of tissue.

Shoes. The good luggage. A bottle of whisky; you never knew, in a fire, who might be hurt or in shock or exhausted. The store accounts, which I hadn't yet got around to. Books and records? Oh no, there were too many, and all of them were precious; she couldn't begin to choose.

When she came downstairs again Ken said, "Look at that sky now. Think it means anything?" The pink glow was stronger. Ken said, "They may need fire fighters somewhere," and went to telephone Kennebunkport.

The voice at the firehouse was peremptory. "Where are you, Goose Rocks? Stay right there. The engines are on their way to the Colony store. You'll be needed."

Now Dorothy began to carry our possessions down and out to the truck. Ken and Marian helped. Ken said, "The wind's blowing down toward Kennebunkport." Dorothy snapped the leads on the dogs and went to the phone to call

Fran. Fran had heard on the radio that the fire was blowing toward her end of the beach. Dorothy said, "I'm coming over."

She turned to Ken. "We'll go in the truck. We'll drive to Mrs. Sergeant's and I'll take her car. Then Marian can go in the truck to get her things, and yours at the store. Marian and I will meet back here and see what to do next."

"Good," Ken said, "then I'll know Marian is with you."

They started out in the truck. Over the hill behind Chilton's farm, where the pink glow had been, a smoke cloud was forming. As they came out of the driveway they saw smoke swelling also at the other end, Fran's end, of the beach. Dorothy drove past the store, where no engines had arrived yet, and straight through town, putting on speed. At every house people were piling children, pets, and possessions into their cars. Some were already swinging out into the road toward Kennebunkport. The sirens were screaming steadily now from every landward direction.

Mary Burke sped by, her sedan loaded with her own possessions and household goods. Even the front seat beside her was stacked high. Mary was alone in the car, driving fast and looking neither to right nor to left. Don was probably fighting fire somewhere, Dorothy thought fleetingly. But there were some families without cars. Shouldn't Mary be taking some of them to safety?

At Fran's house Dorothy swung around and stopped, jumping out with the dogs. She called to Ken at the wheel, "Don't waste a minute! This end of the beach is going!" The wind was rising, tearing her words from her lips, and smoke already stung her eyes. But she had the split-second realization that it was blowing away from the house on the Point, and there would still be safety for them there if they could get back to it. "Don't forget—go back to my house, Marian!" she called.

She struggled against the sucking wind and got into the house. Fran came toward her, leaning on her cane.

"I might have known you'd come. We must hurry, mustn't we?" Fran said calmly. But her calm was a thin mask. She turned from Dorothy and looked vaguely around her beautiful living room.

"Get what you need, Fran." Dorothy made for the sideboard, snatched a white damask tablecloth from a drawer and scooped Fran's silver into it with both hands.

Fran said, "Silver—one can always buy new! Leave it, darling!"

It was not the value but the beauty of it that Dorothy couldn't bear to abandon to destruction. She tied up the bundle and hefted it over her shoulder. "Fran! Where are you!"

Fran's voice came muffled. "A hat—I can't find a hat!"

"You've never worn a hat—come now, Fran!"

Fran backed out of the coat closet, a man's fishing cap from heaven knew where on her head, but she turned again to the living room. "Hal's picture—I just want to take it." She had not said a kind word about her third husband since he died, but she limped to the mantel for his picture and thrust it into her knitting bag. On the way back she stopped and seized a bottle of Scotch from the liquor cabinet.

"I have a terrible roaring in my ears," she said.

"That's not in your ears—it's the wind," Dorothy told her. She opened the door. They were sucked out of the house, flung against the car in the driveway. They got in, and Dorothy pulled out into the road.

She rounded the corner by Albion's house. Albion stood there, stopping cars from taking the road out of Goose Rocks toward Kennebunkport. He jumped on the running board beside Dorothy.

"Fire's jumped the road at this end—you'll be safer up your way," he shouted above the roaring.

"We're going there!" Dorothy shouted back. "Where are your children, Albion?"

"I don't know where they are—"

He dropped off the running board and ran back, his words lost like a wail on the wind. His children must have gone to school, as on any other morning, with all the Goose Rocks children—were they in Kennebunkport? Or marooned in the school bus on the road somewhere, the fire racing around them?

Dorothy drove back past the store—still no engines, but perhaps now they could not get through from Kennebunkport. She came to the Point, to the big house. The truck was there, piled high; Marian had managed to get Ken's things as well as her own. But now she stood beside the truck, twisting her hands, hysterical.

"Ken's gone! I may never see him again!"

"He's needed, Marian. He'll be all right."

"I want to go where he is!" Marian wailed.

There was a bellow from the kitchen steps:

"Come now, you big baby, stop crying and help with these thing—" It was Hedi! "Don was so kindly bringing Cheechee and me here for safekeeping," she explained to Dorothy, "but I think it will not so long be safe, yes?" Her bright hair was tied up in a bandana; her candy-striped pedalpushers and fireman's red shirt were covered by a man's slicker. Cheechee clung terrified around her neck.

Hedi was lugging a hatbox of Dorothy's. "I bring these one more piece of good luggage, you overlooked, I think. Dorothy, all have been driving past here to the sea."

Cars were in fact, strung out down the King's Highway, the overgrown, rutted road, half of it under water at high tide, which wound from the house on the Point all the way to the clam flats. Dorothy counted four cars, five. And here came another, Don Burke driving Bab and Albion's wife and two couples who had no cars, with their children, from up the road.

"Don't stay here any longer, Dorothy," Don said. "My house is burning."

Dorothy said, "Wait, Don!" She rushed into the house, snatched blankets from every bed and an armful from the linen closet. Bab reached out and took some, going on, and Dorothy piled the rest into Fran's car.

Fran was shaking, either from shock or chill or both; it was getting very cold. "Darling, I'm afraid I'm unable to drive," she said through chattering teeth.

"All right." Dorothy got behind the wheel. "Hedi, jump in." Too bad Hedi didn't know how to drive. "Marian, drive the truck! I'll lead."

Marian cried out, "No! I'm going to find Ken!"

Dorothy looked up the hill. The Chilton Farm had disappeared, and a wall of fire was marching down upon them; the wind had shifted again. Burning branches flew before it, and birds with their feathers flaming. It might stop at the tidal river, or it might not.

"Hedi, grab her!" Dorothy cried. Hedi pulled the girl into the car. Dorothy drove away, leaving the house, leaving the truck with everything of ours she had so thoughtfully chosen for saving, with Marian's own things and everything that Ken owned in the world. She headed out after the rest, along the clam road winding through high beach grass toward the sea.

Halfway there, Don turned out of the road for her. He was on his way back into the fire, to pick up more people who were stranded in their houses without cars. Dorothy called to him, "Look for Hattie Black!" Don nodded and drove on.

On the beach they were huddled together against the freezing wind, perhaps a dozen people all told; more cars were coming down the clam road. Old Mrs. Barnes sat on the sand with all the children, a two-year-old in her lap, the others pressing close against her. She had some of Dorothy's blankets snug around the whole group and was telling them, in a quiet voice, the story of Daniel in the lions' den.

Fran got out of the car, still carrying the bottle of Scotch in one hand, her cane in the other. Halfway down the beach she stopped.

"I won't need this," she said, and threw away the cane. Carrying the bottle, she sat down beside Mrs. Barnes and the children.

Phil Smith's wife and her sister were there, Albion's wife Edith, Lucy Gooden, and old Sarah Chilton. Sarah Chilton was standing stiffly against the wind, staring out to sea, muttering to herself. Lucy took a blanket from Dorothy and wrapped it around her.

"Sit down, Sarah. Rest yourself," she said, pushing her gently down by the shoulders.

"Where's Rawl?" Dorothy asked Lucy.

"Dropped him at the store. All the men are there. I called the airport," Lucy said irrelevantly, and she too stared out to sea.

"What's that, Lucy?" Dorothy prodded her. Lucy, who had never ridden in anything but the 1912 Ford—it stood there among the others in the beach grass. "Why did you call the airport?"

"I saw people here—from the front yard I could see them. I called the airport in Portland to tell them there was people on the beach here and they should send planes to get them out from the ocean side—they'd never get out by land. We were going the other way, so I called the airport before we left."

"But you didn't go the other way."

Lucy shook her head. "The sow—Rawl tried to get the

sow. We put all our money in the sow, you know. She birthed twelve, day before yesterday. Rawl couldn't get her. The fire was down to the pigpen. It came so fast. One little pig—he put it in the car."

"You saved one? Good, Lucy!"

"To eat," Lucy said laconically. "He was ready cooked in the fire."

Marjorie Wilkins and Stevie came over, a blanket wrapped around them both. Stevie was crying. Marjorie's sweet, perpetually smiling face was stern and angry. She looked, for the first time, like one of her own Puritan ancestresses.

"Dorothy, did you pass Mary Burke?"

"Yes, come to think of it, she passed me, going toward Kennebunkport, quite a while ago. I wonder if she got through."

"She got through all right. I'll never forgive her. She passed right by old Mrs. Barnes. So we had to leave Stevie's dog. Bob had everything ready and was going to call Hercules. And there stood Mrs. Barnes." Hercules was an enormous dog who took up the space of two passengers.

Stevie said, "Herkie was standing in the doorway. He was wagging his tail."

"Don't worry, Stevie, Herkie is a smart dog," Dorothy said, without conviction. Hercules was no thoroughbred, but he was a favorite on the beach, and everybody knew he would not leave the house when the family was not at home. If he were outdoors he might just escape being trapped—but it was a slim hope.

The smoke was getting bad. Dorothy remembered about wet blankets, and they began to wring blankets out in the sea and put them over people. The roaring of the fire was a constant sound now. They could hear the breaking of branches, and now and again an explosion as gas tanks, fuel-oil tanks caught fire. Branches and burning shingles were dropping on the beach, carried by the wind, which was now a gale.

Suddenly Chris drove up out of the smoke, with his wife in the car. She joined the others on the beach, while Chris, with two Indian fire extinguishers on his back, got out of his car and stayed to stand guard against the fire in the beach grass. Don came with more people and two more children, who moved dazedly toward the other youngsters clustered around Mrs. Barnes.

Mrs. Barnes said, "So now, children, we'll do as Daniel did. We'll pray to the dear Lord to help us out of our trouble."

The children obediently got on their knees and began to pray. Dorothy, coming close to put a wet covering over their dry one, heard them: "Now I lay me down to sleep—" It was not the right prayer but it was the one they knew best.

Hedi had Marian under control; they were together under a blanket. Dorothy crept under the blanket she had thrown over Fran and the dogs. It was hard to breathe. They had to get down low to the sand and hold the wet blanket over their faces.

There was a shout from Chris. The beach grass had caught fire at last, and he was running around and around the cars, pumping one of his fire extinguishers. His shout was about something else: rats!

They ran out of the beach grass, as terrified as the human beings, seeking safety from the smoke as much as from the fire. They tried to crawl under the blankets. The women, frightened for the children, ran up and down, kicking the rats into the sea. The dogs went wild, tugging until Fran could barely hold their leads. And not only the dogs. Suddenly old Mrs. Chilton stood up, threw off her blanket, and ran headlong into the sea.

Lucy ran after her, but Hedi was faster. She caught the old woman waist-deep in the water and dragged her back.

Cheechee was next. Terrified of the fire, terrified of the rats, and now completely panicked with her mistress gone, the little monkey fled screaming into the burning beach grass.

Hedi cried out, "Cheechee!" Don—the very Don who had fired two shots at Cheechee only a few weeks before—turned and ran into the flaming grass after the monkey. And then it was Hedi's turn to run after Don, crying, "Come back, come back, you foolish man!" She beat with her hands at Don's trouser bottoms, which had caught fire.

Hedi scolded, "You should not risk so. You could not save her," while tears streaked the coating of soot on her cheeks. Don, shamefaced, ran back to help guard the cars.

With the fire at their backs, the heat and smoke becoming every moment worse, Fran said, "Some could swim to the island."

Through the smoke they could just see it, the one spot of green still left. She and Dorothy and others there had often made the swim to Timber Island—less than a mile, and at low tide it was possible to walk a good part of the way. The tide was now three-quarters, and rising.

They took council and decided to try for the island. Everyone except Hedi could swim a little, and some were strong enough to carry a child or help a weak swimmer. Hedi said, "Do not worry for me. I have more fear to swim than to stay. I will sit in the water and the fire will not burn me."

Don was to carry little Sukie. He said to Hedi, "I'll come back for you."

They started. They were slow, keeping together, helping each other, and that was their good fortune. They had not gone far when Hedi, watching from the shore, shouted to them and pointed to the island. They looked, and saw their last green refuge burst into flame. Huge brands had flown on the wind, and though it was nearly a mile offshore the island was burning too.

It looked as though they were trapped. They took council again. The water was too cold to stay in for very long. The children and the older people were beginning to suffer.

Hedi shouted again. Where she crouched at the edge of the water she could see that the flash fire on the beach was burning itself out.

"Here! Is better here now!" she called, waving them back to the beach. They made their way back toward the beach and the dark mound which Hedi made in her blanket, like a solitary rock in the blowing smoke.

The beach grass, black and smoldering, was no longer a peril. Thanks to Chris, the cars had not caught fire. The beach was safe except for flying, flaming debris. They crept out of the ocean and huddled again under their blankets, freezing, choking, and waiting, while old Mrs. Barnes and the children knelt again and prayed, their prayers punctuated by choking coughs.

❧ 32 ❧

The House on the Point

On the beach they could not tell when day changed to night, but there came a time when the roaring seemed to recede little by little. Dorothy lifted her head. Again the wind had shifted, and the smoke seemed thinner; she could breathe. She thought she saw the silhouette of the house on the Point, still standing.

Between the house and where she crouched the beach grass had apparently burned itself out. She might be able to make it on foot by the short cut.

She said, "Fran, I'm going to see if I can walk back to the house. If there's a safe place I'll come for all of you."

Edith, Albion's wife, said, "Dorothy, I've got to get back. I must know what's happened to the children."

Don took Edith to his car. Dorothy picked up the dogs and started toward the house.

Carrying the dogs over the smoldering beach grass, she groped through the smoke along the short cut. She saw lawn furniture—the chaise, the table—she saw the bushes and the front steps. Little flames were licking all over them. Down beyond she saw Riverview, the cottage where the aunts had stayed; it was a smoking ruin. But the boathouse near it, freakishly, was still standing, the little boathouse for which nobody had had any use since Dorothy had first taken a job in the city and Dr. Mignault had sold his boat.

In the turnaround she saw the truck burning, and the wild rose bush, and the back steps and the back porch where the oil barrels stood. The porch was burning under the barrels!

She ran up the front steps into the living room, tied the dogs so they wouldn't follow her, and ran down the cellar stairs where hung my Biddeford present, the forty-pound pressure fire extinguisher. The house was full of smoke, but she could not stop to see where else it might be burning. If the oil barrels went, everything went.

She put out the fire on the back porch. She put out the fire creeping around the garage doors. She ran around to the front. Beach grass had burned up to the house wall; the glass of the big picture windows had buckled from the heat. She put out the flames that were feeding on the front porch. Next the roof: asbestos shingles, she remembered, and was thankful. But sparks kept flying, and flaming debris. There were places up high under the eaves that she could not reach with the extinguisher.

The hose was in the garage. Water? She turned a hose spigot: a sucking sound, and nothing. She got buckets out of the garage and ran down to the tidal river.

She was filling the buckets for the third or fourth time when a man in a rowboat came down the river.

"Want any help?" he called.

"What do you think?" He came ashore and took the full buckets from her hands. Some other men came; they were carpenters who had been repairing Phil Smith's garage, which was now burning. Together they went on to fill any vessels they could find—ash cans, garbage pails. People came walking back from the beach by the way Dorothy had taken, and everyone who could carry joined the bucket brigade. When they could see no more live flames anywhere they stood the pails of water at intervals around the house.

Now that they were inside a house, and could feel mo-

mentarily safe, people became less heroic and more human.
Bab helped Marjorie put her Stevie to bed, then they both
helped put the other children to bed. Then Marjorie put Bab
to bed. And finally Marjorie sat down on the bedroom floor
and cried, until old Mrs. Barnes came and found her there
and put her to bed.

In the living room the candlelight was dim and smoky.
Marian sat in a corner, staring at nothing, speaking to nobody. Hedi tried to rouse her, and then Hedi fell into a chair
and went instantly to sleep.

At the windows, strangely dispassionate arguments were
going on. "That's our house going up now." "No, it isn't,
it's Bab's." "You're wrong, I saw the shape of it, it's Carter's." "I beg your pardon. It's my house." Distances were
deceptive in the dark. And values were distorted, or perhaps
they were temporarily restored to what they should be. People wept from exhaustion, from relief, from anxiety about
others who were not there. But none among the refugees uttered one regret that night for the loss of everything they
possessed. They were alive; it was enough. Fran stood at the
window with the others, taking bets on whose house would
make the best fire, her own or some other. When she learned
the next day that the whimsical wind had spared her house
and it was safe, she went all to pieces.

Sometime before dawn made an end of that long night, the
kitchen door opened and Chuck Donoghue from Biddeford,
who serviced our pinballs and jukebox, put his head in and
called cheerfully, "Anybody here want some cold beer?"

And that's what he had, a whole case of it, along with
dozens of other things all immediately usable. He was the
first of the Red Cross caravan that kept arriving from then
on.

He and the others had driven through live flames to get
to Goose Rocks. Their trucks and station wagons were

charred and singed. The fact that the fire had jumped the Biddeford Road and the way was littered with burning debris had not stopped them. The laundry truck, the dry-cleaner's truck, the bakery trucks, the soda and dairy and ice-cream trucks, station wagons and private cars were driving up and down the fire-scarred roads of Maine, loaded with great pots of hot spaghetti, with mountains of sandwiches, with cans of fresh water, with soap and razors and baby foods and milk and cigarettes and matches and lanterns and flashlights and extra batteries and blankets and clothing.

Everybody whose house was not actually burning was out either fighting fire or wearing a Red Cross armband and carrying relief, bringing comfort and news to the marooned and taking messages out to people waiting to hear. The Red Cross thought of everything, morale-builders as well as body comforts. About the only thing they didn't think of to bring was lipsticks to perk up the women.

The Red Cross team went from one to the other of our refugees while they ate hot spaghetti, and took messages. Dorothy gave them a message I would have recognized: "Fran, dogs, and I all safe, house standing, store gone." But I couldn't carp. Hundreds and thousands of messages taken by candlelight or lantern light, in thick smoke, beside burning houses, went out over the wires in those three days. It was a miracle I got any message at all.

The fire fighters began to come in, and they brought news. Freakish things had happened: our house on the Point and Fran's house and some others at her end of the beach stood, but everything from our house to beyond the store had burned. Two families whose houses were deep in the trees had piled their valuables into their cars and driven the cars to a friend's turnaround, which was open and bare of trees. The cars and all their possessions burned, and one house in the trees; the house beside it was untouched.

Albion, fighting fire without regard for his own property, had been saying of his house, "Let 'er burn!" His neighbors' brick houses burned, but Albion's simple wooden house remained standing. The fire ate its way through Goose Rocks, house by house, and skipped the firehouse!

Biddeford Pool, Goose Rocks, Cape Porpoise burned, but Kennebunkport stood in a charmed circle, untouched.

Far up in the woods the Clock Farm stood, a farmhouse with a four-sided clock tower which had been a landmark since Colonial days. It is still a thriving farm. When the fire fighters got there its owner was starting a backfire, a controlled fire intended to form a burned-out barrier against the oncoming flames. As usual in Maine, the debating society took over—"You'll lose everything that way!" "Backfire never works in a wind like this!" "Animals and birds will carry the fire across!" He persisted, and against their expressed convictions they helped him. The Clock Farm was saved.

Sometime during that night the schoolteacher from Kennebunkport arrived, bringing the first of the Goose Rocks children. When the fire had spread to Goose Rocks she saw nothing she could do but take the nine of them home with her, feed them, and put them to bed. As the fire passed their homes she woke them, family by family, and all the rest of the night she spent delivering them to their parents.

Day came, though there was still no light from the sky that could penetrate the heavy black smoke lying over the land. The fire fighters came again, and this time one of them handed a little bundle to Dorothy, a cat he had found in a tree. Its eyes were burned shut, its mouth was burned, but it was alive, and from what was left of its singed fur Dorothy recognized it: Marjorie Wilkins' cat. Stevie's dog was apparently lost. But here was Marjorie's cat. Dorothy said nothing to her, but carried it down to the cellar and made a bed of rags for it there. Every half-hour she went down to drop oil on its swollen eyelids with one eyedropper, and warm milk into its burning mouth with another eyedropper.

That night we came, Eric and I. Along with the many things there were to do, cooking for the fire fighters and our own people, making our refugees comfortable, Dorothy shared her secret nursing job with me.

The next morning the smoke still hung heavy, and you saw the sun as you see an eclipse through smoked glass, but at least you could see it. We went out to discover what, if anything, was left of Goose Rocks.

We walked along the beach, past bare foundations where hardly a timber was left, each with its chimney standing gauntly erect, and andirons still in the fireplace which no longer had the walls of a room around it. We came to the place where the store had been.

It was level, with only a pit where the underground gas tanks had exploded. The town house, the Casino, the garages, the store, might never have existed except in a dream. Only the Mobilgas sign, still swinging desultorily, testified that they had all been there as we remembered.

Walking down what had been the center aisle of the store to the stockrooms, the path we had run so many thousand times on our rounds, Dorothy and I stood suddenly still and reached for each other's hands.

Something fragile and lovely stood there, rising from the black ashes, a tree of glass with twisted slender arms, pink and rose and amethyst and green and violet tinting its glass fingers. It was like a dreamed impression of some strange plant waving its opal-dyed arms at the bottom of the sea.

We gasped, "How beautiful!" and "What was it?" Then we knew: all the empty soda-pop bottles which had been waiting in the stockroom for the company's truck to take them back. Their wooden cases had been burned away, and the fire which had turned everything else into a charred and blackened waste had transformed their insignificance into a thing of beauty, and left it here.

❦ 33 ❦

How to Thumb Your Nose at a Fire

While the fire still burned the men still fought it. But life began to move again, though in improvised channels. The lights came on and the refrigerator and deep freeze began to hum. Water did not yet run in pipes or come out of faucets, but when you picked up the telephone it had a voice.

People could come and go again and plan how they would rebuild their lives. When they saw the black wasteland the fire had left, the women were mostly silent. It was the men, some of them, who wept, out of anger and helplessness before the monstrous uncaring force which had devoured every vestige of their years of living and working, all in a few fierce hours.

The fire fighters—their clothes singed and torn, their eyes red-rimmed circles in sooty, haggard faces with stubble beards—came to eat, rest, and go again on their shifts. They were undone by watching the death of trees, of animals; deer and rabbits and small creatures running from the fire and carrying the fire with them on their burning fur, birds flying in flames until they dropped; barns burning with the horses and cows trapped in them; a mother cat running with one kitten in her mouth.

Ken came with his shift of fire fighters. Marian ran to him with a cry. She fetched his water ration to wash off the soot and grime, exclaimed over a burn on his shoulder where an ember had fallen, bandaged his hand where the hose had burned as he held it. She brought him food and sat with him while he ate. Ken was too tired to talk, but he smiled, and went to sleep smiling on the sun porch.

Then Marian's father came. He had flown in from Boston. He had tickets on the next plane out for Marian and himself, and the taxi from Portland was waiting. He was a courteous man, but understandably tense; he kept putting his glasses on and taking them off, putting them away and taking them out and putting them on again. He said, "Get your things, Marian," and little else, but the mere fact that he was clean and well dressed made those tired and dirty and ragged people in the room bridle, as though he had said, "Look at the mess your foolishness has got you all into."

Marian stood in her ragged jeans and blouse, a sweater from the Red Cross over her arm.

"I said, get your things, Marian," her father repeated.

"I haven't any things," she answered.

"Oh? Then come along."

"But I'm not going with you, Daddy," Marian said.

"I think maybe you'd better go, honey," another voice said.

Every head in the room turned to the doorway of the sun porch. Ken was standing there. "It'll be best all around. And I'll come for you, as soon as I can," he told her. Marian protested, but in the end she submitted to Ken's better judgment and went with her father.

Chris came, jubilant, shouting for Stevie Wilkins. Chris was carrying a huge dog—singed, emaciated, but unhurt— it was Hercules! He had been swimming for two days, perhaps for three, unable to set foot on the burning shore, all the way to Cape Porpoise. There Chris had seen the swimming animal and called to him, and here he was.

The people in the house looked at Hercules, licking Stevie's wet face, and thought of Mary Burke, who had driven away from the fire with her car full of household goods instead of people. They reminded each other that Don Burke had gone back again and again into the fire, bringing people, and especially the children, who trusted him, to safety on the beach. The summer's fierce partisanship swung to its opposite pole: from wicked Don and poor Mary, it was now selfish Mary and noble Don. This is the reason, I suppose, why public-opinion polls must be taken so often.

Meanwhile, in the cellar our little casualty was showing signs of recovery. Marjorie's cat opened its eyes; it lapped its milk. Its coat began to look better; we took to brushing it regularly. (Three and a half weeks after the fire we proudly presented her restored cat to Marjorie.)

Our refugees gradually diminished in number as those left who had somewhere to go. The Red Cross teams came bringing clothing, bales of it. They came again to make lists of what each family had lost.

Dorothy and I listened, deeply impressed. This was not charity. It was businesslike and efficient: farmers had to be put back to farming again, lobstermen to lobstering. The economy had to be restored. But it was also warmly human. Families were to have what they needed to function again as families, to live again as they had lived before. There was no question of a handout, but only of giving back to people their accustomed standard of living. Wherever you had bought your food, your clothing, whatever stores you had dealt with before, there you could go with an order from the Red Cross to replace what the fire had taken. If the Red Cross erred at all it erred, humanely, on the generous side. A lobsterman who had lost a patched-up old dory with a many-time reconditioned outboard might find himself the owner of a fine new boat with an inboard motor. Children who had known nothing but hand-me-downs learned for the first time how it was to wear new clothes.

One felt ashamed, eavesdropping while old Mrs. Barnes named all her worldly possessions: a two-room house, a bed, a table, two kitchen chairs, a rocker, a bureau, one skillet, one saucepan, one stew pot, one house dress, one apron, one good dress for Sunday, black, and a black Sunday hat. The list was quickly ended.

"Except—" She hesitated.

"Yes? Tell me everything you can remember, Mrs. Barnes," the Red Cross worker encouraged.

"The photographs—of my parents, of my husband the Reverend, of my son who died a baby. You're very kind, but I'll have to keep those in my mind."

Lucy Gooden's and Rawl's list was longer: farm buildings, farm animals, Rawl's inventory of his farm machinery and tools; so many hens, two roosters, six ducks, the sow and twelve piglets. "No, eleven," Lucy amended carefully. "We et the one."

The Red Cross worker covered a smile. The cows, the bull, the bull calf and the heifer calves, the cow that was going to calve soon. The household furnishings. And the treasures that could never be replaced: an ancient, capacious farmhouse attic had been full of them. Hand-built cradles and trundle bed, Indian-carved sandalwood box and Spanish shawl and Chinese embroidered scarf and silk-and-ivory fan, the things skillful hands of the past had made, the things seagoing menfolk had brought home "from away" to the waiting Gooden women.

"And the china closet," Lucy ended. What had been in the china closet, the lifelong collection of little figures and animals and miniature flowers in which she had invested so much love, this was gone forever, and she did not waste breath in the mention of it.

Old Sarah Chilton, recovered from her terror on the beach, sat by, nodding to everything Lucy said: "I had one like that. I had them. That's right. I did, too."

Phil Smith's wife Della came next: less farm, more household and tool shed. The new washing machine, the ironer, electric toaster and percolator and vacuum cleaner, the nearly new electric refrigerator, the electric sewing machine —and Sarah Chilton alertly putting in, "I had that. I had one of them. I lost them." Phil's electric drill and sander, all his woodworking tools— "I had them, I lost them," old Sarah Chilton said.

Albion, coming in from a fire patrol, carefully took a sheet of newspaper from the wood box and spread it on Dorothy's upholstered chair before he sat down. Even with fresh jeans or overalls on, the men always did this when they came into the living room and were offered a chair.

"Gawd knows, my house is standing, maybe you can tell me why," he rumbled, amused. "Boat's gone. Maybe six lobster traps I had ashore, and some buoys. A barrel of lobster bait, about half full. Fishing tackle. Didn't lose Edith or any of the children. I guess that's all."

And Chris: "I built my cabin. No reason why I can't do it again."

"But lumber, roofing, window glass, nails?" the worker prompted. "Furniture? Clothing? Your wife's kitchen utensils? And you'll need tools."

"Oh, sure, I don't mind getting 'em new. Can I get new Western boots too?"

The worker looked puzzled. *Western* boots? He was kidding, surely.

"What about canvases and paints and brushes, Chris?" Dorothy reminded him.

At this he sighed. "Eyah. Got to start over again, there too. Fire took two paintings you never saw, Dot—one was pretty good. Be a while before I get time to make some more."

The worker, now beginning to get it, carefully wrote down: "Paints, canvases, brushes," and an estimated figure in dollars.

Don Burke said succinctly, "Typewriter. Writing supplies. One suit of city clothes. One suitcase."

"Your house, Don!" Bab exclaimed.

He flushed. "It wasn't mine."

When Ken's turn came he was inarticulate. He owned literally nothing but the torn shirt and dungarees he had on and his scorched shoes. Dorothy said, "There was cash in the truck, Ken. How much money did you have in your room that day? Try to remember."

He could only shake his head. Dorothy and the Red Cross girl pieced out a reasonable list, but afterward Dorothy said, "I think the best thing we could do for Ken would be to get him a job."

The worker put her papers in her briefcase. "I guess that's all here now. I'll be back to get more as they come in." She looked at Dorothy and me and she smiled. "We'll get around to you two. I'll bring lots of paper and pencils for your lists."

The listing went on and on, all up and down the burned-out coast, and for us it went on and on in our living room, which still remained the headquarters for Goose Rocks. Some people were voluble about what they had lost, some reeled off the sum of their possessions like an animated adding machine, and some simply couldn't remember. For these last, the ones who couldn't remember, we felt a strong kinship. The things you lose that you don't remember, until sometime long afterward—probably a psychologist could tell you why.

Dorothy said, "All those beautiful shorts!"

And I said, "The shoes that we bought so carefully for when our feet would hurt!"

And we both said, "Fran's socks!"

And weeks later, in the middle of a conversation about something else, I remembered with a shock the beautiful heirloom jewelry which had come down to Dorothy through the generations, and which we had almost lost the very first day of the store—gone, now, with everything else in the truck.

The movie projection machine, in the Casino. And five hundred folding chairs. The popcorn machine! We had ordered it at the beginning of the summer, intending to pay for it on time. But it never came until the end of the summer— the last week—and on an impulse, feeling rich, we paid for it outright, one thousand dollars. It had been used for just six days.

Afterward, long, long afterward, when people began coming to us to ask for them, we remembered all the negatives of those picture post cards of people's houses that Dorothy had tracked down right to the photographer in the sanitarium. The houses were gone. And the only records of them were gone, too. People wrote to friends to whom they remembered sending post cards, asking if perhaps they had kept one.

"Who keeps picture post cards?" I asked scornfully when Dorothy began writing, too. But some people do, as we discovered, and that's how we happen to have a picture of the store.

Dorothy got a job for Ken. At least she got a promise that a man would hold up a decision and interview Ken for a job if he got there within twenty-four hours. A hotelman in Maine had telephoned a hotelman in New York who had a small good hotel in Florida. The Maine man recommended Ken on Dorothy's word. But twenty-four hours!

We raced into Biddeford, where the priest who was in charge of the contributed clothing, gathered by the Red

Cross and kept in the community center, helped us pick a suit for Ken.

"It has to be a good suit," Dorothy said firmly, giving Ken's measurements. "Just under six feet, broad shoulders, weighs a hundred and seventy usually—he's thinner just now."

"I'd say, medium large and fairly long," the priest said, seeking earnestly through the second-hand clothing on most of which no sizes were visible, looking for a "good" suit that would conceivably fit.

He found one, a tweed, and a good white shirt and a necktie that would not disgrace a man looking for a job, also socks, underwear, a white handkerchief, and quite good shoes in almost the right size. Fire or no fire, Ken had to make a good appearance. Money for his pocket, a loan, also courtesy of the Red Cross. We raced back again.

Ken meanwhile had shaved and bathed. Five of us gave up our water ration for the day so he could have a real all-over bath.

He came down and stood in the center of the living room to be inspected; he was no fashion plate, nor any model of sartorial splendor, but he looked clean and respectable and, in his boyish way, very appealing. His secondhand shoes pinched a little, he said when we asked him, but he would work them in. Looking at the shoes, all of us exclaimed at once, "A shine!"

I ran for the shoe kit. He sat in a living-room chair, much embarrassed, while we shined his shoes for him. And then we hurried him into the car and drove him to Portland to catch the plane.

He phoned us from New York the next night. He had the job. He had phoned Marian and she was going to marry him and go down to Florida with him. "Thanks to you and the fire," he said, "we're going to make it, this time."

The fire rearranged some other lives for the better. Mary Burke did not come back to Goose Rocks, and she did give Don a divorce. He married Bab and eventually became the father of a baby girl.

As the fire passed from one area after another the fire fighters changed their hoses and fire axes for guns and went on patrol against looters, because wherever there is disaster there are a few who will try to fatten on it. Dorothy and I took our turn patrolling with the men, armed like them.

Eric had gone back to the city. Dorothy thanked him for coming but she would not consider leaving Goose Rocks now, when there was everything to be done, everyone needing help.

Bill came in his place. Back from the West, he caught the first plane up. And—it was absurd, but like Bill and like Maine—this time he came to stay. While we prospered, while the land was beautiful and the community alive and gay, he couldn't make up his mind. Now that there were only corpses of trees, a graveyard of houses, nothing but black waste and debris to be cleared and the future in every way a total blank, no money, no business, no job, no idea which way to turn or what to do—now he came.

We knew by that time that we had nothing. Dorothy had her house, but it was empty of the things you need to live. She had fed the fire crews and the refugees unstintingly from the winter stock, and by now was scraping the bottom of her pantry shelves and her deep freeze.

The Red Cross team had finished everyone's lists and gone away, and they had come back a few days later with long faces.

"We find we can't do anything at all for you girls," the man said unhappily.

They had sent to New York to investigate and had found that we had earned very good livings in the advertising business and could do so again. Our store was not our livelihood but "a venture." True, we had invested in it everything we had. True, we had lost everything; that thrifty Maine custom of reducing the insurance right after the season meant that the bank got its mortgage, and we got nothing. All the money we had made in that fine summer season had gone back into the store.

In a few hours the fire had made the difference between being worth a hundred thousand dollars as owners of a going business, and having a few hundred dollars, no business, no personal possessions, not even a suitcase into which to put the clothes we didn't have!

But, said the Red Cross, a line had to be drawn somewhere.

"We base it on the Texas City fire," they told us. "You wouldn't expect the Red Cross to replace the Monsanto Chemical Works, would you?"

How would we live? They had also verified the fact that both of us had practically unlimited credit for whatever we needed to live, in New York or in Maine.

We looked at each other—and laughed. What else was there to do but laugh? We could find no loophole in the logic. We could raise no argument that we ourselves couldn't argue right down again. It was a colossal joke on us, the best joke in years. We hoped we would not find another like it to laugh at in our lifetimes.

I did not take it with calm philosophy. I was furious, not at the Red Cross, for which I had then and have now and will forever have a monumental admiration. There is nothing to beat the work of their disaster unit, the planning and the thoughtful, warmhearted execution of it. No, indeed, I was not mad at the Red Cross. I was mad at the fire.

How do you get even with a fire? I thought and thought, and then I saw—idiot, it's obvious! You fix it so this can't happen again. You get so well set for it that the next time it begins to burn, you can thumb your nose at it.

Dorothy and I went to the Ford agency in Brunswick and talked about a light truck. We went to the iron works in Bath and talked about a water tank that would fit on a light truck. The men at both places worked with us, and we came up with a fire engine that was cheap to buy and maintain, and would fight fire.

Then, beginning right at home with Goose Rocks and Cape Porpoise, we set out to sell the little fire engine to all the townships that had burned, as auxiliary fire apparatus. When a town didn't have the money, we stayed and raised the money, with street dances, clambakes, church suppers. When we got through, we had left bright red-painted truck-and-tank fire engines in townships all along the coast of Maine. Without quite being aware of it we had also laid the groundwork for a public-relations business.

34

A Community House for Goose Rocks

They elected Dorothy "Mayor."

There was so much work to be done; there were so many community decisions to be made. Goose Rocks itself had no town meeting, no governing body, no direct representation as a community in Kennebunkport, of which it is a part. The nearest selectman was from Cape Porpoise (but the next fall Goose Rocks Beach elected a selectman).

From disaster and relief and fire-fighting headquarters the house on the Point had become the natural center for all arguments and discussions and disputes about rebuilding the community, and Dorothy with her calm wisdom and foresight was the natural moderator. The Goose Rocks Beach Association, formed a year or so before, now had new purpose. Dorothy was elected President by acclamation.

I don't know who started it but from then on, instead of coming in and asking, "Where's Dorothy?" they took to asking, "Where's the Mayor?" Actually the only change was to make it official; they had been coming to her to talk things over anyway. Boundary disputes cropped up everywhere. When every landmark was swept away, it was hard to determine just where one man's land ended and the other's began; few of the old deeds were very clear on these points.

Dorothy's legal training was enormously useful during that time. I shall always maintain that her legal wisdom all deserts her and she is as a babe in arms when it comes to her own affairs. But she is as wise as Solomon in settling other people's troubles.

People began to rebuild everywhere. We had an unforeseen influence in the building: we had talked up the Maine winter so glowingly to our summer-colony friends that most of them, when they rebuilt, built all-year houses. Bill got himself a piece of land and built his own house and then, without quite knowing how, he became the building contractor for others.

When winter shut in and building stopped in late November, there was enough work to do still, and there were not enough carpenters and cabinetmakers to do it. We had an inspiration: adult education. What Bill had taught me about woodworking and furniture finishing he could teach others. We arranged with the neighboring school for the use of its shop one evening a week, and people flocked to the classes with more lively enthusiasm, even, than to a Gary Cooper movie.

Women especially took to it. One woman whose husband had died of overexertion during the fire, though their chinchilla farm was saved, wanted to learn carpentry to make the cages for the little animals. Another wanted shelves and cupboards for her kitchen, declaring that no carpenter had ever made them to suit her and in her new house she was going to have them just right. A woman who mourned a table that had come down to her through her family wanted to reproduce it; she had waxed and polished it lovingly for years and knew exactly its shape and its ornamentation.

Dorothy and I stayed in Goose Rocks until Christmas. We were not going to miss giving our annual Christmas party. But this time we gave it, not in the house on the Point, and not just for the children. We gave it on the store property, for everybody.

Albion found a fine tree—as with the houses, there were patches of woods, too, that had been freakishly spared by the fire. He set it up right in the middle of our land, looking out on the sea, and we trimmed it and strung it with lights. The whole community of Goose Rocks gathered round, and we sang carols and had cookies and hot cocoa, and gingerbread men and candy for the children.

Then we took off for New York. We bought ourselves a few essential city clothes on our charge accounts. We called on our business acquaintances, told them what had happened to us, and asked them what we ought to do. Unanimously, they advised us that since we loved Maine and wanted to live there, we should go back and set ourselves up in the public-relations business there. Between us, they said, we were a business firm, complete: Dorothy a lawyer and market analyst, myself with advertising and public-relations background and special experience in radio. So that was what we did.

We had already repaired the house on the Point. When spring came we rebuilt Riverview, the summer cottage, making it very trim and modern. And we let the bulldozer go over the land where the store and the other buildings had been, clearing it of debris, wiping the slate clean.

We were the only ones who would do this. None of our friends and neighbors would, either the local or the summer people. For some the deciding factor may have been the cost, but from their talk it seemed to me their protest was on more mystical grounds, as though letting the bulldozer in were a violation of nature.

I couldn't see what obligation they owed to nature in this matter. It was nature, after all, that had done this to them. According to the general opinion, no carelessly thrown cigarette, no lighted match, no unquenched campfire had caused the fire. It was caused by spontaneous combustion. It seemed to spring out of the ground itself. After the open winter and the summer virtually without rain, there must have been many low places in the woods where dead leaves and vegetable matter were decomposing in those hot Indian summer days, with no currents of air to carry off the generated heat. Nature perhaps had reproduced the conditions in which an unventilated hayloft will burst into flames.

But when we had cleared the land there was nothing more we could do. We had no money to rebuild. And now we had the mortgage on the house to pay off—yes, as the Red Cross had ascertained, our credit was good, and the fire had accomplished what until then I had been able to prevent. Dorothy's big house was mortgaged.

The Goose Rocks people simply could not believe their Mayor. They wanted their store, their restaurant, their soda fountain just as they had been. More than anything they wanted their Casino. A summer without the Saturday night dances, the bowling alleys, the movies, without a safe place for the children on a rainy day and patient Henry to baby-sit, was unthinkable. Why wouldn't we rebuild the Casino? Why wouldn't we give the land to the community so it could build a community house? Why wouldn't we . . . ?

It was no surprise to me that they thought Dorothy a rich girl and persisted in thinking so no matter what she said. The way she gave away anything she had to anyone who needed it was evidence to Maine people, at least, that the supply was inexhaustible. I reminded Dorothy how she had fed the whole community our winter food during the fire without asking any compensation. All she did was look at me for answer, and I tried to imagine keeping the food and letting the people go hungry, or making them pay for what they ate. The fire fighters, for instance. Or the refugees whose houses had burned with everything in them.

So there was no answer to that. But it had been a hard thing, that Christmas, when we found the cards we had forehandedly bought while ordering greeting cards for the store, and didn't have the cash for stamps to send them out.

Somehow at last—and perhaps I helped a little to convince them—Dorothy's "constituents" accepted the fact that though she was unboundedly generous she was not rich, that at the moment, indeed, she was stony, and that she always had worked and probably always would work for a living, although when she made a living in her own profession it was generally a handsome one, at least by local standards.

A woman whose land lay a little farther back in the country offered an acre for the community house. Another owner offered a right of way, provided the community would build a road in. That summer we ran money-raising events one after the other. The people wanted dances: we had street dances. Andrew Austin's boy Jim, back from M.I.T., hooked up a loud-speaker system from the high-fidelity phonograph he had built himself, and we took turns sitting there, diskjockeying from our quite good collection of records.

We ran clambakes and lobster bakes. The ladies who liked bridge organized bridge parties. The good cooks cooked and baked and sold what they made. With the firehouse miraculously spared, Andrew, who was also our fire chief, built a kitchen on it, and we organized suppers there at a dollar a head. When we had the eight hundred dollars for the road we began building it. And we went right on raising money.

But when we looked into the cost of building the community house we lost heart. We had all been thinking in prewar terms. To rebuild anything like the Casino, they told us, would come to fifty thousand dollars. Well, and if it weren't like the Casino, if it had no bowling alleys but was just a shell with a dance floor? Built the cheapest way? Then, they said, maybe it could be done for half.

Where was twenty-five thousand dollars to come from?

Dorothy said, "We could buy a building and move it."

We were at a party in someone's house one night when a man said, "I've got a house I want to get rid of. I'll sell it cheap to anyone who will take it away."

The house he was talking about was the old community house of Kennebunk Beach, out of use these many years because it sat on a plot of ground just big enough to fit its foundation, and people who had built homes almost up to its walls wouldn't stand for the noise a community house generates.

It was a big shell of a house with a good dance floor. Dorothy asked, "How much?" and when the man said a thousand dollars we knew there was a community house for Goose Rocks.

Then the fun began. The best figure for moving it that we could get was $22,500. Again it looked hopeless. Then one day a man came from northern Maine who said he was in the house-moving business and what house did we want moved where?

He was a French Canadian, quick but a little scrambled in his English, his thoughts tumbling ahead of his tongue. In his city clothes he looked somehow helpless, certainly not like a man who could move houses. Before we showed him the house, where it was, and where it had to go, we mesmerized him into listening to a public-relations spiel. It was a Madison Avenue trick, but we had to do it. We were desperate enough to promise him anything to keep the price down. We promised coast-to-coast publicity for the house moving and asked him to make a price we could pay. We drove him to Kennebunk Beach to look at the house and back to Goose Rocks to look at the site, and he said without blinking, "Hokay. Four t'ousand dollars."

We looked at him unbelieving. From $22,500 this was quite a drop.

"Yes, yes, I do it. We go by sea."

We asked around. By sea? A fifty-ton house on pontoons, in the open ocean? Get him to insure it for plenty if you want to see any part of your money back.

We asked him how much he would insure the house for. His answer took us completely by surprise.

"I 'ave never lose a pane of glass from any 'ouse moving!" he exclaimed, deeply offended. " 'Ow motch I hinsure? I do not hinsure for nothing!"

So we would have to insure it ourselves. How much would that be? The insurance men looked and named an astronomical figure. That settled that. There wasn't that much money in the Association treasury after buying the house and paying for moving it. The house would float or it would sink, but without benefit of insurance.

Getting it down to the beach was routine, our house mover said, and that we could believe, having seen houses moved before. He got it down there without mishap. Getting it onto the water was also routine, he assured us. Now that he was in working clothes, shouting orders to a crew, he inspired respect. Dorothy even professed to feel confidence.

We did our part. The leading national picture magazine sent a team of photographer and writer to cover the story.

The house stood on the beach. The towboat would come, and then the house on its pontoons would be floated off by the next tide.

The towboat didn't come. A lobster boat came in. The skipper said, "Passed a towboat from up north, said he was looking for Kennebunk Beach."

"Didn't you lead him in?" we asked.

"Me? No affair of mine."

And the story went up and down the beach: "Fine chance

that house has ever gettin' to Goose Rocks, with a towboat
that don't know how to find Kennebunk Beach!"

It seems callous, but all the lobstermen felt that way. They
said, "The sea will be full of timber by morning." And they
wanted no part of the project, not even to leading in the towboat that couldn't find Kennebunk Beach.

That night our good Frenchman slept in his car, but I
doubt if he slept. When the tide began to rise he went down
to watch over the house. What he would have done, how he
would have held the house back if the tide had threatened
to float it off, we didn't ask and he didn't say. The lobstermen
and the Coast Guard went about their business, but no one
spoke to him. He was alone with his responsibility.

Two tides came and went, washing around the pontoons,
but the house stood firm. At last the towboat came. Twenty-
two thousand cars came from all over to watch the house go
to sea. The beach was solid with people as the tide rose again.
The towboat tugged, the house moved—it was afloat!

Dorothy and I stood on the beach listening to people telling us what a foolhardy venture it was. The trip would be
made in darkness because of the towboat's delay; it was already getting dark. A sou'wester was rising and the seas
would be high. Everything was against the Frenchman. The
lobstermen had already turned their backs on the project,
and now the Coast Guard strongly advised against it.

The hardy man didn't pause even for breath to answer.
Once begun, the house moving would be carried through.
Somebody had thrust flowers into Dorothy's arms, and a
bottle of champagne, and that plus the Frenchman's dogged-
ness, I think, decided her. She said, "Well, Skipper, shall we
go aboard?"

"In the 'ouse? You want to ride down?"

"Yes," said Dorothy. "You say it's safe. I want to show
all these people I believe you."

His eyes opened wide and he turned a little pale. We discovered later that he had never been on salt water, not even in a rowboat.

But he said, "Wait, I get boots."

He strode to his car and brought back a pair of high waders for Dorothy like the ones he had on. She stepped into them, and without more ado they waded out and climbed into the house.

Still there was delay. Lines had to be tied and checked and untied and retied and checked again. Aboard the Coast Guard cutter anchored near by the men were eating their supper. They waved to Dorothy in the house and called companionably, "Can we do anything for you?"

Neither of us had eaten since breakfast, and only a cup of coffee then; we had been too excited to think of food all day. But now Dorothy was setting forth on a journey, and the house she was in had neither kitchen nor pantry. So she answered without hesitation, "Yes—send over some food!"

And they did. Dorothy supped on hamburgers, courtesy of the United States Coast Guard, while she waited.

At last they were ready. The towboat started. The house lunged, hung back, gathered way, and began to move smoothly out of the harbor. I waited until I could no longer see its awkward bulk, like Noah's Ark with red and green running lights, or the faint blink of Dorothy's flashlight from the doorway that opened on black Atlantic water. Then I got into the car and drove, weaving through the twenty-two thousand sight-seers' cars, talking to the dogs to keep up my spirits, home to the Point.

I tried to think what Dorothy would need when she came ashore (I suppose, to keep from thinking that she might not come ashore). She would be cold; she had had no jacket or sweater, only her thin blouse. I filled a thermos with hot coffee, filled a small medicine bottle with whisky, got her

warm jacket, went back and got a blanket besides, and the
dogs and I went down to the beach.

All Goose Rocks was waiting there. It was like a death
watch. People said solemnly, "Hello, Mac," and drew away.
They left me alone, like the chief mourner, bowed under
my blanket with the dogs huddled beside me, hugging the
thermos bottle and Dorothy's jacket. Dorothy is a strong
swimmer, I kept telling myself. But the water was bitter cold;
there were high seas; she might find herself far from land.
And what if the house, sinking, sucked her down? Or it
broke up, and a timber hit her? What if a thousand things?
And a skipper who couldn't find Kennebunk Beach—how
would he ever find Goose Rocks? I wondered how I could
have been so crazy as to let her go.

I looked up the road, where the sight-seers were lined up,
bumper to bumper, all the way back almost to Kennebunkport, headlights blazing. I thought bitterly, "They came to
see a show. They'll go away not caring if the show fails, and
forget it."

But those sight-seers had their use. The line of headlights guided Dorothy through the night, and with her flashlight she in turn guided the towboat skipper, who did not
know this southern coast. Timber Island, sand points, rocks,
shallows, she of course knew them all, and with the road out-
lined in brilliant light to steer by, she brought the house in to
shore. One man, I don't know who, rowed out in a dinghy to
meet her in the pitch-black night; nobody else dared.

She came ashore wet, chilled, but jubilant, concerned only
with whether the salt water might have harmed the dance
floor, because seas broke and washed through the house the
whole way.

"Good 'ardwood," the Frenchman assured her. "A little
water, it is nothing." He was in high spirits, too. He had
taken his first sea voyage, and although the house had rolled

more than a little he hadn't even been seasick. Since then and as a result of that house moving he has had enough business to keep him prosperous for the rest of his life.

And so Goose Rocks got its Casino, or a lineal descendant of it, a seagoing house that was tough enough to take anything. Like the store, like so many of the things that had happened to Dorothy and me since I had detoured on my way to Arizona for a stopover in Maine, it was a wild gamble that had paid off.

I have only one more note to add: on the outcome of my own relations with the State of Maine. These had begun to improve perceptibly during my first winter there. A Maine winter is beautiful, exhilarating—and tempering. Many people know Maine in the summer, but to know Maine in the wintertime is a privilege shared by few. Only the mercury falls; everything else in the country and the people rises to the magnificent, challenging season.

A shared Maine winter also makes a bond that's hard to break. When people asked, in the store in July, "How was the winter?" if one of the local men was near by he would catch my eye and answer for me.

"Not for them soft folks, eh, Mac?" Or, "We made it, didn't we, Mac?"

Then there was the fire, and going on patrol, and then there were long months of rebuilding when people came to the house and, if the Mayor was out, they'd sit down and discuss whatever it was with me. Some of the confidence they had in Dorothy rubbed off, maybe, on me.

Then, after the end of this story, there came a time when I went to the hospital—nothing serious, a couple of impacted wisdom teeth, but I'm a baby about pain. I stayed there three days. I had visitors.

Not our city friends, those who were still on the beach. Our Maine neighbors. Albion, of course, and Chris, both making excuses about having to be in Biddeford that morning for something or other. But Phil and Della Smith came without making excuses, and Lucy Gooden and Rawl, and Andrew and Mrs. Austin. And Mrs. Keene and Mrs. Cobb and Abby Peace and all the women.

They sat and commiserated and told me lugubrious tales about people they knew who didn't get out of a hospital alive no matter what they went in for. Typical Maine talk, full of doom and disaster.

I loved it. Because by this time I can almost believe I'm a State of Mainer myself.

Afterword

All those good and bad times happened fifty years ago and—as I write—are more vivid to me than anything I did this morning. Since this book was first published, more than forty years ago, people have been asking what we did in later years. Most recently, the question has come from the folks at Down East Books, who are bringing our Maine story to life again during this fiftieth anniversary of the 1947 fire.

Briefly, here's what happened to us:

After the fire, Dorothy and I, like many of our neighbors, had to start over—from scratch. We began by setting up our own public relations firm, Mackenzie & Mignault, with two regional clients in the Northeast and one national client in New York City. For a while we shuttled between Maine and New York, which was tiring, but worth it, because we didn't want to leave Goose Rocks Beach. But the time came when we had more clients in New York and the Southeast than we had in the Northeast; we had to say good-bye to Maine and move closer to our bread and butter.

Dorothy and I worked together much the way we had in the store, each doing what she did best. I developed corporate public relations programs for television, magazines, pharmaceutical companies, and management organizations. Dorothy specialized in resolving union and management disputes for automotive companies and textile mills, and in sorting out problems for not-for-profit organizations.

Which brings me to an exchange between us that readers of this book will find familiar. One evening, while Dorothy was working on a project with the Girl Scouts of America in New Jersey and I was working on NBC's early efforts to establish a viable educational channel, I was tearing my hair and beating my breast over the frustrations of trying to nail down the financing for a television documentary. I raved and ranted, and Dorothy, as usual, patiently heard me out.

Finally, she sighed and said, "I know how it is. I've had a frustrating day, too. We're trying to make our sales goal for Girl Scout cookies; we'll make it all right, but we've run into a problem."

"A problem selling *cookies?*" I exclaimed. "Dorothy, I'm talking real money here. I'm talking about $350,000."

She smiled. "I know."

"Well, what's so funny?" I said, with some irritation, "How much money can you expect to make selling cookies in New Jersey?"

"About a million and a half."

Ah, well.

In 1952, I found myself telling the story of our Maine adventure to Ruth Goode, who even then was well-known among publishers as a gifted teller of other people's tales. Simon and Schuster published our book in 1955. It was taken up by a couple of book clubs, published in England (as *We Bought a Store*), and optioned as a Broadway musical (which never came to pass, because I hated the lyrics).

Around 1958, Dorothy decided to devote all her energies to not-for-profits and accepted the daunting challenge of becoming Director of Detroit's YWCA, where she plunged into groundbreaking community relations work in that then volatile city.

Ten years later, she retired and moved to Green Valley, Arizona, where she lived in a handsome house and had an active social and civic life. I, too, moved, this time to the Caribbean, where I lived for seven years. (Dorothy was one of my frequent visitors.) Caribbean island living was almost as challenging as living in Maine, but not nearly so much fun. (I found myself writing a book about *that* stay, too.) I loved having brown feet all year round, but in 1975 I was ready to go home, back to where I could read the *New York Times* every morning.

In 1976, Durrell Publications published a softcover edition of *My Love Affair with the State of Maine,* introducing it to a new generation of readers. We were all pleased with that. Maybe, we thought, it should be reborn every twenty years.

In 1978, Dorothy died of cancer. A sad, sad day.

As for me, I'll be eighty this year, and I live, happily, at the top of a tall building on the East side of Manhattan overlooking all the busy doings down below, feeling blessedly free of the pressures I used to cherish.

Scotty Mackenzie
January 2, 1997

About the Authors

SCOTTY MACKENZIE is a New Yorker by birth and temperament with the native's urge to get out of New York and the equal compulsion to return to it. But Maine, she declares, is her spiritual home. She also maintains, "If it hadn't been for the perception, humor, and warmth of Ruth Goode, the luxury of getting this Maine adventure on paper would never have been mine."

Scotty's first book was RUTH GOODE's thirteenth. Her thirty-three fiction and nonfiction titles sometimes bear her name alone, and sometimes her name and a collaborator's. Some of her works—in education, medicine, and psychiatry for the general reader—were ghostwritten and do not bear her name at all. Also a born New Yorker, she learned her trade in the city room of a metropolitan newspaper. Of all the other people's experiences she has written, Scotty's is the one she would most like to have lived.